Antarctica – Both Heaven and Hell

ANTARCTICA
Both Heaven and Hell

Reinhold Messner

Translated by Jill Neate

The Crowood Press

First published in Great Britain in 1991 by
The Crowood Press Ltd
Ramsbury, Marlborough
Wiltshire, SN8 2HR

Title of the original German edition:
Antarktis – Himmel und Hölle zugleich
© R. Piper GmbH & Co. KG, Munchen 1990

British Library Cataloguing in Publication Data

Messner, Reinhold
    Antarctica: both heaven and hell.
    1. Antarctica. Travel
    I. Title II. [Antarktis]. *English*
    919.8904

ISBN 1 85223 704 X

The author's thanks go to all who helped with the book,
especially Ralf-Peter Märtin for compiling the historical
chapter.

Typeset by Chippendale Type Ltd, Otley, West
Yorkshire

Printed in Great Britain by Redwood Press Ltd,
Melksham, Wilts.

When I set off for the South Pole, my daughter Magdalena could not yet talk. When I returned, she asked me lots of questions:

– What did you find down there?
– Infinity.
– What's infinity like?
– White, peaceful, still, and everything moves slowly.
– So, is that like Heaven?
– Perhaps that is Heaven.
– Did you look for Heaven in the Antarctic?
– No, I wasn't looking for anything there, but I discovered white infinity there.
– What do I have to do to see white infinity?
– Fight all your life to make sure that people don't put up buildings and electricity pylons, or burrow around or divide up the last wilderness amongst themselves.

Dedication

To Magdalena, for whom the Antarctic should remain
as Shackleton, Scott and Amundsen experienced it.

Contents

I. The Journey

1 'Don't go!'

It was autumn. Autumn not only on the mountains around Juval, also down in the valley. The fruit gardens were no longer colourful and made me sad. I wanted to be off. One way or another. In the Schnalstal behind me, where the winter snow lasted throughout the summer, I sensed coldness and storm. Fears too? Yes.

The first snow lay on the outlying, usually black summits of the Ortler group. The coldness illuminated the valley. It was autumn, the grass brown and yellow. The smell of decay, autumn in the forest. The leaves had fallen from the birches and lime-trees. In the meadows the tinkling of cow and sheep bells. Already weeks before the cattle had come down from the upper pastures. Now the small herds grazed near the brown farmsteads. The farmers were gathering fruit and happy to see the cattle grazing off any unmown summer grass. Thus it had been in my childhood. Here I was at home.

For three months I had been almost exclusively occupied with preparations for my Antarctic expedition. I read, planned, negotiated with sponsors and talked things over with Wilhelm Bittorf of *Der Spiegel*, who was reporter on our journey on the ice. Equipment was tested. Then again I was busy day after day, somewhere on a glacier, practising how to handle the sail that was to help us pull our sledges in the Antarctic. I learned quickly. Now and then I spent the night in the open. At home I often got up at dawn and made myself run, from Schloss Juval where I lived, up the road into the Schnalstal, up to the Altrateiseralm. As a rule I don't train, haven't done so for years, but anxiety always got me on my feet. It roused me and drove me on; it did not let me sleep.

It was a steep rise of 500 metres as I hurried up the mountain, then a

Juval's mountain peace and ruins. The northern end is restored but not habitable.

traverse which brought me back to the Juval farms and into the castle, panting and sweating. Soon I felt myself bodily fit; nevertheless, the anxieties remained. I noticed the excess weight I was carrying and my worry about breaking down on this trip. I had acquired a cushion of fat by overeating, so as not to freeze in the Antarctic and to have reserves for the months of grind. A team of doctors had advised me to put on fat and observe moderation in training. My joints had to be spared for the 3000-kilometre march.

Autumn was everywhere, not only in my mood. I was absent-minded, full of curiosity. Above all, I was restless, tormented with fears. This expedition was associated with notions of terror and loneliness. They attacked me ever more frequently the nearer the time of starting came. So long as an adventure exists only as an idea, it is easy to be a 'hero'. Of the reality, however, I was afraid. The planned Antarctic crossing would be a new dimension of adventure for me, perhaps with too many unknowns. Time and again at night I started up out of sleep, plagued by anxiety dreams, with the sensation of being left alone like a foundling, exposed to the terrors of ice and storm.

Why exactly did I want to go there, where Dante had placed the worst of his enemies, in the deepest inferno? This endless ice, 'where the sinners stuck in the cold', projected its horror. When, half asleep, involuntarily I conjured up pictures from Dante's *Divine Comedy*, I froze:

> So, to where modest shame appears, thus low
> Blue pinch'd and shrined in ice the spirits stood,
> Moving their teeth in shrill note like the stork.
> His face each downward held; their mouth the cold,
> Their eyes express'd the dolour of their heart.
>
> Straightway their eyes, before all moist within,
> Distill'd upon their lips, and the frost bound
> The tears betwixt those orbs, and held them there.

When, whilst running, I sensed my energy, the Antarctic turned in my imagination from a 'sea of ice', which looked like glass and not

12

Schloss Juval, steel engraving after a painting by Johanna v. Isser (1821). On the home farm below I do organic farming.

water under the cold sky, into a realm of stillness, peace, infinity. That was Dante's paradise:

> Thus in the sun-thaw is the snow unseal'd;
> Thus in the winds on flitting leaves was lost
> The Sybil's sentence, O eternal beam!
> (Whose height what reach of mortal thought may soar?)
> Yield me again some little particle
> Of what Thou then appearedst; . . .

For five years Juval had been my home. In 1983 I had acquired a ruin and, with the help from local craftsmen, I had managed to preserve it and restored it so that we could live there – Sabine, Magdalena and I. I loved them both and felt good at Juval.

But how long could I bear it here? A year perhaps or two. I was still too young to become a stay-at-home. Much as I prized this middle-class security, it could not hold me. Perhaps later on I would have the

13

strength and endurance to stay at home and write down all that I had experienced in my life. Perhaps I could settle down and manage the mountain farm under the castle, without always having to go off again. Yet I could not.

What did I know already about life, but that which was mirrored in the faces of the mountains and ice deserts, when a thunderstorm or a blizzard swept over them and me? Not one soft bed or good meal remained in my recollection. The days and weeks which I had spent in the wilderness, cold and hungry, were those which had marked me. I longed for that as much as I feared it.

My journeys had nothing to do with tourism, the greatest commercial enterprise on earth. Neither did they serve science. They led away from all paths. For me, travelling in the wilderness was not about the outside world, rather about the world within me. I was the master of my own soul and felt myself a pupil of St Augustine, who had spoken of nature as a means to self-experience:

People go to wonder at the heights of mountains and the tides

Roald Amundsen. This Norwegian is without doubt the most successful of all polar adventurers. A 'pupil' of Nansen, he was the first to traverse the North-west passage and to fly to the North Pole.

14

of the sea, the currents of the rivers, the circumference of the ocean and the pathways of the stars and outgrow themselves thereby.

My journeys were intended to discover no riches, they were to prove nothing to mankind. I had always advised the tourists who followed me against their schemes. Perhaps I had succeeded now and then in giving back to the ice paradises in the wilderness of the Himalaya at least a part of that myth which the conquerors of the turn of the century – Sven Hedin, Fridtjof Nansen, Roald Amundsen – had destroyed with their Victorian spirit of discovery. More and more on my journeys I renounced technical aid, because I wanted to make people conscious of the value of protecting the wilderness into which I, as a human being, went. Antarctica, the Himalaya, Greenland were a potential for human dreams and, for that reason, of inestimable value. Nevertheless, often it was almost impossible for me to get my message across. However, the lack of understanding which I encountered before each new journey could not hold me back.

> Most people think of 'adventure' when the word 'discovery' comes up, so I want to pin down the difference between these two concepts from the standpoint of the explorer. For him, adventure is only an unwelcome interruption of serious work. He does not seek titillation, rather previously unknown facts. Often his journey of discovery is nothing more than a race against time, in order to escape death by starvation. For him an adventure is simply an error in his calculations, the fact of which the 'experiment' has exposed. Or is it a very unhappy proof that no one can take into consideration all eventualities? . . . Any explorer experiences adventures. They excite him and he looks back on them with pleasure, but he never seeks them out.

Thus the discoverer of the South Pole, Roald Amundsen, had explained the apparent contradiction between 'adventure' and his 'work'. For me it was the other way round. I sought the 'titillation' in order to discover myself as a person. Adventure as an end in itself. In that I am neither masochist nor potential suicide, not even subconsciously. I agree with Robert Edwin Peary, discoverer of the North Pole:

> Frozen and bleeding cheeks and ears are the unpleasant things which belong to a great adventure. Pain and discomforts are unavoidable but, seen in the context of the whole, they are scarcely important.

I felt good at Juval. I had arranged the historic building to my taste, according to my concepts. Nevertheless I had to get away. My farmer-neighbours observed my comings and goings with scepticism. I knew that there could be no friendship between us as long as I did not stay there and live like them. But time and again I had to leave. Perhaps one life would not suffice in order to become 'homey', perhaps I didn't want that anyway.

In Villnöss, where I had grown up, I had suffered from the proximity of the village inhabitants – my school friends, and the innkeepers who enlisted my celebrity for their *pensions* and hotels and, in bad weather, sent their tourists to my home. They disturbed me in my quiet and brought my rhythm of life into confusion. At Juval there was a wall around my domain. I had not only the feeling of being shut off, I had the security of being able to live *my* life, as it corresponded to *my* concepts.

And yet I must away Toni didn't understand it. Toni, my nearest neighbour, was a dear friend to me. Earlier, when the castle was slowly falling into disrepair and the walls were crumbling away, he had had charge of the building. Then, during the restoration, he had helped with diligence and skill. He was a mountain farmer, sixty years old, with a natural talent of a stonemason, who could handle stones like an artist with colours. He was always there to construct a pathway or to patch up fragments of walls. Often he had helped me replace stones correctly or to build tables and benches out of rock slabs. Toni came to me with his ideas, Toni advised me, he loved Juval. When he gave me advice, he always began: 'It's not for me to say . . .'. 'Only I thought . . .'. Between us a silent friendship had developed.

When Toni heard that I was setting off for the South Pole, he did not know exactly what to make of it. He watched my training with

16

shakes of the head. The loading of the car, with which I continually took equipment to Munich, where the expedition headquarters was, pleased him still less. His mistrust grew. He did not know when it was to happen; and what was I to tell him? Give him the definition of the South Pole?

The geographical South Pole is the mathematical point, which the imaginary axis of the earth's rotation passes through, at which the meridians unite, where the only direction is north, where the wind comes out of the north and blows north and the magnetic compass always points north, where the centrifugal force of the earth ceases and the stars no longer rise and set.

Why was the Antarctic so foreign to the 'simple man'? Certainly, it was far away. So inaccessible. Media discussions about Antarctica were almost exclusively about ecological, political and scientific problems. Who had been there already?

The first land expeditions, which had taken place at the turn of the century, were forgotten, apart from the death of the 'immortal' Captain Scott. And the nations, which maintained their scientific bases there, and thereby marked out their claims, managed brilliantly to keep the Antarctic out of the public eye. This continent was for most of us as far away as the moon and colder than the universe. We could develop no feelings towards it. We believed the experts when they said that the Antarctic was important for water economy, the climate, life on this planet, just as we believe in Einstein's theory of relativity. But it meant little to us. The South Pole was a geographical neuter.

By our journey, I wanted to bring home a feeling. A feeling for the landscape, hope for its survival. I wanted to give the Antarctic a human dimension. Only when millions of people developed feelings for this part of the earth, could a 'Nature Park Antarctica' be enforced.

The South Pole was for Toni the opposite of the North Pole, something on the other side of the world, far away. 'Is warm there?' Toni asked now and then. 'Are there polar bears there?' Thus he wanted to know when and how this expedition would take place.

At the beginning of October, as once more I filled my car with boxes, cases, skis and tents, Toni watched me again. I winked at him. Perhaps he took my greeting as a leave-taking for months. Toni came up as I was about to drive off.

'Are you off then?'

'No', I said, 'I'm coming back but only briefly.'

'Where are you off to this time then?'

'To Antarctica, as I told you already.'

'Not to the North Pole then?'

'No,' I said, 'Exactly on the other side of the world, to the South Pole. We want to go to the South Pole and cross the Antarctic.'

I noticed that the geographical data had no significance for Toni. He had been to elementary school and knew not much more than the farms roundabout, plus Bolzano and Meran. Nearly forty years ago he had taken over the home farm with his father and spent his life there. He had not been far away in his life but he knew what it meant to repair a fence in thirty degrees of frost, to drag stones or to handle iron with bare hands. He could handle tools. Also in winter, he knew what it meant to struggle against the storm in the cold, icy Schnalstal wind. Toni was a practical person. He could picture to himself what it meant to survive in forty degrees below zero.

'Stay at home!', said Toni tersely. It sounded like an order. 'Now that you have everything, now the castle is repaired, where you have a child. Stay here!'

I said it was too late to stop this expedition now, everything was already fixed.

He shook his head and said: 'If you want to stop at home, you can stop at home.' And he was right.

The preparations for this expedition had been going on for three years. I had found sponsors, developed the logistics and rigged up the items of equipment. Two years previously I had found the ideal partner for this journey; the North German adventurer and seaman Arved Fuchs, who took on responsibility for that part of the expedition for which I lacked experience: navigation, radio sets, detailed assembly of foodstuffs.

'You've been at Juval five years now', Toni continued the conversation. 'Yes, five and Juval has become beautiful.'

Toni Pichler. My next-door neighbour at Juval, Toni, the 'old' castle restorer, didn't hide his worries about my Antarctic expedition. I took his objections seriously.

'Yes,' I said, 'I'm very pleased with it.'

'Then stay here!'

'I'm coming straight back.'

Toni looked at me with disbelief. He still didn't want to believe that I was not to be stopped. 'Why must you always be off again, then? Juval is the second most beautiful castle in South Tyrol.'

I laughed. Then I asked back. 'Which is the most beautiful castle in South Tyrol, then?' He didn't answer. Toni, who had borne the responsibility here for decades, who had watched that the beams, the last inlays did not disappear out of the ruin, loved this eighth-century building as much as I did. Originally, a sort of fortress had developed on the hill at Juval, erected by the Langobards who passed through from north to south. Then, in the thirteenth century, noblemen had built a stronghold on the rock and resided there. In the sixteenth century the *kellermeister* (cellar master) of the gentlemen of Tyrol, Sinkmoser, had acquired the ruined citadel and restored it. He had travelled to northern Italy and had been in Tuscany and had transformed the gloomy castle walls on the sunny granite hill at Juval into a proud Renaissance building. Later the castle fell into disrepair again.

For two hundred years it was in the hands of mountain farmers. Only the foundations and walls remained. Luckily, in 1913 it was acquired by a Dutch colonial gentleman who had owned rubber and tea plantations in Malaysia. On a ski tour in the Schnalstal he had seen it and bought it at once. After he gave up his estates in Malaysia, he came back to Juval in 1924. With much empathy and taste he had built up the construction again and thus given to the former Renaissance building that proud and simultaneously playfully romantic appearance which had struck me at once. When, in 1983, I spotted this hidden hill for the first time from the valley, I went up there and fell in love with it at first sight.

I put a great deal of energy, enthusiasm and creativity into the old ruins. This castle lent wings to my imagination, not only because it was to become my 'home', my 'stronghold', my 'nest' but, above all, because it had a history. I needed a haven for the times between expeditions, for later years, for the months after returning. Again and again. This piece of South Tyrol also lay in my heart because it belonged to that natural and cultural landscape which I, despite my journeys to Tibet and South America, to the most beautiful spots on earth, liked more than any other region.

Here then I was at home. Despite everything, I saw my nomad-like journeys not as a contradiction, for I needed them like I needed this home. I knew every stone, every tree, every bush at Juval. It was my ambition so to preserve this castle hill as it had been hundreds of years before. Such calm, such obvious elegance I had noticed only in Tibetan monasteries.

I wanted to say goodbye to Toni, to drive to Munich. As usual, I was in a hurry prior to an expedition. 'Don't go!', Toni said suddenly. It sounded like an entreaty. I knew that this old man liked me and for that reason his concern disturbed me. It would have been superfluous to ask 'why'. So I said once more: 'The expedition has started already, it can't be stopped'.

'Don't go!', Toni reiterated. 'You have experienced everything. Up to now everything has gone well. Think of all that could have happened. Don't go!'

Toni was right and he was not the only one who tried to warn me.

Before this expedition, I received numerous telephone calls and

The Englishman Robert F. Scott voyaged to the Antarctic twice. Despite many training runs with the huskies he was unable to get on with them.

letters from friends whom I trusted. Always the same concern came across, above all from those who thought well of me. They had more fear, more doubt than before earlier expeditions, before journeys which I had undertaken in Africa, to the seven-thousanders in the Hindu Kush, to the Himalaya. The eight-thousanders in Tibet had been dangerous. The march to the South Pole meant still more loneliness, forlornness, danger to life.

There was this endless vastness of the Antarctic. Perhaps the earlier expeditions of Shackleton, Scott and Amundsen played a part too. When I read these books and my worries welled up, even with sleeping tablets I could not get to sleep for a long time.

Perhaps with this expedition my doubts and fears were also greater than in the ten previous years, in which, year after year, I had regularly set off for the Himalaya because I lacked experience in ice travel. To put it another way, in the last five years I had noticed that exactly this tension, which increasingly failed me, the doubts, the fears on the earlier eight-thousander expeditions, had not only held me back, but also borne me up and inspired me. In this arc of tension between enthusiasm and fear, between knowing the dangers and fearing the dangers, that energy had developed which had let me outgrow myself.

I had dreamed of adventures all my life. For forty years no one had been able to deflect me from my projects; not my parents, not my teachers, not my critics. Have I not the right to stake my life in order to be able to live it?

But Toni's words got under my skin. Perhaps because he knew more about life than I did. His objections weighed more than those of an intellectual. Despite his naïvety, he knew more about the Antarctic than any desk johnny or bureaucrat. Toni did not think about a person dropping out of middle-class life to seek adventure. This other existence of mine did not interest him. He could well imagine such a life as men had had to lead for thousands of years in order to survive. He knew too that man was capable of surviving for months under such hard environmental conditions as were to be expected in the Antarctic: −30°C, constant wind, always alone. His whole life had been proof of that. For him it was about not losing his neighbour. Also about keeping here the father of a daughter whom he saw every day out walking.

There was in South Tyrol little tradition concerning the Arctic and Antarctic. South Tyrolean folk had been competent mountaineers for two hundred years, mountain guides too, and tourism in the country went back to these early pioneers. Everybody knew the mountains to some extent. No one from South Tyrol had ever been to the Poles. Three people had crossed Greenland in 1983 and 1872 two mountain farmers from the Passeiertal, Johann Haller and Alexander Klotz, had accompanied Julius Payer, the famous explorer of the Ortler group, in the direction of the North Pole. That was all. They had been members of the subsequently famous Tegetthoff expedition which was to discover Franz Josef Land. We South Tyroleans had not been attracted to the Poles.

In the weeks before departure it frequently happened that someone in the street, in the bank, in the restaurant spoke to me and asked: 'Aha, off to Alaska this time?' Patiently, I replied, over and over: 'No,

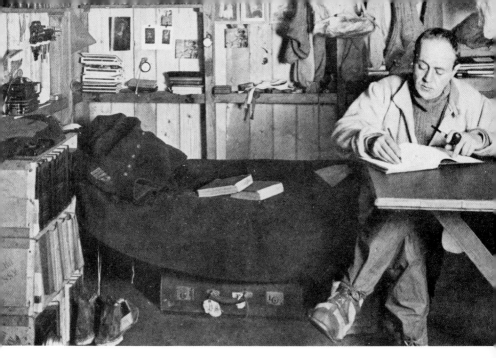

Robert F. Scott spent four winters in the Antarctic. At the start of the fifth winter he perished with his team.

to Antarctica'. So as to make it short and sweet, and the explanation unequivocal, mostly I emphasized I was going to the South Pole.

The South Pole was only a staging post on this journey, though naturally a key point. We wanted to march across the Antarctic continent from the South American to the New Zealand side, to reach the sea at McMurdo. Part of this route was that by which Scott had reached the South Pole in 1912 and on which he had lost his life whilst returning.

Toni was not to be shaken off. He remained standing by the car. He wanted an answer. Questioningly, he gazed at me with his youthful eyes. Still he thought he could restrain me from this Antarctic adventure. 'I'll be back in the spring', I told him. It was meant as a comfort. He was not satisfied with it. 'Toni, it will soon pass.' And, after a bit: 'I'll make it.'

Toni insisted: 'Don't go!'. And again: 'It's no longer necessary. You have shown that you know everything. You don't have to prove it.'

'Yes', I said, 'you're right. I have nothing more to prove. But I must go there.'

'You don't have to at all!'

'I *must* go', I went on after a while. 'I can't sit all my life here in Juval. Juval is finished. It is a fantastic place. In Juval I am at home, but in the long term not happy. I shall return, for Magdalena's sake, for your sake, for Sabine's sake. For all your sakes. Above all, for my own sake. I am attached to life, and', I said grinning, 'I enjoy it here so much, Toni, you can be sure I shall return!'

I took my leave and drove down the steep mountain road into the valley. To the south I could see part of the mountain castle. There the ruins stood which I had designed as a Zen garden and otherwise left as they had been. A standing stone among them symbolized the mountain, a prone one the desert. From there I could see the movement of the clouds and gaze at the stars at night, as I lay amongst the walls, thinking of nothing. I was not leaving Juval for good now. It was definite that I would return in a few days to fetch some more bits of equipment and to take my leave. I drove past the home farm from which I managed my affairs and a wine shop with some local helpers. Here I had created a self-sufficient oasis which gave me security, free of all fears and cares.

I was sleeping badly and for days had been taking sleeping tablets. They didn't help. It was many years since I last used such expedients! Now I was waking up about three o'clock in the morning, sometimes bathed in a sweat of fear, sometimes despairing, and not getting to sleep again. Imagination played tricks on me about the Antarctic. Like in a film. No amount of planning was proof against so many impressions. My own experiences and my Antarctic studies mingled in my subconscious into an alpine dream. The fears came ever more frequently. Fears such as I had experienced as a five-year old below my first peak. Then at age fifteen beneath my first big Dolomite face, before my first extreme climbing route. Fears like that time when, at twenty-five, I had set off in 1970 for the Rupal Face on Nanga Parbat, to the highest rock and ice wall on earth, my first eight-thousander. Again, ten years later, I had experienced similar fears when I had climbed, alone and without artificial oxygen, to the summit of Mount

Everest during the monsoon. Now, at forty-five, these fears gripped me at the thought of the Antarctic crossing.

It was interesting how the change from one sort of adventure to another gave me a lot of energy, a thrust of enthusiasm. Simultaneously, I experienced these retarding fears.

Because I needed to sleep, I took tablets. I wanted to be rested. For that reason I remember only some of these anxiety dreams. There I saw myself with someone, who was not identifiable, going into an endless snow plain. It was not the size of the landscape, nor the whiteness, which terrified me. Rather it was the inner emptiness, the forlornness, the hopelessness of there being no path. Never before had I experienced futility so vehemently. On a mountain there was an up and a down, the country lane had a direction, but Antarctica was endless and without direction. I did not know from where these images came. They occupied me not only in dreaming. I had come to know the Antarctic only as a mountaineer and it had thrilled me. For the time being everything was only a project, developed from my idea. My planned expedition, which was to begin in a few weeks, dominated me completely. Yet I was no ice traveller. Also I did not know from whence came the many fears which would not let me sleep.

I have two daughters. A nine-year old who lives in Canada and a two-year old with me at Juval. Magdalena, my second child, could run but not talk. So she asked no questions. She gazed at me with great eyes as I packed cases. For months now she had known that packing cases meant going away. I sensed that later on she would ask questions about my journey and I was glad about it.

Was I justified in going to the Antarctic now? That question did not trouble me. Only a fool could exclude death on such a trip from the outset. I knew that I could perish in the Antarctic but I did not believe it. Faith is stronger than knowledge.

After studying the history of the geographical 'conquest' of Antarctica, my fear of failure increased. The early explorers, above all those who, at the beginning of this century, had attempted to get to the South Pole and back, were familiar to me: Shackleton, Amundsen, Scott. In similar manner as they, we wanted also to get to the South

'Man-hauling': or, pulling the sledge full of provisions oneself. By this method Nansen and his team crossed Greenland's inland ice in 1888.

Pole and further: under our own steam, with the simplest means. Exposed to the storms, the cold, the loneliness. In the same endlessly great vastness.

During my earlier years of adventure I exposed myself to growing criticism, part of which came from nature lovers, who considered I would make the last primeval landscapes on this earth attractive to the tourist industry. I understood their concern and tried to leave behind no evidence of my passing. A second part came from citizens, who were indirectly angry with themselves, when they saw one person living out his dreams to the ultimate. But, above all, I understood a third group of critics: my nearest neighbours. They considered my activities irresponsible. That somebody should think it right to evade his middle-class responsibilities was an affront to their morality. That I, despite my family commitments, for months escaped from day-to-day pressures, in order to follow my private ambitions, was for them not justifiable. Therefore I did not try. I accepted the criticism and

26

stuck to my individualism. I would have to stand by it further when, time and again, I led my body and mind to the limit of their possibilities. Only then am I satisfied, well-balanced, bearable. I am convinced that mankind would be a more peaceful race if, now and then, each person had a chance to stretch himself to the limit of his capabilities. Peace presupposes not only free nations, but is only possible when *all* people can develop themselves as *whole* people.

In my final school years I had already perceived that my path to knowledge would lead not via libraries and professors, or universities and intense studies. My path was life and raw experience. I could only learn so much second hand – nothing surpassed my experiences in the wilderness. All my knowledge of social, natural history and religious matters was based on experiences which I myself had had. That was one of the reasons why I forced myself again and again to take up a new expedition, to begin a new journey. How often had I said to myself whilst away that enough is enough! Yet, weeks later, when the exertion, the worries and the drudgery were forgotten, I began to dream of a new challenge, a new journey to plan. Soon I was on my way once again and, invariably, it was a dangerous undertaking. No, I did not want to risk life and limb! But I knew that, if I were one day no longer to dream, no longer able to travel, I would be old and despairing.

2 The Plan

Three times I had tried to get to Antarctica: in 1983, 1984 and 1986. In December 1986 I landed at last at the foot of the Ellsworth Mountains. In order to be able to climb Mount Vinson, I had flown half-way round the world with two friends, Oswald Oelz and Wolfgang Thomaseth. At just 5,000 metres above sea-level, Mount Vinson is the highest mountain in the Antarctic. It counts as one of the seven peaks which a few climbing freaks designate as the 'Seven Summits': respectively, the highest mountains on the continents of Europe, Asia, South America, North America, Africa, Australasia and Antarctica. For years a few prosperous alpinists played a game which was as silly as tourists ticking off the number of countries they were able to visit. I joined in the game too. I had climbed South America's highest peak, Aconcagua, by its South Face, and Mount McKinley by the 'Wall of the Midnight Sun'. Elbrus, highest summit in Europe, I had experienced in a snow storm. Twice I had stood on top of Mount Everest and twice on Kilimanjaro. In Australasia I had climbed the Carstenz Pyramid in New Guinea. Now I also had to 'do' Mount Vinson if I didn't want to fall behind in this childish game. The sum total of these ascents resulted in no special performance, but they impressed the media public.

Six of the seven mountains I had known for years. My ambition, with Mount Vinson, to climb the seventh, was greater than my wish to experience the seventh continent.

The Antarctic occupied my imagination but I did not know much about it in practical terms. Vaguely, I knew the books by Scott and Amundsen, the expeditions by Filchner and Shackleton who, at the beginning of the century, had tried to cross Antarctica. For the rest, my knowledge of the Antarctic consisted of clichés: sterile, unimaginably big, cold. The only emotional attraction to the South Pole I had was a recollection from my time at school. We had read Scott's diary,

*My friend Oswald Oelz, one of the 'Seven Summiters', and Wolfgang Thomaseth,
who traversed Greenland, at the foot of Mount Vinson in the Antarctic.*

an heroic and sad story, the end of which had stuck in my mind. On
29 March 1912 Robert F. Scott died in a snowstorm, eighteen
kilometres away from his next supply depot. With thirty opium
tablets in reserve, the Englishman gradually succumbed to death in his
tent from exposure.

I was fascinated by Shackleton's third Antarctic journey. After his
failure to reach the South Pole, this old hand had developed the bold
plan of crossing the Antarctic. The polar-experienced 'Shack', as his
men called him, was the second man who resolved to traverse the ice
continent from one side to the other. For 'Shack', the outcome was
much worse than for the German Filchner. When, in the closing
months of 1914, he sailed for the South Atlantic in his reinforced ship
Endurance, there began a singular odyssey. Not once did the ship get as
far as the *Deutschland* under Captain Filchner. Without erecting a shore
base, without even seeing the Antarctic coast, Shackleton's *Endurance*
stuck fast in the pack ice, was frozen in, then crushed by the towering
ice floes until she sank. How Sir Ernest and his men coped with the

Ernest Shackleton and the wreckage of his Endurance *in the Weddell Sea. The ship was destroyed by the pressure of the ice.*

months of dragging their boats, spent the winter under lifeboats on the drifting ice, survived on storm-whipped rock islands, and at last were all rescued, is one of the most exciting adventure stories of all time.

I had organized my 1986 trip to Antarctica through Adventure Network International (ANI). This private Canadian organization, which flies mountaineers and tourists to Antarctica, is still young. In order to open up the interior of the Antarctic, a handful of outdoor specialists and pilots had built up a logistical chain which allowed them, with two-engined Twin-Otters, to get from Punta Arenas in southern Chile as far as the Ellsworth Mountains. We flew along the Antarctic peninsula to a base camp at an altitude of about 2,000 metres. Thus Mount Vinson was accessible to mountaineers with only two weeks to spare.

After I had reached the summit with 'Wolfi' Thomaseth, a South Tyrol cameraman, and Dr Oswald Oelz, my expedition friend of

Test run (December 1986) with a sledge weighing 80 kilos, in the vicinity of ANI Camp at the foot of Mount Vinson. Was 'Shack's' idea realizable?

many years, there was still plenty of time in base camp before the experienced polar pilot Giles Kershaw could fetch us with the 'Twotter', as he called his red and white aircraft.

I was sitting in the middle of the Antarctic. Mount Vinson had been easier to climb than I had expected. To be sure, the wind had torn at our clothing constantly and the cold had crept under our skin but, nonetheless, the Antarctic was accessible. That was the impression which remained with me. In base camp, I discussed with 'Wolfi' Thomaseth the possibility of putting Shackleton's plan into practice. Together with Robert Peroni and Sepp Schrott, two more South Tyroleans, 'Wolfi' had crossed Greenland in 1983. In eighty-eight days they had covered a stretch of nearly 1,100 kilometres, pulling the provision sledges themselves. Was it possible to walk across the Antarctic continent in this style: 3,000 kilometres in 120 days? With ANI as logistical support? Perhaps so.

During these days I began to experiment with a sledge which was lying around in camp. I loaded it with eighty kilos and pulled it across the snow surface. I made a good 4 kilometres per hour. The theoretical calculation showed that I could pull an approximately eighty-kilo sledge 3,000 kilometres across Antarctica in 100 days. I began to calculate further: in four months, assuming two depots, I could get from one side of the Antarctic to the other. Via the South Pole. The march, which Shackleton had called 'the most fascinating land journey on earth', was conceivable. And it was still available. A singular situation! In 1989, seventy-five years after Shackleton's start, I wanted to make a journey in such a way as no one had attempted it before. I wanted to traverse Antarctica, which is bigger than Australia, under my own steam: not with dog sledges, as Filchner and Shackleton had intended; not with aircraft and chain-driven motor vehicles, like the modern conquerors; but rather on foot. On skis, pulling the sledge with provisions and equipment myself. No exhaust fumes, no noise of engines, only the rustling of the skis and sledge runners on the snow crust. That was my style! A march through the unpredictable white desert.

At that time, on the homeward journey from Mount Vinson, I heard for the first time of the idea 'World Park Antarctica'. On our overcrowded planet, the Antarctic serves as a sort of dream-land. The air there is pure, the summer sun shines longer than in southern Europe. In winter it is always night. What would happen if the protectors of the environment did not prevail? The tug of war over the Antarctic had long since begun. The resources, which were presumed to be under the earth, enticed ever more nations to the seventh continent. But who was showing people how singular and, for that reason, worthy of protection the Antarctic was? Certainly not its exploiters.

Antarctica is the coldest, driest, stormiest, most inaccessible and hostile region on earth. At the same time, the most peaceful of all the continents: heaven and hell alike. Next to nothing grows there, although 70 per cent of the earth's fresh water is stored in the gigantic ice-cap.

Previously, only 'official expeditions', that is scientists who worked in the national research stations, could survive on the ice continent. Nevertheless, this ice desert at the edge of the world had remained a

Ice mountains and the continental mainland beyond the Ross Sea. The exploitation of Antarctica's natural resources is inexcusable, above all on account of the transport danger.

paradise. Here world peace was still a reality. The Antarctic has been a weapon-free territory for thirty years, and there is a working treaty which regulates the human presence. Every state which is a member of the United Nations Organization (UNO) or which is invited by one of the Treaty signatories can accede to the Treaty. Nearly thirty states have done this so far. Of these, so far only the twelve original signatories and those who actively research in the Antarctic hold the status of Consultative member. Currently, these nineteen states are: USA, USSR, United Kingdom, France, Norway, Belgium, Argentina, Chile, Japan, Australia, New Zealand, South Africa, Poland, India, Brazil, Germany, China, Uruguay and Italy. They vote on controversial issues.

The first success of the co-operation was a convention about the preservation of animal life of the Antarctic sea and an attempt to exchange scientific data among one another. The Antarctic Treaty is to be renewed in 1991. Is it not threatened by too many materialistic

33

considerations? Some believe that from the natural resources, which lie under the Antarctic ice-cap, gigantic profits are to be made. Others figure out returns with the sale of technology for the drilling of oil or through tourism.

Big oilfields, precious metal deposits and tourism are the magnets which ever more entice people into the Antarctic, not the original, the unadulterated landscape. Already the question is being discussed as to how the potential resources can be fetched out of the ice.

In the Antarctic Treaty the question of what belongs to whom is shelved. So far claims have not been committed to paper. No one had the courage to exclude a territorial division for all time. Now the twenty supervising powers of the Antarctic Treaty want to regulate how discovered or potential natural resources can be developed and whether they can or should be developed. Instead of excluding all usage from the outset, on account of the ecological threat from mining and transport, a game of poker is being played.

New stations, ever bigger research ships and airfields have been built. Poor countries, for example Peru, fear the Antarctic could come under the hammer without their presence. They have quickly set in motion some research in order to secure for themselves a future say in the matter.

Antarctica is the common heritage of mankind, like the sea and the air. Who defends this heritage? In Antarctica, where apparently men have never lived in earlier times, there should be no rights of sovereignty. It needs only an environmental police; still better, an environmental consciousness. Control of the Treaty community through the UNO is not only important on account of the riches of the undisturbed continent but, above all, on account of its sensitive ecological balance.

Two hundred years ago, when the British explorer James Cook sailed around the Antarctic for the first time, it was 'Terra Incognita'. Whether a hundred years ago an American seal hunter was the first to set foot on the ice or a thousand years ago a South American aborigine suffered shipwreck on the Antarctic peninsula, is irrelevant. National symbols of this sort are a farce in the 'home of ice and storm'. Norwegians were the first to endure a winter on the ice. Norwegians were the first to reach the South Pole. Americans sent the first aircraft there. The British were the first to traverse the continent. The first Antarctic child was born in 1978 in an Argentine station. Regional claims cannot be derived from that. Nevertheless, since 1943, seven countries have claimed wedge-shaped portions of the Antarctic continent for themselves: the United Kingdom, France, Norway, Australia, New Zealand, Chile and Argentina. Australia claims almost half the continent. The principal research base of the US stands on the piece claimed by New Zealand on McMurdo Sound. The situation on the Antarctic peninsula could become explosive where the regional claims of the United Kingdom, Chile and Argentina overlap. The peninsula is so important because it rises in the relatively ice-free water near the South American land tip. On King George Island, off the tip of the peninsula, seven research stations lie together like eggs under a hen.

To be sure, the Antarctic Treaty leaves all territorial claims in suspense, but who defends it? The former Chilean President Pinochet has kissed the ground of Antarctica, given stirring speeches there, without the claimants for the peninsula declaring war on him. The Argentines have held a cabinet meeting on the ice and no one took offence. Were it not a protest against all country names if one were to walk right across the continent: without passport, without permission, without ministry back up? With this background I wanted, by my journey, to demonstrate the wilderness of Antarctica, its beauty. To point to the problems of its development, exploitation and division. There is no fair arrangement for its possible use. There can be only renunciation for the benefit of the wilderness. So long as no one really knows the commercial value of the continent, a world park can still be enforced. Thus my haste.

The old Antarctic Treaty does not run out irrevocably in 1991. It can be revised, however, in this year at the request of a contracting party. That is both an opportunity and a danger. Meanwhile, a growing fleet of support ships negotiate their way summer after summer through the girdle of drift ice. In the research stations are stored millions of litres of oil. Each leak in a tank means a catastrophe! How big would the ecological risks become if the transport of drilled oil from the Antarctic began? Unthinkable.

Like a patchwork quilt, in summer a gigantic girdle of pack ice swims around Antarctica. In winter the ice-floes freeze together.

The American and Soviet commitments in Antarctica are so far comparable. No one has promoted tourist activities until recently; in many cases people have tried to hinder them. Now tourism entrepreneurs stand in the starting blocks with ambitious projects. Chile has built the first hotel for Antarctic visitors. It is to be the tourists' doorway to the South Pole. Argentines celebrate weddings on the ice continent. Germany, only lately acceded to the Treaty, draws level with the superpowers in its research endeavours. Its ice-breaker *Polarstern* is one of the most modern research ships on the high seas.

The Alfred Wegener Institute (AWI) for Polar and Ocean Research, according to its leader Prof. Dr Hempel, 'wants to contribute to the exploration of the Antarctic. It feels itself jointly responsible for the future of the South Polar region.' We hope that it remains so. In the season 1986–87, Italy set up its station in Terra Nova Bay, which is to be further developed. Until now any reclaimable raw material in Antarctica is of relatively little commercial value, for the opening up of the 'riches' is unimaginably difficult. In each case, it is ecologically irresponsible. The route from the ice to the rest of the world is very risky and the ice continent with its surrounding waters exceedingly sensitive ecologically. Thus, not only the high costs of reclamation should deter us from fetching fossil fuels from Antarctica, it is above all the transport through the ice which no one can justify.

The future of the continent depends on the question of who is to protect it. For that reason the Antarctic must not be shared out. In order to hinder an international race for exploitation ravaging the virgin land, the Greenpeace protestors do not suffice. Most people must feel something for their heritage, and we can only defend the Antarctic when we grasp its beauty. The true worth of the still undisturbed continent to mankind is not measured in dollars. It is measured only by the quality of wilderness, which is naturally peaceful, endless and beautiful. To experience wilderness is my calling. For three decades I have followed it with enthusiasm, obsessively. Whosoever listens to me experiences my respect for the wild, my worries about earth's last reserves; not my records, victories or discoveries. I am no conqueror and no geographer. I am a person who gets on well in the wilderness, who can thereby convey to other people insights and outlooks, which they can never experience for themselves. I try, when travelling in the wilderness, to be a spokesman for this wilderness, prompting millions of people to learn to esteem, love and defend it.

On the homeward journey from Mount Vinson, I began to reflect on the financing of my new expedition. I needed sponsors, special pieces of equipment, the right partners. The practical preparation of such an Antarctic crossing was certainly harder than all other things afterwards. For a year I worked at my plan sporadically. Thus I got to know from Jürgen Lehmann, a friend with Bavaria Film Gesellschaft in Munich, who had made several documentary films with me, that a German adventurer was pursuing another project in the Antarctic: an expedition with dog sledges. He was called Arved Fuchs, was from North Germany and a seaman with Arctic experience. I knew of him from outdoor activities literature. He had crossed Greenland in 1983. His difficult water and land journeys in Canada and South America had impressed me.

As yet I had not decided on my team. One thing, however, was obvious: for this journey I needed a partner who had experience in ice travel, could navigate and was ready to go through hell. Was Arved Fuchs the right man? He was a skilled seaman, thirty-five years old, had extreme trips under his belt. With dog sledges he had crossed the Greenland ice-cap. In a one-man canoe he had paddled around Cape Horn in winter. As a member of an international expedition, in spring 1989 he marched across the brittle drift ice to the North Pole.

I mulled over it before I asked Lehmann to let Fuchs know about my scheme. If Fuchs wanted to join the party, he was to get in touch with me. I would have been delighted to go with a 'mountain man' again. I was familiar with them. My climbing friends were all very fit and were enthusiastic about the Antarctic. However, the more intensively I occupied myself with my Antarctic project, the clearer it became to me that a seaman was better as a partner. He had to be a specialist in ice travel, not a mountaineer, and also a navigator and radio operator. There was no doubt: Arved Fuchs was the ideal partner for an Antarctic crossing. Would he join me?

While I was planning and organizing, I read more and more about earlier Antarctic expeditions and suddenly I noticed that, subconsciously, for many years I had been interested in the ice continent. There were some Antarctic books in my library. I had collected maps and pictures. I yearned for reality. The beginnings of this longing I could not remember exactly. First, in 1986, after the ascent of Mount Vinson, a subconscious wish had become a day-dream. A few weeks later I had developed that concept of an Antarctic traverse which was to become a fixed idea. For four months, from the end of October 1989 to mid-February 1990 I wanted to travel in the Antarctic summer, to make the 3,000-kilometre plus crossing from the Filchner Shelf Ice via the South Pole to Ross Island on the other side. Each further study of my literature strengthened my conviction of having to make this journey.

At the end of his voyage in 1774, Cook, the discoverer of Antarctica, summed up the results of the expedition:

James Cook was impressed by the overwhelming ice scenery of the Antarctic.
Nevertheless, more than one hundred years were to pass before anyone set foot on the
ice continent.

38

Shackleton got to know the Antarctic with Scott. On his own first expedition – using pony sledges part of the way – he got almost as far as the South Pole.

Thus, after we had luckily escaped from innumerable dangers and had had to battle with countless difficulties and resistances, we brought at last our journey to a happy conclusion; it had lasted three years and eighteen days, in which time we have made by our reckoning a voyage longer than any other to date. If we add up all our reckonings, we arrive at a distance which corresponds to more than three times the circumference of the globe. We were likewise lucky enough to lose only four of our ship's company, of whom three died through unlucky accidents, while the fourth suffered a disease which, had he remained in England, would have perhaps carried him off even sooner. The most important task of our journey, to be on the look out for a southern mainland of moderate climate, was resolved. We had even investigated the frozen sea within the southern polar circle, without being able to find that extensive mainland which one had earlier supposed must lie there. At the same time we had made yet another scientifically significant discovery: namely that

nature forms large ice masses in the ocean which, devoid of all salt particles, have the useful and wholesome properties of water. At other times of the year we crossed the Pacific Ocean between the tropics of the temperate zone, where we discovered for the geographers new islands, for the naturalists new plants and birds and, above all, for the friends of humanity new races with unknown living customs.

Although Cook advised against further voyages of discovery in the direction of Antarctica, Amundsen praised him highly:

A great act of seamanship was accomplished here and rightly one names Cook the greatest sea hero of his century.

Cook wrote of the 'unspeakably terrible sight' of this ice continent, 'never to yield to the warmth of the sun'. He was quite certain that no man would ever venture further than he had done, and that the region in the extreme south would never be investigated. Amundsen was able to refute Cook, but nevertheless, he respected this splendid seafarer:

Few people nowadays have a proper understanding of this act of heroism, only a few grasp what courage and contempt for death was necessary in order to take on themselves such a great risk. With two heavily manoeuvrable ships – by today's notions veritable boxes – these people travelled into the heart of the pack-ice and with that did something which, by the unanimous declarations of all earlier polar travellers meant certain ruin.

Earlier explorers were often, once underway, involuntarily overtaken by adventure. They had then to risk everything in order to come through unscathed. We, who today know much more, intentionally attempt to bring about circumstances in which we can perish. The rules and the art of survival, behaviour outside the usual norms of society – inner experiences remain the same as for the adventurer in the classic mould, whether he goes only to sea as in Cook's day or makes a sledge journey to the South Pole.

The books by Ernest Shackleton about the interior of Antarctica captivated me more than all the others. I read the report of his 1907–09 expedition, which had been published under the title *The Heart of the Antarctic*, several times. His description of the landscape, the daily problems, the sweating, grinding drudgery – all was so vividly described that it became graphically comprehensible. Shackleton loved the Antarctic with a love I had not considered possible:

> The sunsets in the beginning of April [1908] were wonderful; arches of prismatic colours, crimson and golden-tinged clouds, hung in the heavens nearly all day, for time was going on and soon the sun would have deserted us. The days grew shorter and shorter, and the twilight longer. During these sunsets the western mountains stood out gloriously and the summit of Erebus was wrapped in crimson when the lower slopes had faded into grey. To Erebus and the western mountains our eyes turned when the end of the long night grew nearer in the month of August, for the mighty peaks are the first to catch up and tell the tale of the coming glory and the last to drop the crimson mantle from their high shoulders as night draws on. Tongue and pencil would sadly fail in attempting to describe the magic of the

Marshall, Shackleton, Adams and Wild back on their ship Nimrod. *The four almost got to the Pole.*

colouring in the days when the sun was leaving us. The very clouds at this time were iridescent with rainbow hues. The sunsets were poems. The change from twilight into night, sometimes lit by a crescent moon, was extraordinarily beautiful, for the white cliffs gave no part of their colour away, and the rocks beside them did not part with their blackness, so the effect of deepening night over these contrasts was singularly weird.

When, on 29 October 1908, Shackleton, Marshall, Adams and Wild set out on their march of discovery – the South Pole was by their reckoning about 1,400 kilometres away from the point of departure – there began one of the most dangerous adventures in the history of mankind.

29 October 1908. A glorious day for our start; brilliant sunshine and a cloudless sky, a fair wind from the north, in fact, everything that could conduce to an auspicious beginning. We had breakfast at 7 a.m., and at 8.30 a.m. the sledges that the motor was to haul to Glacier Tongue were taken down by the penguin rookery and over to the rough ice. At 9.30 a.m. the supporting party started and was soon out of sight, as the motor was running well. At 10 a.m. we four of the Southern Party followed. As we left the hut where we had spent so many months in comfort, we had a feeling of real regret that never again would we all be together there.

After four months the men were back. They had not reached the Pole but they were alive. When, three years later, Scott and his men got to the Pole by the same route, Amundsen had been there already. The South Pole was 'conquered'.

Thereupon Shackleton developed his plan of crossing the Antarctic but this attempt was to flounder before it even started.

Vivian Fuchs, a British geologist, and the New Zealander Edmund Hillary, first man to climb Mount Everest, were able to translate this old plan into action at last in 1957–58. With tractors and Sno-cats, they drove across the Antarctic. This first overland crossing, however, was so far removed from Shackleton's original idea that I could not respect it. In the old style, as the pioneers had of necessity practised it, the traverse had still not been done.

Arved Fuchs called me. We had a long conversation and I liked him straight away. We reached the decision to attempt the journey with just the two of us. This proposal came from him. Originally, I had thought of a three-man group because an additional man meant more security. But two's company, three's a crowd. I gave way. With two the trip was a bigger risk. Should one injure himself, the other could not help him. However, even with three members, in an accident two would not have been able to drag the injured man as far as the other side of the Antarctic. Arved's argument that the inner peace of two gave greater security, convinced me. Three men were not a good combination. In difficult situations, over many weeks, three or four of us would certainly have got in each other's hair. I did not want to quarrel, I wanted to succeed. In a trio there is always one who feels left

Arved Fuchs in Antarctica. He is without doubt Germany's most experienced 'ice traveller'. Robert Swan invited him to join his North Pole expedition.

out in a discussion, weaker. Quickly we united ourselves into a joint expedition for the 1989–90 Antarctic summer.

Slowly, I initiated Arved into my exact plans, whereby it was confirmed from the start that navigation was to be his job. Only because *he* too had wanted this journey from the outset, did I consider him to be my partner. That was presumably why later on he was able to feel that this journey was his idea; and that was important for success. We were no longer two individuals, we were two adventurers, who wanted the same thing. We were a team.

Arved was not someone who constantly risked his life. He went on 'journeys'. The crossing of Antarctica under his own steam, on foot, was to be his big, his 'maximum trip'. Arved lived in Bad Bramstedt, a middle-class brick idyll between Hamburg and Kiel. For the inhabitants of Bramstedt, Arved Fuchs was neither a 'drop-out' nor a daredevil. He was a cosmopolitan who was plagued with the wander-lust sickness. His grandfather had been to sea, likewise his uncle. Arved had experienced the heat of Borneo and the cold of Labrador in his search for locations which suited him. Now he knew where he belonged: in the cold, in the north and the south. Time and again he had to travel – to Alaska, to Greenland, to Tierra del Fuego. He became a polar fox. Soon he knew what it was all about. A pragmatician, holding back, slow, but determined.

Were his expeditions childhood dreams come true? No, rather flights of fancy which he organized with compass and map, away from the metropolis, where nature had become for most people something abstract. His journeys were also a protest against capital-ized nature. Environmentally conscious, he travelled without material interests. 'Nature does not need us, we need nature.' With this dictum we met and became partners. We wanted not only to complement each other in the ice of the Antarctic, we had to gel beforehand, as it were, to make the expedition possible.

Again, there was much criticism before this expedition. But I under-stood those desk-bound folk, who sat out their time at home or in an office, yet would rather have walked across the Antarctic with me. As they consciously experienced neither a budding self-criticism nor the summons to alter their lives, they had to react aggressively towards me. Not because I was a 'superman', rather because I provoked them by my actions. As time and again I placed my life in question, I called into question their lives also. Despite family, despite my forty-five years, despite that questionable fame which, in the middle-class mind, guaranteed me an existence, I was again once more ready to put my life on the line.

In Spring 1989 Arved marched to the North Pole – as a member of Robert Swan's Icewalk Expedition. I first experienced Icewalk and their programme later on. However, I knew nothing of the people who tried to establish the dubious German branch of Swan's 'Icewalk' idea in Hamburg as an 'environmental organization'. My expedition was not an Icewalk initiative, Arved being my only partner. We both had our concepts concerning the environmental problem in Antarc-tica. Arved was an environmental protector from the start. He advanced his concerns with such clarity that I never doubted that they were important to him. Nevertheless, in summer 1989 people warned

Spherical compass, Magellan-GPS device, ice-axe, inner boots, piss-pot. Arved and I shared the job of obtaining equipment.

me: 'Look out, he is a member of Icewalk'. 'So what?' How often I had been warned about partners because someone would gladly have taken their place. Only one thing disturbed me. Arved entrusted a 'manager' with his business affairs and public relations work. Whosoever needs a manager and lets him attend to his image, facelessly, is suspect to me. Except for Arved. 'In the end he won't be fit, will leave you dangling and then play the hero', warned Paul Hanny, a friend of mine. 'As usual', I laughed, firmly convinced that in Arved I had found a persevering and intelligent partner.

'Reinhold, take care that it doesn't happen again.'

'I know, Paul, it could happen again but ought I to stay at home for that reason?'

'Every time backers have intervened in your expeditions, they have been falsely represented afterwards. You, the star, are only taken advantage of.'

'You're right.'

'Look for a partner without a manager.'

'There's no one better than Arved Fuchs.'

With that the discussion ended for me. No, this time it would turn out otherwise. The poachers could go and jump in the lake. How I despised them, these backers to whom, ultimately, it was all about business; and the best business was in any case my good name.

It has never mattered to them, to mark me with lies and half truths. The aim of these backers had always been to put me down as the publicity-seeking slave driver, who gained in stature after each successful adventure at cost to his partner. That this was untrue, because I had planned, financed and organized the journeys myself, was understood only by the objective observers. Best of all, the managers and friends of some of my climbing partners had denounced me so thoroughly in the media after the respective expeditions, that they could 'make' themselves Number One. And, because they did not succeed in taking away my self-esteem, I sought new partners time and again. And always the best.

Arved, the navigator, seemed to understand. Moreover, he was an organization freak. Fascinated by the play of forces – fear, ambition, inertia, will – like me, he looked for problem situations in nature. Yet, he did not want to be a hero. He could handle his adventures excellently, better than all those with whom I had climbed.

But, did he like people?

He liked giving lectures but felt himself easily isolated in a crowd. 'Fundamentally I am not a man the masses like.' We were similar in many respects, also in this one. We were spared the masses too for the most part. Best of all, both of us went the long, lonely, icy way. Harmony between action and thinking led to accord with nature and, if all bridges were demolished, we found our own way.

> Worst are the first few hours. To know that I shall not see my girlfriend for weeks. No one to talk to but myself. There remains only my diary, the only material thing which I take on each journey.

Arved was a lone wolf, subject to his own laws. A tiny, warm speck in the icy landscape, free in the Schopenhauer sense:

On his march to the South Pole, Robert F. Scott had support teams for transporting supplies. Seventy-six years later, Robert Swan renounced this.

Each of us is only complete in himself when he is alone; whosoever, therefore, loves not loneliness, loves also not freedom.

This profound sentence separated us. Two persons isolated in a world without time, are two alone. Day after day, for better or worse, eyeball to eyeball, each with himself. I knew all the masks would come off.

Navigation was Arved's responsibility, also the procurement of the necessary apparatus. As radio operator, he was to maintain contact with the outside world. Moreover, he wanted to bring to the expedition his experiences concerning foodstuffs. My job was the financing of the trip, testing the tents, skis and crampons for crossing the areas of crevasses. I was to organize the journey out to our destination and back home again. We wanted to develop the logistics together. It was clear from the first that Arved was free to look for his own sponsors, without having to contribute a single Deutschmark to the expedition coffers. Also, each of us was to be free to exploit the expedition according to his own ideas. There was no expedition contract between us, no expedition leader. We were equal partners. Before, on the ice and afterwards.

After we had exchanged our experiences and 'probed' each other, it was confirmed we would realize the plan together. We met from time to time. There was a mass of things to work on. Not much time remained, for each of us had other expeditions in mind which required preparation. We both had prior obligations. Gradually, we accustomed ourselves to our common idea, with sketches of sledges, lists of foodstuffs and bulging folders full of maps and letters.

In Sulden am Ortler, we met for the first time to test the tent that was to be our 'home' for four months. Unfortunately, there was too little wind to try out the sails which Arved had brought at the suggestion of a German amateur inventor. They had proved a success as an aid to traction in Greenland and were to be a big advantage in the Antarctic.

Again, I studied old expedition reports. The books by Robert Falcon Scott, Roald Amundsen and above all Robert Swan now comprised all my reading. Swan, from Great Britain, had gone to the South Pole on foot in 1985–86 with two friends, in order to re-enact the stresses which Scott had taken upon himself in 1911–12. This 'Footsteps of Scott' expedition told us how we could overcome an almost twice as long stretch. With his comrades, Swan had been flown out from the South Pole. Nevertheless, we could model ourselves on them; but not on any expedition which had crossed by aircraft or tracked vehicle.

Robert Swan, Roger Mear and Gareth Wood wanted to repeat the adventure of the early polar travellers in the machine age. They renounced machines. They decided to walk from McMurdo to the South Pole 'in the tracks of Scott', pulling their own provision sledges. Distance: 1,420 kilometres.

Exactly seventy-five years after Scott, on 3 November 1985, the three set out. They had rations to get them to the Pole and no advance dumps. They went without radio sets. They wanted 'to feel the same isolation' as Scott and his men who, on their death march, had not been able to call for help.

Like Shackleton, Scott and some of those who crossed Greenland used Siberian ponies as draught animals. Not good tactics in an icy climate.

On the seventieth day of their journey – Scott had taken seventy-eight days – Swan, Mear and Wood reached the South Pole. The American station was the culminating point of their unprecedented march. They spared themselves, however, the hardest part of Scott's expedition: the return march. Too exhausted to go on, and also not prepared for it, they let themselves be brought back to McMurdo by air.

Arved and I could identify ourselves with a string of previous expeditions. In 1902–03, Scott had undertaken the first journey into the interior of the Antarctic. For him it was only the beginning. He deplored uncertainty in relation to tactics and organization: 'To start with we knew neither how much food we must take with us, nor how our cookers worked, we were not once able to erect our tent properly and put on our winter equipment correctly. Nothing had been tried out and the general uncertainty and lack of organization affected us most painfully.'

Ernest Shackleton, one of the three men on Scott's first Antarctic journey, organized his own trip to the ice continent a few years later. His goal: the South Pole. In the summer of 1908–09, together with Marshall, Wild and Adams, he reached the high plateau for the first time across the Beardmore Glacier. Only 87 miles away from the South Pole, the four men gave up, tiredness and lack of rations compelling them to turn back. Suffering from scurvy, with stiff joints, swollen gums and emaciated, four months after setting out, they appeared to their comrades in the coastal base like 'nightmares out of Hell'. They had covered 2,100 kilometres. On the first section – marching over the Ross Shelf Ice – Siberian ponies had pulled the loads which not only reduced the exertion but, above all, made possible the construction of supply dumps for the return march.

In this 'heroic age' of polar exploration, all expeditions took draught animals as aids. On their ships they brought Eskimo dogs and Siberian ponies from the Arctic to the Antarctic. On the ice continent there were no draught animals, not even polar bears or other mammals. The last pony slaughtered, the support team sent back with the decimated dog pack, the men pulled their sledges themselves. Now they had – like the Shackleton expedition – only to feed themselves. 'Man-hauling' was the name of this drudgery whereby loads were moved by human muscle power.

In the race for the South Pole in 1911–12 between Roald Amundsen, the polar expert from Norway, and the British naval officer Robert Falcon Scott, no one asked about the *how*. Questions of style played no part. All that counted was who reached 90° south first. Both men would have used aircraft if they had had them. Amundsen, who had settled for dog sledges, won. He arrived at the Pole with a whole month's lead because he had solved the transport problem better and his route was shorter.

Captain Scott experimented and set out with dogs and ponies. The motorized sledges had already broken down beforehand. The supply organization was soon hopelessly muddled. Scott and his companions still had to drag their provision sledges without help 600 kilometres to the South Pole. On the return march, the prearranged depots were too far apart and they perished.

Scott (second from right) with his tracked vehicle. The machines were not reliable.
Nevertheless, Amundsen feared for his success because of this 'trick'.

Arved and I wanted to pull our sledges ourselves all the way. Between the South Pole and McMurdo Sound there was to be no laid-out depot. If successful, our expedition of more than 3,000 kilometres would be the longest 'man-hauling' one. However, we were not interested in this 'record'. It was necessary on tactical grounds. On Captain Scott's longest and last journey the sledge-pulling had come to an end close to 2,200 kilometres.

How differently Amundsen had travelled! With fifty-two dogs, the Norwegians set out on the conclusive march. Four sledges each with thirteen dogs. They returned with only eleven dogs. Had they so wished, all eighty-six animals which had been employed for load transport to the Pole and back would have survived but, in this case, the sledges would have had to be so heavily laden with dog food that the pack would not have been able to pull them. Already a year before, the Norwegians had begun to lay in food dumps on the route to the Pole; otherwise the journey could not even have been started.

Amundsen's condemned huskies – likewise the condemned ponies

53

COMMEMORATING
THE FIRST
TRANS-ANTARCTIC CROSSING
1957-8

Mr.J.O'Carroll,

20 Balgay S

Ricca

of the Scott expedition – made the gigantic ice world seem fearsome. The terrors of the Antarctic, however, were forced into the consciousness of people through the deaths of all the men of the Scott expedition. Myths developed and fears arose. Only technology was to expel these myths from Antarctica again: the combustion engine driven Ski-doo, aircraft, radios and satellites.

In 1929 the American Richard Byrd was the first to fly to the South Pole. He returned without having landed there. It took him sixteen hours. Captain Scott had been underway 142 days by the time he got to his last camp site.

Lincoln Ellsworth and his pilot Hollick-Kenyon flew over the Antarctic in 1935 in a single-engined Northrop. Because their machine ran out of fuel prematurely, the fliers had to walk the last 200 kilometres back to their base, Camp Little America. They dragged their sledges with the most essential equipment and rations themselves. With that, adventure had acquired a new meaning. An adventure was that which became vital when technology failed. Why

ROSS DEPENDENCY

ROSS DEPENDENCY

ANTARCTICA

SHACKLETON 4d SCOTT

EREBUS

20 JA 58. 1

ROSS DEP.

SCOTT BASE

[STCHURCH   W.1.   N.Z.

Envelope with special postmark of the Fuchs 1957–58 Expedition. With aircraft support and dog sledges as vanguard, the ice continent could be traversed with tractors and tracked vehicles.

should a person pull a sledge across the gigantic mass of ice when he could use a heated snow-mobile or, equally, could fly? The 'man-hauling' expedition had become a joke.

In 1947 President Truman wanted to demonstrate to the Russians that the US Navy could operate in the toughest region on earth. Cold war in the double sense of the word. With thirteen warships and supply vessels, a whole squadron of aircraft and 4,700 men, the US invaded Antarctica with all their technology.

A decade after this 'Operation High Jump', the Antarctic land route was traversed for the first time from coast to coast. The British geologist Vivian Fuchs had organized, with government assistance, a large-scale operation: the Commonwealth Trans-Antarctic Expedition. In the 1957–58 polar summer, it was to 'master' the ice continent with tractors and tracked vehicles! However, the eleven men from Great Britain and New Zealand did not set out on Shackleton's 'last great land journey in history' as he had envisaged it, but rather with two columns of vehicles which rolled across the ice like tanks.

'Shack' had certainly not pictured his journey thus, although he too had settled for technology. He had had a tracked vehicle specially made for the crossing, a forerunner of today's Ski-doo. But such expense! Vivian Fuchs and his crew sat in 'Sno-Cats' which were driven by Chrysler engines and had heated cabins. Four 'Cats' roared with rattling tracks over the ice. The scene resembled a tank offensive. On the other side of the Antarctic, the New Zealand team, led by Hillary, travelled in tractors in the direction of the South Pole. That was no classic polar journey. Crevasses and technical breakdowns were the main problems for Fuchs and Hillary.

> On 27th October there was a white-out and no flying was possible, nor could we guide our slow advance by the mountains, which were now obscured by cloud. We therefore lined up stakes with a compass, and worked towards each other in pairs. Each pair worked side by side, separated by a distance slightly greater than the width of the vehicle tracks. Shuffling forward, each man plunged his wooden or aluminium pole to a depth of five feet every yard, a distance sometimes reduced to a foot or to six inches if there was reason to suspect the area. When a crevasse was found, the cracks along its edges were opened up at one or more points, so that the nature of the filling could be observed. If it appeared unsafe to cross, a diversion would be made to avoid the dangerous part and to return to the original line of march. Fortunately, the curious wide but short nature of the crevasses made this fairly easy; even so it was often necessary to probe routes in three or four directions before a safe passage could be found.

Moreover, there were communications difficulties. And also problems between the star performers Hillary and Fuchs. On 22 December Vivian Fuchs sent a memo to Hillary, who had already pushed on much further towards the Pole:

> Personal for Hillary. We arrived South Ice 21st December after severe crevasse trouble and three major recoveries of Sno-cats. Distance travelled in 29 days 349 miles but consider this worst

One of the tracked vehicles of the 1957–58 Trans-Antarctic Expedition stands today in the museum in Christchurch, New Zealand.

stage of journey and expect rapid travel from here on. Thanks for your information and proposed crevasse recce. Hope you will be able to mark route through or limit of area with snow cairns or stakes. We leave here with four Sno-cats three Weasels one Muskeg will probably reach you with four Cats and one Weasel. Two dog teams will travel ahead. We expect leave South Ice 25th then Otter and four RAF fly there to await suitable day for flight to Scott. Hope for radio contact with you as arranged 26th onwards. Happy Christmas to you all. Bunny [Fuchs].

Hillary arrived at the Pole on 4 January. He stayed a few days and flew back to Scott Base on McMurdo Sound. In a memo to Fuchs he advised him against continuing the Trans-Antarctic expedition:

Dear Bunny. I am very concerned about the serious delay in your plans. It's about 1,250 miles from the Pole to Scott Base, much of the travelling north from D700 being somewhat slow and laborious, with rough hard sastrugi. Leaving the Pole late in January, you will head into increasing bad weather and winter temperatures, plus vehicles that are showing signs of strain. Both of my mechanics regard such a late journey as an unjustifiable risk and are not prepared to wait and travel with your party. I agree with their view and think you should seriously consider splitting your journey over two years. You still probably have a major journey in front of you to reach the Pole. Why not winter your vehicles at the Pole, fly out to Scott Base with American aircraft, return to civilization for the winter, and then fly back into the Pole station next November and complete your journey? This plan would enable you to do a far more satisfactory job of your seismic work, and I feel fairly confident that Admiral Dufek would assist with such a flying programme. Personally I feel the need for a break from the plateau after nearly four months of tractor travel, and there's a lot to do. I prefer not to wait at the Pole station, but will get evacuated to Scott Base as soon as possible. If you decide to continue on from the Pole, I'll join you at D700. Sorry to strike such a sombre note, but it would be unfortunate if the sterling work you've put into making your route through to South Ice and the Pole should all be wasted by the party foundering somewhere on the 1,250 miles to Scott Base. I will go ahead with the stocking of D700, and I will leave at the Pole station full details plus maps of the route from Scott to the Pole. Hillary.

This exchange of views was made public and although the Fuchs group continued their work, the affair escalated in the press into a *cause célèbre*.

Hillary Pole Station. Appreciate your concern, but there can be no question of abandoning journey at this stage. Innumerable reasons make it impracticable to remount the expedition after wintering outside the Antarctic. Our vehicles can be, and have been operated at minus 60 but I do not expect such temperatures by March. White-out and drift will be our chief concern. I

Today tracked vehicles are still used in Antarctica, similar to those used successfully by the Fuchs expedition: ponderous steel giants.

understand your mechanics' reluctance to undertake further travel, and in view of your opinion that late season travel is an unjustifiable risk I do not feel able to ask you to join us at D700 in spite of your valuable local knowledge. We will therefore have to wend our way, using the traverse you leave at the Pole. The present field of giant sastrugi has extended 57 miles so far, and continues with ridges up to 4ft. Are we to expect similar fields north of D700, and approx. how many miles *in toto*? Main damage is to sledge tow bars, which have to be electrically welded causing delay. Am shortly abandoning second vehicle as planned, leaving us four Sno-cats and two Weasels. Max. interval seismic stations 30 miles, gravity stations 15 miles, rammsonde once or twice daily, meteorology includes fluxplate and radiation measurements. Present position 83°43′S, altitude 7,000ft. Bunny.

Nonetheless, Vivian Fuchs met Sir Edmund Hillary, the first man to climb Everest, at the Pole. He, meanwhile, had constructed all the fuel dumps for Fuchs with his motorized support troops from the Ross Sea onwards, had flown back to McMurdo, and returned by aeroplane to the Pole, in order to meet Vivian Fuchs and his crossing crew there.

Despite the advanced season, Fuchs ventured the entire crossing of the Antarctic. With his Sno-cats, he followed Hillary's reconnoitred route towards the Ross Sea. When they entered the American–New Zealand base on McMurdo Sound on 2 March 1958, they were received by journalists who had been flown in. They had covered 3,472 kilometres and taken ninety-nine days. In an irony of technology, one of the Cat drivers appeared to have been poisoned by engine exhaust fumes.

This crawler tractor trip of Vivian Fuchs was certainly a pioneering performance, yet an anachronism. Was it not absurd to undertake a journey in the vastness and stillness of the Antarctic sitting down and thereby constantly exposed to the noise and stink of engines? Trapped in cabins in the purest air on earth, almost to the point of suffocation? In point of fact, 'what technological civilization does on the ice continent, becomes a caricature of this civilization'. This sentence from the American environmental protector, Michael Parfit, held true completely here; and it still holds true.

By my expedition, I did not want to demonstrate the British readiness for sacrifice – I wanted to make relative the use of technology. Therefore the 'revaluation of the value'. 'Man-hauling' versus engine power. For me it was about the human dimension and not about the unlimited possibilities of technology. Whosoever moves in the Antarctic with motor vehicles, helicopters and aircraft, is like a car tourist who squats in his capsule and feels nothing of his surroundings. Arved confirmed: 'He who wants to experience the Antarctic intensively must get far away from aircraft and snow-mobile; even though we need aircraft to get to the ice.'

Already in 1986, when I had developed a definite plan for crossing Antarctica on foot, I found out that in 1989–90 we would have 'competition': an international expedition, led by Jean-Louis Etienne, a French alpinist, and Will Steger, an American dog-breeder, was to be underway at the same time as us, trying to cross the Antarctic with huskies. The six-man team wanted to cross the continent by the

Scott, in the middle, ready to start. His expedition to the South Pole led to tragedy, partly because he was not absolutely in control of any of his three transport methods.

longest possible route; from the Antarctic peninsula to the Pole and on, via the USSR station Vostok to Mirnyj. That was a gigantic stretch of more than 6,000 kilometres, but possible perhaps with dog sledges. Arved and I perceived this expedition not as a competitive undertaking, although the media attempted to present it as such. My plan went back to an historical model. The length of the journey played a subordinate role. Geography prescribed it for us. Shackleton's historical idea of 1914 must be carried out today with the tactics of yesterday. I wanted to prove this hypothesis and with it demonstrate a journey 'by fair means', as I had already done by my ascents of the eight-thousanders without artificial oxygen.

When Arved repeated his proposal to fit out the expedition with sails, which the German Wolf Behringer had developed, I initially remained sceptical. Not on account of the technical aid. No, on account of logistical considerations. What if there were no wind? These sails had been used in Greenland with success and worked in the manner of a kite. They were to help to pull the sledges. With sail assistance, faster progress was possible. Ought we to rely on sailing, however? Without the necessary experience? Only if we could also make it without sail, were our logistics correct.

On the first trial with sail and skis on a South Tyrol glacier I confirmed enthusiastically that the wind indeed was a big help. Although, according to the statistics, we could count on predominantly following winds on the longest stage of our journey, from the Pole to McMurdo, I remained sceptical, not least because Scott had foundered on his death march despite sail assistance. He had mixed several methods of transport together: horse-power, dog-power, man-power and wind-power. Finally, he succumbed to hopelessness. I knew that, on the first crossing of Greenland, Nansen had used sails as a welcome aid. As the basis for movement, however, sails seemed too risky to me.

A second time – this time in mist and wind – I tested this coloured monster which was more similar to a parachute than the classical Nansen sail. The sail swelled like a spinnaker and climbed obliquely upwards like a kite; already I was moving away on my skis before the wind, drawn by the parachute sail which fluttered above me. This 'wonder instrument', which I had tried out first with its Schwabian inventor in Remstal, pleased me more and more. When a strong breeze blew into the sausage-like air pockets, which it comprised, there was no holding it. I had to let down the sail in order to stop. In a good wind it was not difficult to have oneself and the following sledge pulled along. The hardest part was getting the sail off the ground. I fastened the sail in front of my chest with a special harness. The sledge hung from a pulling harness which I wore around my hips. The colourful, feather-light Perlon cloth I steered with cords and a sturdy bar which I held with both fists and could tilt. With the natural energy of the wind I progressed without great exertion, almost 'as in flight'.

So much for theory. Yet what would happen if we could not use the sail on the way to the Pole? If after the Pole there were no wind or the ground did not permit gliding? This means of locomotion could be a help on the riven and bumpy surface of the ice continent but not a permanent means of locomotion. Arved and I agreed on a compromise and two kites for sporadic sail assistance were purchased. Arved placed his faith almost exclusively in sailing. I hoped he was right.

The tactics of our advance altered gradually. By our conversations. By our tests. Neither Arved nor I had developed from the start a correct, unassailable system. Time and again we had to alter it, right up to the last moment. We could not and did not want to organize ourselves according to an inflexible standard. In reality, the difficulties in the Antarctic were to force tactics upon us.

My original plan had been to start from the Filchner Shelf Ice and to get to the Pole by the shortest route across the high plateau. I wanted to reach McMurdo on the other side by Scott's route. However, this variation was expensive. Adventure Network, the only organization which flew private expeditions into Antarctica, demanded a fortune for it. And the Canadians had a monopoly. As I would have had to pay too much to be flown from Patriot Hills, the Adventure Network camp on the edge of the Ellsworth Mountains, to the mainland edge of the Filchner Shelf Ice, I put up with a longer route. Hugh Calver, the manager of ANI, offered to take us to the German Filchner Station for a smaller sum. This summer station at the edge of the Ronne Shelf Ice would also have been an ideal starting point for us. After crossing the Ronne Shelf Ice we would have arrived at Patriot Hills, packed our sledges with fresh food supplies there, and gone on. The next depot was scheduled to be at the Thiel Mountains, almost exactly half-way between Patriot Hills and the Pole. For the second part of the journey, we left undecided for the time being whether we wanted to have an expensive dump installed at Gateway, half-way between the South Pole and McMurdo. Perhaps it would be possible to walk this long stage without help, as Robert Swan had shown. The longest stage ever covered by people without a depot.

In the three years of preparation from 1986 to 1989, I occupied myself not only with the historical opening up of the Antarctic and its geography, but I studied ecological problems too. Winter and sum-mer stations had been operating in the Antarctic for three decades. Only after Greenpeace had established its own tiny station, did the environmental damage become more widely known. In their ship, the Greenpeacers cruised from station to station, taking water samples to test the pollution of the sea water. They observed the behaviour of the wild animals in the vicinity of people. I did not want to increase

Rubbish dump on the edge of Antarctica. As removal is difficult, empty oil drums, parts of prefabricated buildings and muck of all sorts remains in many places. The interior remains wild.

the pollution by my journey. No rubbish was to be left behind – only a track in the snow.

In the hundred years in which man has travelled and 'exploited' the Antarctic continent, the coastline has suffered badly. We wanted to point to that also with our journey.

For Arved and me adventure was our first concern. But we wanted by this traverse also to advocate a standard: respect for wilderness. And we hoped to be able to make clear-cut statements about Antarctica afterwards.

Thus we had four aims. Firstly, we wanted to cross the Antarctic from the American to the New Zealand side via the South Pole. Secondly, we were trying to realize an historical idea. Thirdly, by our foot march, I hoped to give the Antarctic a human dimension. Fourthly, we wanted after our expedition – if we made it – to use our publicity for a 'World Park Antarctica'. But how were we to win people over to the protection of Antarctica? By showing its singular beauty! Only that which we love do we also conserve.

64

In the Antarctic there are thousands of unclimbed peaks. It is definitely harder to reach the foot of these mountains than to climb them.

The wild, white continent, which was only occupied by people at a few points, had to remain so, as it had been for millions of years. So long as Antarctica had been *terra incognita* for mankind, it had been left in peace.

The more I occupied myself with it, the more it became clear to me that the singularity of the Antarctic consisted of values which we all had forgotten long ago: stillness, peace, undisturbed vastness.

The Antarctic increasingly took possession of me. I slept worse than ever. In my short dreams I lived more and more on the ice. The great mountains, which had engaged me for twenty years, were memories. The deserts of Asia and Africa, which I had got to know, no longer absorbed me. Nothing made me so curious as the ice desert. And nothing gave me more fear. Pictures of the Arctic, which had been explored and travelled much earlier than the Antarctic, mingled in my dreams with impressions of the Antarctic. Scenes, related by Shackleton, Scott and Ransmayr, developed into impressions which I myself might experience. Hostile to man as the two Polar regions are, they

65

have drawn people time and again. At last I wanted to go there. Also, I wanted to grasp why the Polar sea and South Pole exercised such a spell on all who had once been there. The question of why the most hostile of all parts of the earth, Antarctica, is so important for the survival of mankind, had become again a matter of secondary importance.

None of my mountain expeditions had been as expensive as the planned crossing of Antarctica. When I reckoned the costs of my eight-thousanders – all in all thirty attempts with eighteen successful ascents – I had not spent more money than this single journey was to cost. Had not Reinhold Würth, a young industrialist from Baden-Württemberg, spontaneously undertaken a sort of patronage for the expedition, I would have already foundered at the outset. Würth was ready, for public relations purposes, to underwrite half of our outgoings. When I got to know Reinhold Würth closer, I understood why he wanted to support us. His business was conducted with traditional performance objectives:

> The workers are knowingly encouraged as far as that very fine and filigree line, beyond which challenge and motivation would collapse under demand and manipulation, that is none of the workers invest pyschological or physical personal reserves in the business: it suffices, if the male and female workers experience pleasure in work and a common joy in success.

On German Marketing Day, Reinhold Würth gave a lecture in which he described working conditions such as I had in mind for my expeditions:

> If a business succeeds in offering the workers a certain home with an ambience that is marked by harmony, optimism, plain dealing, calculatability, trustworthiness and respect for the per-formance of workers and colleagues, people will develop a We-feeling in the sociological structure of the business; the workers will take pleasure in the common success, in the growth of the undertaking.

Had not Shackleton thus led his men? Was it then, in 1989, still possible to organize an expedition in such a climate? To transfer my motivations to others, to my partner, had never been difficult for me. Although we had to be called the 'Würth Antarctica Transversale', we were each free to exploit our success. But for the time being the sponsors and I carried the risk. Not Arved Fuchs, who contributed no cash funds to the expedition.

This traverse cost more than DM1,000,000. Of that, the flights alone, including setting up the depots, made up 80 per cent of our budget. The Würth sponsorship was the financial basis for the expedition. Now I had to find further sponsors and interest the media in my plans. At a meeting with Wilhelm Bittorf, a sensitive *Der Spiegel* journalist, whom I had known for more than ten years, I noticed his interest in the plan. In 1979 Bittorf had accompanied me to K2, the second highest mountain in the world. He was so enthusiastic about the idea of crossing the Antarctic, that he convinced *Der Spiegel* to take up exclusive coverage. It was also then he who pressed strongly for a three-part television film with ARD.

With that, Arved and I had the funds to start the expedition. Naturally, sponsors, press and television meant obligations. These we took upon ourselves gladly. Without them we would never have been able to set out on our dream journey. I had promised Würth, as principal sponsor, to do four press conferences: two before the start and two after the end of the expedition. *Der Spiegel* naturally insisted on world-wide exclusivity of coverage. The video films, which Arved and I were to shoot during the expedition, belonged exclusively to ARD. Arved signed the same *Der Spiegel* contract as I did. Beyond this he undertook no sort of obligations. He was to be free to do as he liked.

We could not afford to make any mistakes in the planning, in the assembling of equipment and in the logistics. Any error could have had fatal consequences or at least jeopardized our success. It lay with both of us to complement one another. Each must prepare himself for the expedition.

Shortly before departure I met Wilhelm Bittorf and Giles Kershaw

Giles Kershaw in the Twin-Otter run by Adventure Network International (ANI). Giles played a large part in building up this business.

in Munich. Giles was ready to fetch Arved and me from McMurdo and to fly us out to South America if we arrived there too late.

Five months later, on 5 March 1990, on the day on which we were to return to Europe, Giles Kershaw crashed in the Antarctic. Giles was one of the most experienced polar pilots. He and only he had been prepared to fly us out in case of emergency – which, in the end, was not necessary – but not remotely had I thought that we were never to see each other again. While attempting to fly a gyrocopter he crashed into Jones Sound near Rothna from a height of 100 metres and was killed.

Giles had flown Oswald Oelz, Wolfgang Thomaseth and me to Mount Vinson in 1986. He had told me about his adventures and so awakened in me that enthusiasm for the Antarctic, which was the precondition for the Antarctic traverse. Giles had completed more than five thousand flying hours over the seventh continent without serious accident. I liked his dry English humour. His ability impressed me. He was bold enough to return to Antarctica again and again.

My leave-taking had begun weeks before. Although I was still in South Tyrol, people looked at me as one who is condemned to death. Yet I went voluntarily to the ice. Always, when someone wished me luck, my thoughts flew ahead. The day of the outward flight was confirmed: 16 October. The leave-takings became more serious. At last we started in the direction of South America. In the capital of Chile, Santiago, we met the press crew: Wilhelm Bittorf, cameraman Jürgen Bolz from Southwest Radio and Ulrich Jaeger who, as Wilhelm Bittorf's assistant, was to follow as far as the South Pole. In the next three weeks we were to become a five-man expedition team.

3 Punta Arenas

It was late evening when we landed in Punta Arenas in southern Chile. The airstrip glittered in the rain. Out of the aircraft's window I could only see glaring lamps and, as we disembarked, it was so dark that I was unable to orientate myself. Martyn Williams of ANI was waiting for us. Was everything ready for the flight to Antarctica? We drove to Hotel Cape Horn and went to sleep.

There were six of us: three reporters, Arved, me and Sabine who wanted to spend a few days with me. Wilhelm Bittorf was to report for *Der Spiegel* on the spot how our journey was progressing. As a youngster he had been very interested in the 'conquest' of the South Pole and knew the books on the subject. Scarcely second to none, he could recall the stories of the 'home of ice and storm', as vividly as if he had been there himself. Wilhelm was an excellent writer and committed protector of the environment: the ideal reporter for our purpose. He had also agreed to work on the documentary film about our crossing of the Antarctic which was to be shot. Ulrich Jaeger was his assistant and as far as possible he was to give Bittorf live reports. Jürgen Bolz was everything in one: cameraman, sound technician, director. This good-humoured and lively extremist was to accompany us to shoot a film on the ice for Southwest Radio.

Next morning Arved and I went to the customs house. We had sent our expedition luggage on ahead and some 500 kilos of foodstuffs had to be redeemed. There were no difficulties. I executed the customary bureaucracy – a form here, another official there – everything went faster than we had expected. Now, from choice, Chile was experiencing a foretaste of democracy. Pinochet was to step down. There was noticeably more freedom than before, at the same time more chaos.

The Antarctic is not part of Chile, although Chile claims the Antarctic peninsula as its territory. That meant that we were neither importing nor exporting our expedition goods; we were in transit.

Our team: Arved Fuchs and I in the Antarctic. I had not tested Arved on his fitness before the start. It was my mistake.

After we had completed the customs formalities in this sense, we took our equipment to a small camp at the edge of the town and were allowed to camp in a joinery, helped by Alejo Contreras, a Chilean mountaineer. The items of equipment and provisions that we wanted to take on the long trip on the ice were listed, weighed and counted. After three days everything was packed. We were ready to start and waiting for our flight to Antarctica. Where was the heralded DC–6, a machine which ANI and 'Antarctic Air' had purchased specially for the 1989–90 Antarctic summer? It had not arrived in Punta Arenas. We took our time. Before the start we wanted to check through everything once more.

Arved and I also now had plenty of time to talk with one other, and I got to know him better day by day. We were coming together as two adventurers obsessed with the same idea. Now it was time to become a team. That was only possible if we mutually respected each other, warts and all. We weren't 'friends', we were two self-confident lone wolves who knew that they would be dependent on one another. I was curious as to how Arved had become the person I had got to know?

'How did you come to dream of adventure?'

'As a small boy, although exactly when I can't say, as I can't remember. It seems as if it had always been in me. As a child I could not define my dreams in such concrete terms. Then, as a youngster, when I could read, I got seriously interested in adventure literature. At that time I read *In Night and Ice* by Fridtjof Nansen. For a child that was a really dry adventure book but I enjoyed it. Factually written, good to read. True stories have always fascinated me more than 'Winnetou' and 'Old Shatterhand', although Karl May's books captivated me, also *Lederstrumpf.* But I found real stories more fascinating. It was in me, although not clearly defined, what I would do. For myself I knew it. By the grown-ups it was dismissed as childish dreaming.'

After a pause, he continued:

'I was always curious. Other people interested me, other customs, other countries. Above all, things and situations interested me. What I never liked was sitting around. I was no desk man. Probably that's why I wasn't a good pupil. I felt my school-days to be an unpleasant restriction of my time. No, I did not go to school gladly. The outdoors always called to me. How much time I spent outside as a youth! I was lucky to have tolerant parents who let me live out my dreams. As a child I was on the go somewhere from morning to night. In addition it came about that I got interested in open air sports. Not ordinary school sports, rather types of sport which I had chosen for myself, like canoeing which I did with enthusiasm. I began canoeing as a small boy and learned everything connected with it.'

'And you learned to ski in the Dolomites?'

'Yes, that's right. I was there by chance. My parents had been to the Dolomites before, to Armentarola in the Gadertal. Often they spent their winter holiday there, and I usually went with them. At that time I was fourteen. So I found out about skiing; in the heart of the Dolomites.'

'Your father was a doctor. When you were growing up did he try to hold you back? Did he not want to steer you into a middle-class life-style?'

'Yes and no. I believe my father was himself divided concerning life

72

Arved Fuchs is a skilled seaman. He has his own ship with which he can operate in Arctic waters. He would like to voyage in the Antarctic.

and profession. He died young. On the one hand he showed a great deal of understanding for my desire for freedom, while at the same time he would have been happy to see me as a doctor. At all events he supported me in my ambition to realize my dreams and I was allowed to live out my desires. As I got older my ideas and plans became clearer. Early on I knew what I wanted to do as well as what I didn't want. Travelling in whatever form was my passion. My father belonged to a generation which had been cheated of its youth by the war; thus he had not been able to live his dreams to the full. Perhaps that is why he showed so much understanding for my adventures. He understood why I wanted to do it. He made my first trips possible, financially and emotionally. "Do it, go off on your bike, do what you like most", he said, and I did. On the other hand he was worried about his son's future. He didn't want me to drop out. I was to have a professional training. To begin with I tried to make a solid professional career, to please my parents. Perhaps at some stage I could have given up my dreams but this time was so far off as to be in effect never. My father had set himself up as a specialist in internal medicine.

73

Medicine was a profession which had also interested me but the obligations of a doctor simply were not compatible with my other passions. Doctor or adventurer, the question answered itself.'

'You had a proper seaman's training?'

'Yes. You know, seaman is not an unusual profession in northern Germany. Many people go to sea, also in our family. In my mother's family this profession was traditional. My grandfather and my uncle went to sea for at least part of their lives. So eventually I was finished with school and faced with the decision as to what to do now? I had to do something. For a long time I had flirted with seafaring. Now came the decision. I wanted to combine the necessary with the congenial. As a sailor I could travel and at the same time build a career. On this basis I chose the sea. I began my training in the merchant navy as a cadet. As I was also interested in scientific things, I went into the technical branch and worked my way up through the ranks. Then I went to sea and completed a course in ship operating systems. My ultimate goal was to make ship's engineer but I did not pursue this career to the end. I had got to know the amenities and difficulties of sea life. At some point I came back to my old dreams. The two didn't go together. So I asked myself the question: what do you want then? Adventure or profession? I couldn't work as an engineer and make long journeys. I had to decide on one or the other. And I decided on adventure.'

'What was your first Arctic journey?'

'It was an experiment, a hesitant, curious seeking. In the late summer of 1979, I travelled alone up the west coast of Greenland, just with a rucksack, not a real expedition. I simply wandered. Going along the inland ice, I peeped in at settlements, learned, lived. I was there just two months. I was fascinated by the landscape, by the people, by the ice. This time was decisive for me. I had previously undertaken expeditions to tropical regions, now I had begun to come to terms with polar travels. In Greenland I became infected with the 'Arctic bug'.

'How many Arctic trips have you made? How did it build up?'

'Each trip was built on a previous one. I started on the first serious expedition in 1980. It was an ambitious goal: I wanted to get to the geographical North Pole. This expedition promptly foundered, which

Sledge dogs in a snow-drift. Arved Fuchs had experience with huskies and could handle them. However, we wanted to cross Antarctica without their help.

certainly made me think, but after a little while I noticed that I had learned a lot through this failure. I spent a lot of time with the Eskimos. From them I learned the art of survival in the polar world. They showed me everything: how one drives dog sledges, how one builds igloos, how one hunts seals. All that was necessary in the long run if I wanted to live in the Arctic. Building on these experiences, I planned and carried out my journeys. In 1983 I traversed Greenland with dog sledges. This expedition was successful because I knew the Eskimo way of life.'

'On your Greenland expedition you followed an historical model; Wegener's crossing of the inland ice. Later on, did you research old histories?'

'Yes. Depending on the literature. I read polar literature and I was fascinated. Under what conditions those historical polar explorations took place! With great human stakes and simple means. The polar explorer of forty, fifty, sixty years ago, is no more. He was scientist and adventurer all in one. Modern researchers don't care to hear that.

For one thing, the early polar travellers were excellent scholars. They tried to combine both research and survival. These historical aspects interested me. I find a peculiar excitement in following in the drifted up track of a pioneer, which survives only by repute. Especially in the Arctic. The previous presence of people becomes more desire than reality. This is how legends spring up. Yet, suddenly you find a stone cairn. And you know, at some time, perhaps eighty or hundred years ago, an expedition was there. Only one person could have erected this cairn. If you're lucky, you find an account of this expedition. It doesn't happen often. For that reason this search remains exciting. To follow the tracks of an historical expedition is, I feel, like the magic of a fairy-tale, even more exciting because the story with which I empathize was true, or could be true. There is a bit of detective work in historical research. This historical aspect was important on my expeditions. There are, however, also other aspects. Today I study primitive races with the greatest respect. I like these people who are often regarded as primitive. When I can look a little behind the scenes, as with the Eskimos, I am full of wonderment. They have not only preserved their race over thousands of years but, moreover, have developed a unique culture. And this is not as lowly as it is always represented. These people's understanding of nature, which is lost to us, the civilized races, has opened my eyes in many respects. I would like to learn from them; I would like to learn about their history.'

My own motivations lay elsewhere. In earlier years my curiosity and readiness to learn from the primitive races face to face had been a basis for my travels. For that reason I understood Arved well.

Meanwhile, however, wanderlust had become a necessity for me. The feeling upon setting out was like a release. Was there anything more beautiful? Were I to remain at home, it would be a betrayal of my nature. I had to continue as I had started as a child even if it were wrong. I knew how much one can experience and always I had to give way to my dreams. It was impossible for me, always to be doing something 'proper', something 'sensible'. There was no disgrace in doing something 'wrong' now and again if everyone else was doing something 'proper'. There was room for one or two 'madmen' alongside so much usefulness in the world.

I had suffered everyday life in central Europe, with its universal banality and familiarity. How lifeless our world was. I could not have endured it anywhere. Juval was fantastic but only if I could get away occasionally. The notion of just sitting at home, of writing, of gazing out of the window, was worse than thinking of death. No, this world was not the real world. Europe seemed to me artificial, the cars so available, the telephone so audible, the picture on the television screen so conspicuous; so scandalously little I experienced here, so much artificiality pained me. The further I was from central Europe, the more this artificial world seemed like hell to me, and made me fidgety, dissatisfied, tired. I thought of heaven on earth in other terms: quiet, peaceful, perhaps even devoid of people. Not to want to be noticed – but was that also flighty?

At last Adventure Network announced that the aircraft was ready for the flight to Antarctica. There it was, standing at Punta Arenas airport, battered, patched, inspiring little confidence. A tin box, a DC–6 from the beginnings of commercial air transport: 18-cylinder radial engines, built 1952, 53,000 flying hours. Once upon a time it had been a PanAm Trans-Atlantic Clipper. Who would not like to have flown everywhere with it then? Now it had come from a weird place in Miami, Florida which the pilot called 'Corrosion Corner'. There old machines were cannibalized and rebuilt. Five old ones into one new airworthy one. Normally these spare-parts machines were used exclusively for air freight, until they could no longer get off the ground or fell out of the sky. But with 'Antarctic Air' people were to be flown to the most inhospitable part of the world.

'The aircraft is "structurally sound"', chief pilot and part owner of the DC–6, Colin Campbell, assured me with a confidential wink. Like the owner of ANI, he was Canadian, and sixty-eight years old.

'And what if it falls apart over Drake Passage?'

'I've flown as many hours as the DC–6 and not forgotten how to swim. I've only forgotten how to quit flying.' We laughed.

Campbell, assisted by two young pilots, was to fly us in the next few days to Patriot Hills, the ANI camp in the Antarctic. We were ready but our plans were interrupted. The machine from 'Corrosion Corner' had arrived in windy Punta Arenas too late and exactly at the

'Antarctic Air': the forty-year-old aircraft on the airstrip at Punta Arenas. From a distance it seemed trustworthy. On account of its deficiencies, we lost weeks.

moment a period of bad weather began in the Antarctic, which was to last seventeen days – from 21 October to 6 November.

Twice Campbell tried to fly the 3,200-kilometre route from southern Chile to Patriot Hills non-stop. Both times he had to turn back half-way. On the first attempt we had been confident. Soon, however, the head wind over Drake Passage increased, above the 'shrill sixties', to 185 kilometres per hour. The air speed of the DC–6, which is normally around 450 kilometres per hour, dropped to nearly half and all the fuel would have been used up before Patriot Hills. We would have plunged into the sea if Campbell had not turned around. Besides, the oil was leaking across our right wing. On the second attempt mist closed in over the Antarctic camp while we were airborne. The thin mist was sufficient to blur the outlines of the ice landing strip and the mountains behind into invisibility. There was no question of a landing. Again the machine turned around, without the honest explanation for the repeated failure to which we felt we were entitled. This delay threw out our timetable: things didn't look good.

Magellan Statue in Punta Arenas. Magellan explored the strait north of Tierra del Fuego and discovered the passage from the Atlantic to the Pacific.

Arved and I were angry. We had to wait, day after day, hoping for a fresh, conclusive start. In front of the Hotel Cape Horn the deciduous trees became bushier. More and more they shaded the bronze statue of Magellan, who stood there with outstretched arm, as if he wanted to command the sea and the 100,000 inhabitants of Punta Arenas. With spring came wind too. In the evening it drove garbage and people along the broad, straight streets. It blew from the south, from the ocean.

Arved and I ate three meals a day, read, discussed alternative plans. We drank 'vino tinto' and finally pondered what to do if things were to come unstuck even before starting.

'If you had to belong to a professional group', I asked Arved over a meal, 'or if you had to state your occupation in your passport, what would you put?'

'I describe myself as an adventurer. That is deliberately provocative. I believe that adventure is a splendid thing. In Germany this notion has a negative smack, I know. Nevertheless it pleases me. With us, for many people an adventurer is someone who is now here, now there, a person in suspense; a giddy fellow. In Germany "adventure" counts as something non-serious. That is tommy-rot. Certainly, there are grounds for this opinion. The adventure concept is elastic like everything else. It is very complex and I try to approach it straight-forwardly. Classic adventure is a creative art expressing itself. Every-body can be creative in his own way; one plays music, another paints pictures, a third makes interesting journeys. I too can express myself in this way. I can relate a journey, I can represent myself through it, I can also criticize when I get on the subject of, for example, environ-mental destruction.'

'Don't you think, too, that in Germany that is why the concept of adventure also has a bad smack, because it is provocative? Many people who lead a middle-class life, which I respect, feel somehow restricted when they witness someone like us. Restricted in their freedom to live fully that which I would like to call the creativity of the simple life.'

'Yes, certainly. We are often understood as a living provocation. A prick to their own existence. On the other hand, not everyone can be an artist, shoemaker or doctor. There must be a talent there. When I now consider the journey, which is ahead of us, the Antarctic crossing, adventure becomes more a profession than a romance.

'When you plan it is exciting and when afterwards you sit by the warm fireside, with a noggin in your hand and talk it over, it is pure adventure. Then there is a special charm to danger and an anticipation of departure, call it romance, and all needs, the fears and hardships, which such a journey entails, are forgotten. But when, a few days later, we are underway the adventure for us, the actors, recedes into the background. Our journey is then a matter of struggling all day long. We get through our daily performance, cooking, trying to sleep. We shall march and at the time it will not be dramatic. Adventure is not exciting when it is reality. Many people would despair at that because it would become clear to them that adventure dissolves in activity. At home you can picture it all as lovely, in reality it quickly becomes everyday life. And you must be prepared for that. I know that many people appraise such a journey wrongly.'

80

'Nevertheless, the idea came to you – I want to go to the South Pole. When?'

'It was not immediately the South Pole or the North Pole. At the beginning of the eighties I asked myself, do you break off your studies or what? I was coming up to my examinations. I would have been able to finish without any problem but everything in me bristled. I said to myself, either you forget your travels or you make them. This moment at the start of the eighties was so important for me! As I said to myself, if I chucked away studying, that was a sort of blow for freedom. The decision for adventure. Everyone said at the time: "You're crazy: chucking up everything just before the exams to go off travelling! Complete your studies, then you can look to the future." But I knew that the danger consisted of being swallowed up by the system. The next step after the exams would have been earning a living. A "career". One is swallowed up so quickly. I did something which all the world held to be irresponsible: I went on expeditions, despite all the warnings. Naturally came the reproach that I was ungrateful *vis-à-vis* my mother. Yet she was the one – my father was by this time no longer alive – who showed most understanding. She didn't hinder me from travelling. Nevertheless, it was a difficult time. Little money, hardly any experience and a head full of ideas. But these years have formed me personally. Since that time I have been wholehearted about what I wanted to do.'

'And the definite plan to travel in Antarctica, when did that develop? When did you negotiate with the Alfred Wegener Institute (AWI) and the German researchers?'

'About four years ago. Since childhood I have always dreamed of the Antarctic. But I saw no realistic possibility of getting to this part of the world. Four years ago I began to think about it in concrete terms. After the Greenland expedition I intended to travel with a dog sledge in Antarctica. I wanted to reach the South Pole, also eventually to attempt a crossing. This dog-sledge trip became an obsession. At that time I established contacts, negotiated, corresponded with the AWI. No one saw himself in a position to transport me to the edge of the ice. And with dogs enormous costs arise. One would have to fly the dogs in from Canada or Greenland, and more besides. Tons of dog food would have been needed. Such an undertaking would have gobbled up millions of dollars. My idea was not realizable. So I dropped this plan again. Then came our contact and your proposal to ski across Antarctica.'

'How were your contacts with the German research community, with the Alfred Wegener Institute? You still wanted to carry out your sledge trip with them. Why didn't that come off?'

'I offered the Alfred Wegener Institute a joint venture. However, the people there have especial difficulties with the idea of adventure. For them our doings seem pretty awful, as I understood it. They didn't say so to my face but I could read it between the lines. No interest in private initiatives. I asked for no direct consideration, neither cash nor transport possibilities. Naturally, I would have been delighted if I had been able to travel to the Antarctic on the *Polar Star*.'

'But that would have been a tremendous help, the greatest possible support.'

'I offered to take a scientist with me. He would have been able to accompany us for a while, my expedition would have led him safely through dangerous areas. At will he could have been picked up again anywhere by an aeroplane from the research station. I would have arranged the logistics. Always there came back the laconic answer that there was no demand for such experiments. No one was interested in that. The ship was booked up for years, I was told. Not once would they have taken so much as a rucksack to Antarctica for me. That was the policy that was carried on in the AWI.'

'And now, do you see the march across the Antarctic combined with both the other big trips which you have made on the ice – the crossing of Greenland, the march to the North Pole – as the hat trick in ice travel?

'Not absolutely. What is the ice-travel hat trick? But you're right: they are three big trips one can make on ice. The traverse of Antarctica, carrying out Shackleton's historic idea, would be a high point. It is really the complete big adventure. The ultimate which can be done in Antarctica, yes, even on ice generally. The Arctic ocean has been crossed, on skis and with dog sledges; the Antarctic without machines so far has not. In that this problem represents for me a tremendous attraction. This task, again with an historical background, absorbs me totally. I see at the moment no more attractive aim than tackling the big traverses. There are certainly other journeys which I could suggest. Nevertheless, Greenland–North Pole–South Pole remain the three outstanding "ice walks" which I wanted to do.'

'And afterwards? After these three big trips, will you go to the jungle or stay on the ice?'

'The polar regions, Arctic and Antarctic alike, have in no way lost their fascination for me. On the contrary, the more time I spend there the more enthusiastic I become. Naturally, I shall be glad to be home again after the Antarctic, to see different surroundings, greenery, a house, and notice other smells. But already I am planning a new ice trip, for summer 1990. I shall travel to Greenland in a sailing boat and, if the ice conditions permit, in 1991 I shall attempt to get through the Northwest Passage. I shall certainly spend more years in the ice.'

'Perhaps I shall too. But on foot, not on board ship. Depression grips me when I can't travel. When I'm away I often dream of home and that is lovely. I have two children and live in a peaceful place. But I cannot remain there too long. At home I become tired and dull-minded. Staying at home is for me synonymous with growing old. You are almost ten years younger than I am, perhaps you don't appreciate that. Moving through wilderness is like bygone life for me and, besides, there is always home to come back to.'

Although the waiting in Punta Arenas was tedious, I was in a very good mood, waiting for the off. We met to eat in the town, read and drank in the evening. Gladly I sat together with Wilhelm. Over a glass of white wine, he often told me his versions of the Scott, Amundsen and Shackleton expeditions. This melancholy Wilhelm Bittorf could in writing – like another person on a real excursion – lay aside his sadness. I liked that in him. And his accuracy, his incorruptibility, his imagination. He suspected that I was afraid, because he understood this stirring transition from the depression of growing old at home to the hazardous enterprise in the Antarctic.

Even if it were wrong to make this trip, something good could still come out of it. For me at least. The condition in between, the now, proved to me that I was alive. Since departure from South Tyrol on 16 October I remembered exactly how the individual days had been

Robert F. Scott (middle) in his hut in the Antarctic. Our reporter, Wilhelm Bittorf, had mulled over these tragic heroes a lot.

spent. I needed notes to jog my memory only when the days became alike. I knew exactly how Toni had said goodbye to me, how the wood in front of his farm was stacked. The leave-taking had remained vivid.

Although I had taken the trouble to explain my trip to the South Pole to him, Toni always shook his head. Of course, he didn't want to tell me I was crazy; he only thought it. Only when he knew that I was so serious about the South Pole that nothing in the world could stop me did he shake hands with me across the car roof. We had looked at each other a long time without speaking – each from another planet.

Being underway in itself, without communication, without compulsion to succeed, without ulterior motives, was not only the most useful, it was also the most liberating life-style for me. To live only against one's own and the resistance of nature. I could be so antisocial. Were there places without any moral standards? In my daydreams they occurred and I sought the corresponding reality: the wilderness without people. The Antarctic, where heaven and hell seemed to be one, belonged to that. This land was not divided up. Everyone could do what he wanted there. Nature alone avenged mistakes and man made the mistakes exclusively.

From the beginning, I was against placing our adventure under the mere cloak of environmental protection. Just as I didn't like vindicating my doings as a mountaineer with scientific aims, I found suspect those expeditions which needed an ecological justification. He who does not feel comfortable with the absurdity of his actions should stay at home. Go to the North Pole for the environment's sake – what a laugh! A slogan but not sincere. I knew that our activity, the crossing of the ice continent, testified more than all the maxims before and afterwards. Naturally, I undertook this expedition because I was curious and was seeking adventure again. Moreover, I was a person with a hunger for recognition, with ambition and the need for enhancement – just like other people.

Greenpeace, the most successful environmental organization in the world, which has my total respect, has been active in the Antarctic for years. Greenpeace has constructed its own station on McMurdo Sound. The voluntary helpers on the spot do the dirty work year in, year out. They test the sea water near the scientific stations. They take away rubbish, where those responsible do not. And they make the whole world aware how endangered the ecological balance is in the Antarctic.

Arved and I wanted to do something with these ecological activities and scientific research: we wanted to walk across Antarctica and demonstrate thereby how fine, inaccessible and peaceful the ice continent was. We wanted to travel 'cleaner' than the pioneers who had not troubled themselves with ecological questions.

It was 1911 when the idea was first conceived to cross Antarctica by one Wilhelm Filchner, a Royal Bavarian Artillery officer, who was later to become a famous Tibetan explorer. Not only outwardly was he the type of man who faces up to all opposition, but with his close-cropped blond hair and clear, defiant eyes he was the conqueror *par excellençe*. In his youth he had undertaken exploration in Asia. His first and only Antarctic expedition, however, was to spoil the ice continent

The Deutschland *was a state-of-the-art ice ship in 1912. Today the German* Polarstern *is one of the best equipped research ships for polar waters.*

for him for ever. To begin with Filchner was very lucky. On the steam-assisted *Deutschland*, a sailing vessel which had been specially equipped for the Antarctic, he sailed with his crew through the girdle of drift ice and fog banks to the edge of the continent. When the expedition settled in on the edge of the shelf ice, which today bears Filchner's name, they did not know what to expect on the planned crossing of the enormous continent. Men, horses and dogs had to be accommodated safely for a long time. The place where the ship was lying is an enormous bay which carves a large chunk out of the Antarctic land mass.

On 'land', a hut had to be constructed which would offer shelter to the adventurers during the long winter. This prefabricated construction had been practised often back home. But just as the barracks had been fairly comfortably fitted out, suddenly it began to rock and the beams came crashing down. The men were lying in their sleeping-bags on the plank-beds when underneath them things began to rumble. 'A din like a hundred heavy guns giving rapid fire broke out', Filchner reported later. Artillery officer Filchner reacted swiftly and

Wilhelm Filchner. Artillery officer Filchner became an important explorer. In Om mani padme hum *he writes about my beloved world of Tibet.*

gave the order to dismantle the hut. A platform of ice the size of Paris had detached itself from the mass of the shelf ice and was drifting out towards the open sea, carrying with it the hut and crew of the *Deutschland*. Everything from the base was collected up and all the men got safely aboard ship. The *Deutschland*, however, lay fast in the ice and not until nine months later did she break free. 'The Devil himself has sealed our fate', wrote Filchner in his diary. The Antarctic crossing had come to grief before it had begun. Any advance on the continent seemed unthinkable. After a long Antarctic night of winter, cold and anxiety, the *Deutschland* and crew sailed back home.

After this Antarctic expedition, Wilhelm Filchner had had his fill of the cold regions. He warned the kaiser and the German people firmly against further travels to Antarctica. His final conclusion:

The Scandinavians, Russians, British and Canadians should explore this region; they are specialists in the Arctic and thus also in the Antarctic.

The second man who thought seriously about crossing the Antarctic was the experienced polar adventurer, Sir Ernest Shackleton. 'Shack'

Building winter quarters from prefabricated parts for the members of the Filchner expedition. A little later the ice cracked underneath and drifted away. Rotten bad luck.

was a man with great personal magnetism. He had rare leadership qualities: modesty, ability to enthuse, everyone trusted him. Shackleton had been to the Antarctic with Scott at the beginning of the century. Then, a few years later, in 1908–09, he had marched on his own account with three friends almost to the South Pole. After Amundsen and Scott had reached the South Pole, 'Shack' planned to cross the Antarctic continent in 1914: from the Filchner Shelf Ice to McMurdo. What he planned as 'the last possible land journey on this earth' was a large-scale undertaking with two ships and a hundred helpers. From McMurdo Sound, a support team was to set up dumps on the Beardmore Glacier, while he advanced from the opposite side of the ice continent. As Shackleton was about to leave England, war broke out. No one guessed that his fate and that of his men would become an odyssey full of drama and last almost as long as the First World War. 'Shack' was certain the war would be over in a few months. Notwithstanding, he departed for the Antarctic with a bad conscience. There he quickly forgot his homeland. The ship with the

88

For 400 kilometres the Endurance *crew dragged their lifeboats with provisions and equipment across the Antarctic ice. More bad luck.*

promising name *Endurance* was to suffer a far worse fate than the *Deutschland*, for she was crushed to pieces by the ice. While Europe threatened to disintegrate, 'Shack' and his men fought for survival for three long years. What they experienced in the Antarctic during these war years, far from the shooting, was perhaps not less terrible than that which a soldier at the front suffered. Nevertheless, on the Weddell Sea, Shackleton did not lose a single man. The support team away in the Ross Sea lost their ship and two men. The survivors were not rescued until 1918.

Without being able to reach the Antarctic coast, the *Endurance* was frozen in the pack ice. She was squeezed, pushed, and more and more damaged by the gigantic pressure of the ice floes. Eventually she was cracked like a nut by the ice. With that there began one of mankind's most exciting voyages since the times of Odysseus. The unbelievable wandering of Shackleton and his men who stowed away all the equipment in the lifeboats, dragged them across the pack ice and forced themselves on for months in order to reach the open sea ended

While the team overwintered, 'Shack' sailed with some companions to South Georgia, in order to fetch help from a whaling station.

two years later. Magellan and Captain Cook experienced a great deal; 'Shack' perhaps more. Although to the wrecked crew of the *Endurance* it was no longer about the conquest of land, rather exclusively about life in the raw, they responded: hunger, cold, a winter under upturned lifeboats. They were condemned to inhuman strains and came through – perhaps only because they trusted their leader.

After the *Endurance* expedition, nobody tried to carry out Shackleton's plan. Arved and I had decided to take up this idea. We wanted to cross Antarctica, which is the size of Europe and Australia put together, under our own steam, without dog sledges, without motor vehicles, without aircraft. Of course, it was a compromise, in that we were to install two depots *en route*, as well as having to use aircraft to get to the Antarctic in the first place. The approach by ship would have been much more expensive. We had no troop of helpers on the other side of the continent, in the way that Hillary acted for the Fuchs expedition.

My original idea of getting from the German Filchner Station on the edge of the Ronne Shelf Ice to McMurdo on the Ross Sea between 21 October to mid-February 1990, was no longer possible after the abortive flights with the DC–6. Arved and I rearranged the plan. The original Shackleton route was shorter: Filchner Shelf Ice–South Pole– McMurdo Sound. ANI guaranteed us without surcharge the longer flight via Patriot Hills to the landward side of the Filchner Shelf Ice. They had finally bungled our transport into Antarctica. New maps had to be procured. Again Charles Swithinbank helped us with bits of advice. What, however, if it remained impossible to get to Antarctica until 10 November?

The four-engined propeller machine looked, after the two abortive starts, as if it had already been engaged in the Second World War. When the maintenance work on the DC–6 in Punta Arenas was complete, Patriot Hills again announced bad weather. Our confidence in aircraft and pilot dwindled. It needed only a clear sign and I would have given up.

Our doubts were now greater than the hopes. Perhaps we had failed on the second run on 2 November because of an engine problem and not on account of the thick mist over Patriot Hills, as had been explained to us. Could this aircraft really land at Patriot Hills? Had the two attempts been only pretexts? The ice landing strip at the ANI camp, which had been laid out in 1986 by Charles Swithinbank, is bumpy and situated in the immediate vicinity of rocks.

On 6 November we were called to the airport once more: the aeroplane was ready to start. According to the last radio conversation, the weather at Patriot Hills was good. For the fifth time I got into my polar clothing. It was hot in the hotel. Clumsily, I stood in front of the mirror. Shapeless as I appeared, I felt secure under four layers of artificial fibres: underwear, pile, anorak and overtrousers. My glacier spectacles held my long hair off my forehead. Even sitting down it was hard work putting on the double boots. I found myself cramped and sweating. Would this approach run succeed? I wanted to but could not believe it. My confidence in ANI was at zero.

The fact that a string of journalists came on board too, wanting to report on the dog-sledge expedition, was no guarantee of a successful flight. Twice already we had been airborne for eight hours, twice in vain. Hour after hour we flew southwards. The replacement dogs for

Charles Swithinbank in the ANI Camp at the foot of Mount Vinson. This glaciologist advised me as to choice of route and provided maps.

the Steger/Etienne expedition became increasingly unruly. The journalists from the USA, Australia and France also put questions to us. We had nothing to say: our adventure had still to begin.

During the night of 7–8 November the DC–6 at last made the flight, yet came within a hair's breadth of foundering. Beneath us, a grey soup of mist. Suddenly a few glimpses of a mountain. For more than an hour, Campbell and his co-pilots searched for Patriot Hills in the mist. With their on-board radar they probed out the Ellsworth Mountains. By the time they had found the ANI camp, there was hardly any fuel left in the tanks. A thin layer of cloud lay over the white infinity. The ice strip below was featureless. We circled and circled.

4 Patriot Hills

I had fallen asleep. When I woke up and looked around I was terrified. I was still sitting in this battered DC–6. Everything was patched. The wind whistled through. Only the deep sound of the 18-cylinder radial engines was soothing. In which direction were we flying? Was the machine all right? The old PanAm Trans-Atlantic Clipper flew on over the Antarctic. On and on. Like an hour ago. This time everything seemed to be working out well.

We were circling over a solid cover of cloud. The Antarctic climbing camp lay somewhere beneath us. Where was the ice strip on which the DC–6 was to land? A few mountain peaks. Now and then dark scraps were recognizable between the fleecy spotted grey of the mist. Rock islands. The remainder of the mountains lay buried beneath a tremendous covering of glacier. Cold shivers ran up and down my back. So much lifelessness! Our flight over the ice had already lasted for hours. We had flown almost 3,200 kilometres from Punta Arenas in southern Chile over Tierra del Fuego and the raw South Atlantic.

At last Colin Campbell found a hole in the clouds and prepared for landing. Everybody held their breath. After nine hours of flying the machine skidded across the ice, turned half round and abruptly came to a halt. We had arrived! Now we were not only two weeks behind schedule, we had lost much of our energy through waiting, hoping and irritation. The crew of Patriot Hills entered the aeroplane. When we had greeted the men, I asked at once: 'When can we fly on? Arved and I must get to the Filchner Shelf Ice as fast as possible.'

Mike Sharp, responsible for ANI in Patriot Hills, shrugged his shoulders. Scarcely had Arved and I climbed down the wobbly aluminium ladder out of the aeroplane than we were surrounded by six courageous men: the members of the 'Trans-Antarctica' expedition. Their cheeks were burned, their clothing dirty. They had been on the go for three months. Coming from the Antarctic peninsula,

'Antarctic Air' in the Antarctic. Behind are the Patriot Hills. After the machine had been unloaded, it flew back and was forced to make an emergency landing.

they were trying to cross the continent by the longest possible route. They were freezing. Apparently more than we were. Although they were definitely hardened after so many weeks on the ice, they were suffering from the cold more than us newcomers, a contradiction which at first I had still to grasp. They had my total admiration.

When the pilot Brydon Knibbs emerged, I asked again: 'Can we fly on tomorrow?' This Canadian pilot with Arctic and Antarctic experience was to fly us to the starting point of the land journey. 'There's not enough fuel for the Twin-Otter here', he said briefly, laconically.

I was furious. The little, two-engined propeller machine had been stationed at Patriot Hills for some days. I saw myself cheated. I felt like a prisoner in this great, endless ice continent. From now on I could change nothing. I could not believe the statement by Brydon Knibbs. I waited. After we had unloaded the expedition luggage and sledges, Arved and I trudged into camp. I was now angry and quiet.

Ulrich Jaeger had flown with us to Patriot Hills, as intermediary between us and Wilhelm Bittorf in Punta Arenas. Jürgen Bolz, the

94

Photo call on the ice. Six men of the 'Trans-Antarctica' expedition and some of their dogs pose for photographers before setting out on their journey.

cameraman from Southwest Radio, shot our 'arrival on the ice'. While Arved and I counted the containers and checked whether everything was present – only our snow saws were missing – the six men of 'Trans-Antarctica' were interviewed, photographed, questioned.

A strange feeling, taking part in a press conference on the ice. It makes you smile when you see how important others consider it. The troop of journalists had travelled from afar, had submitted to a dangerous flight, in order to film the actors of the dog-sledge expedition and to confront them with preformulated questions. How can you win distance for your expedition when your goal becomes clearly defined before departure and announced to people by the morning newspaper and sports reports on television?

Six men from six nations – a Frenchman, an American, a Russian, a Briton, a Japanese, a Chinese – are travelling 6,000 kilometres in six months with dogs and sledges through Antarctica – the longest crossing of the sixth continent.

95

The dog-sledge party spent three days at Patriot Hills. Now was not the right time to reflect on adventure without spectators and to complain about our exclusive contract. Also, without the interest of the media in our journey we would not have been there. Just as little as 'Trans-Antarctica'. My respect for these six men was great. They had already spent difficult months on the ice and passed on much experience to us.

Rested sledge dogs for 'Trans-Antarctica' had also been flown in with our DC–6. They had spent their rest time on a farm near Punta Arenas. The dogs howled with relief when they were once again on the ground. The ten huskies had impregnated the tail of the DC–6 with urine and the smell of excrement during the flight. With fresh strength they were now to help pull again on the longest dog-sledge journey in the history of mankind, an idea conceived by an American.

Will Steger, the initiator and driving force of this expedition, was an adventurer and dog breeder from Minnesota. He, Geoff Somers and the Japanese Keizo Funatsu each led a dog team. How these men could handle the dogs! By comparison Scott had been a sheer amateur on his first Antarctic expedition. On 10 December 1902 he had noted in his diary:

> Yesterday we covered only two miles and to get the second load on at all we had to resort to the ignominious device of carrying food ahead of the dogs. 'Snatcher' died yesterday; others are getting feeble – it is terrible to see them.

Using Scott's tactics, Steger would not have got far. In the camp I met Jean-Louis Etienne, the radio operator and spokesman of the 'Trans-Antarctica' expedition. 'Here you have endless time to think' was one sentence which he was always repeating.

After we had deposited our equipment in the instrument tent, we plodded to the team tent in which cooking was also done. A group of Canadians with Arctic experience had constructed this camp. For three years it had functioned for the short duration of the Antarctic summer. It had several sleeping tents, a stores tent and a cooking tent.

At a long table sat the members of 'Trans-Antarctica'. Will Steger was writing letters, Jean-Louis Etienne reading. As I entered, he winked at me: 'You'll have plenty of time for meditating!' That's what occupied him. Victor Boyarsky, Geoff Somers, Keizo Funatsu and Quin Dahe were having a vehement discussion. The men were tired, absent-minded. Their cheeks were frost-burned. Their faces looked old, much older than they really were. If I were to meet one of them in the street somewhere in Paris, in Minnesota or in Moscow, I would certainly not recognize him, I thought.

Next day – we had slept on a plank-bed in the instrument tent – I began new negotiations with ANI. 'I shall break off the expedition if we are not set down at the promised point.' I insisted upon our rights. Otherwise, I wanted to claim all advance payments back and compensation. Hugh Calver, the Adventure Network manager responsible had assured us in writing he would have us flown to the edge of the Filchner Shelf Ice. Only here no one was ready to redeem his promise. After I had determined for myself that the fuel would not suffice for the 1,200-kilometre flight, I decided to alter the route a second time. Arved agreed. We wanted to be flown to the extreme edge of the mainland. We wanted to start from a point nearer to the camp, between the Ronne Shelf Ice and the mainland, and from there to march to the Thiel Mountains and the South Pole. Had Arved not gone along with this compromise, I would have cancelled the expedition. We would have failed before we had been able to commence the crossing: like Filchner and Shackleton before us.

In order to arrive on schedule, at latest on New Year's Day at the South Pole, we had to be fast. Faster than originally calculated. If we wanted the slightest hope of being at McMurdo on the other side of the Antarctic before the onset of winter, we could not hesitate any longer. We must start with the first fine weather. Days passed before I could accept the compromise. In the quarrel with Adventure Network, carried out over the radio, the talk was about repayments and new dates, about damages and loss of face with the public. It helped nothing.

How much preparation, how much reputation, how much energy was at stake during these days! Just because ANI had not filled up the fuel dump at Patriot Hills sufficiently. 'For what did I pay a year in advance?' The Antarctic crossing appeared to be foundering through

Team tent at Patriot Hills. The stable tunnel tents were dismantled after the season, stored in an ice hollow and erected again. They can be heated.

dependence on technical matters. We had developed the best possible equipment. We had studied the Antarctic literature. We had trained. But we couldn't fly ourselves.

For example, the tent had been made to my design by Signor Ferrino, an Italian tent manufacturer. I had got the basic ideas from Amundsen. The third prototype came up to our expectations: a double tent in dome form. Interior dark, exterior bright, so that the 'summer warmth' would be stored between the two tent surfaces. With provisioning too we had followed Amundsen.

All our provisions were so packed that we could count them instead of having to weigh them. Our pemmican consisted of single pieces each of half a pound. The chocolate was divided, like all chocolate, into small pieces, we knew also what each piece weighed. Milk powder, biscuits. The whole stock consisted of these four sorts of foodstuffs.

98

We wanted to live less frugally – with black coffee for breakfast; bacon and hard bread for the pleasure of chewing; freeze-dried food prepared with hot water for a simple meal each evening, in seven varieties: meat plus potatoes, vegetables, beans, noodles with different sauces; olive oil; and always pemmican, an old Indian food. We had also taken up Amundsen's idea of a beard trimmer:

> Our beards were cut quite short each Saturday, less from vanity than regard for expediency and comfort. Ice gets into a beard and that is often really disagreeable. In my opinion a beard in the polar regions is as impractical and uncomfortable as – for example, if one wanted to walk around in a top hat. After beard trimmer and mirror have made the round of the polar travellers, one after another disappears into his sleeping-bag.

Arved and I had seldom met before the expedition. Nonetheless, we had discussed every detail. As with Amundsen's South Pole expedition, the democratic principle served also with us. Otherwise, I could not have carried out this expedition. The final decision, despite great delay and starting on an altered route, was not easy. During the long hours in my sleeping-bag I brooded over it. Of course I could have terminated the contract with Adventure Network. Whether I would have got my money back from those responsible was written in the stars. I could bargain for a new contract, nothing else.

Arved and I had only two alternatives: either to renounce the crossing or to change the route a second time. Despite everything I wanted to start. 'Let's fly from Patriot Hills to the edge of the continent as far as the fuel lasts,' was Arved's proposal. My first thought of a way-out had been to start between the Ronne Shelf Ice and Antarctica, in Hercules Inlet near Patriot Hills. Arved's idea was better and more logical.

Although by our Trans-Antarctic journey I wanted to demonstrate less dependence on technology and more on our own power, I had to realize how very dependent on technology I was in decisive points. Because of the lack of a few drums of fuel, we had to give up beginning the route from the coast. To get to the Filchner Shelf Ice at 79° south latitude we would have needed two fuel dumps for the

Two long years I had negotiated with ANI. Wilhelm Bittorf travelled specially to Canada for a discussion. Nevertheless, our expedition came within a hair's breadth of failure.

Twin-Otter. From there it would have been a 1,200-kilometre stretch to the South Pole by the shortest route. What was the use of my rage over Adventure Network's 'slovenliness' and 'unfulfilled promises'. We couldn't possibly wait longer for sufficient fuel. Because of an unfulfilled contract we had to shorten the pure continental 'Würth-Antarctica-Transversale' crossing. Also, if we were to reach the other side after marching 100 days, it would be no longer a complete traverse of the Antarctic. This curtailed project was indeed difficult enough for we now lacked starting momentum. Would we get to the Pole on schedule?

Arved and I had become modest and quiet. We would have been satisfied even with reaching the South Pole. If only we could start. My feeling that Arved, who a few months before had reached the North Pole, would have been satisfied with the South Pole, was confirmed in conversation: 'For the great mass of people, the South Pole and Antarctica are synonymous', he said. He was right.

We climbed a peak near Patriot Hills to release our frustration. We wanted also to be together, to be alone, to feel the wind, to get to know the immediate surroundings. We did not want to squat around in camp waiting until news came from Punta Arenas, as to when our start was possible. We wanted to build up strength, motivation, confidence. Nowhere was that more possible than on the mountains roundabout. The elevation gave a clear view of the great ice desert. As I stood up there in the wind, I thought of Dante's hell. To me came the suspicion that the poet had once experienced the Antarctic:

> . . . A thousand visages
> Then mark'd I, which the keen and eager cold
> Had shaped into a doggish grin; whence creeps
> A shivering horror o'er me, at the thought
> of those frore shallows. While we journey'd on
> Toward the middle, at whose point unites
> All heavy substance, and I trembling went
> Through that eternal chillness . . .

The mountain peaks here looked like Dante's damned: stuck in the ice up to the neck. In the frost wind I stood there, gazed, was full of doubt.

The impetus and the confidence we had brought with us from Punta Arenas was expelled from us. If we were to get through, we must, as laid down in my original plan, accomplish 30 kilometres per day, without any time reserve. In order to be able to start this trip, we could not dwell on the suffering which awaited us. Not on the sledge load which was to bow us down. The self-imposed task and the white infinity before us were fascinating. Back in camp, we began to pack the sledges. Once more we checked the equipment. Every single item.

Full of admiration, we watched the 'Trans-Antarctica' depart. With their dog sledges they pulled away in the direction of the Pole. Three dog teams and the six-man team quickly vanished over the horizon. The white space had swallowed them up. Arved and I were frustrated but still full of curiosity. We too wanted to get on the ice at last and march away.

Again I slept badly. I had carried this expedition idea around with

Victor Boyarsky and Jean-Louis Etienne with their dogs just before departure from Patriot Hills. Victor was the front runner and extremely likeable.

me for so long that now it had to be realized. It had become a compulsion. Withdrawal would have brought a pile of problems: financial problems. The expedition was announced. How would I have explained the failure to sponsors and friends? No one would have wanted to believe me. That all weighed me down.

I alone carried the responsibility *vis-à-vis* the sponsors. The stake which had led us this far, the organizational and financial stake compelled me to attempt it in spite of everything.

Eventually, on 13 November we were to fly out. The weather was good. 'Trans-Antarctica', on the move for days now, needed rested dogs and supplies. Journalists were to be collected and dogs brought out. Suddenly there was news in camp, we were to make ourselves ready. 'If you want to fly, you can fly now.' The flight to our departure point had to be combined with a support flight for 'Trans-Antarctica'. In this way there could be economy of fuel.

Everything moved very fast; too fast for Arved and me. We got dressed, for the last time, as if for an execution. We stowed our

'Airport Patriot Hills' with a Cessna and the Twin-Otter which flew Arved Fuchs and me to our starting point. Our base radio was to be in this camp.

sledges in the aircraft. We stuffed full the containers which had to go back to Punta Arenas and Europe. We said goodbye to everybody and simulated nonchalance. Together with Jürgen Bolz, the cameraman from Southwest Radio and Ulrich Jaeger, the *Der Spiegel* man, we climbed into the Twin-Otter.

On the flight map Arved had marked a spot as our starting point. An imaginary spot in the white snow desert: 82° south 71° west, exactly on the edge of the continent, about 500 kilometres behind the edge of the Shelf Ice. It was more than 1,000 kilometres away from the Pole. The length of the section from there to the 'Thiels' was unknown. The fuel would reach that far. So start at this point.

We flew over the ice which seemed endless. Beneath us a single, glistening white surface. It was as if it did not concern me. Suddenly I saw crevasses. Innumerable crevasses underneath us! That was the edge of the Ronne Shelf Ice! I was scared. The fear broke out, that terror, which for weeks had been dormant in me. Now, suspended above these crevasses, my fears found their practical confirmation. How were we to find a way through these many glacier crevasses? How to march? How to lug the heavy sledges weighing eighty kilos over the snow bridges, without breaking through? How could men overcome a stretch which ran zigzag? Amongst these great glacier crevasses progress would be nearly impossible. From above, I imagined us going across the ice, a stretch many times longer than the bee-line which we had measured! Panic paralysed arms and legs. My heart pounded. Like an animal driven into a corner, I peered once left, once right out of the aeroplane window. The ground beneath us was not immediately visible.

5　Setting Out at Last

The journalist Ulrich Jaeger and the cameraman Jürgen Bolz sat quietly next to Arved and me. It was 13 November. We were flying eastwards from Patriot Hills in a two-engined Twin-Otter, to latitude 82°S where we were to set out.

The machine was stuffed full with the two sledges and our equipment. Next to that masses of boxes of dog food. Four huskies, each weighing a hundredweight, pattered and slavered between the seats. They were to be flown on to 'Trans-Antarctica'. One tried to lie across my lap.

After setting us down, the Twin-Otter had to provide Will Steger and Jean-Louis Etienne with supplies and refreshed animals.

The noise of the engines decreased, we flew lower. The machine began to circle. Arved played with a husky which was licking his ear. His face was pale.

I was still full of disquiet, looked hastily at the dog in front of me and out of the right-hand window, stretched myself towards the opposite one. There was only this 'dumb wind-swept immensity' as Captain Scott had called the Antarctic. Snow everywhere. Nothing but an unimaginably immense snow surface.

No more crevasses below us. Suddenly a whistling and crackling. As Brydon Knibbs set the Twin-Otter down on the snow crust with a crunch, I came to again. My anxiety attack was over. Once on the ground and in action, I forgot at once where we were. We had landed. We all got out and unloaded the sledges. Arved determined our position. I measured the altitude. Jaeger photographed, Bolz filmed. We had no time to lose. Everything was much too hectic, a precipitate departure. We put on our skis. Jürgen Bolz continued to film, running hither and thither. Jaeger stood there and jotted down 'last' impressions. Brydon shouted that he must get on. A hasty handshake, then he climbed aboard. The engines roared. They seemed far away. One

The Twin-Otter ready for the off. Our two sledges (in foreground) are laden with equipment and provisions for more than three weeks.

more wave, a salute from the aeroplane – and we were alone. The Twin-Otter made a few loops over us. We ran together as if to prove unity; confidence that we would make it. Then the red and white aircraft disappeared into the milky haze on the horizon. Never to be seen again. Arved and I stood at the beginning of a 2,800-kilometre march through the most hostile wilderness on the globe. Ahead of us, ninety days without 'night'. Ninety days of cold, ninety days of sledge pulling. Ninety 'nights' in the tent on a shelterless plain, with the knowledge that there was no turning back.

I had difficulty in pulling the sledge with its initial weight of 80 kilos. I had to strain in my harness like a horse on the dry drift snow in order to progress. It didn't feel good. Progress resembled the wretched creeping of a snail. What a change! Climbing captures all your senses. The abyss keeps you on your toes. Suddenly this immense distance! And march, march, march. The 'snow lion', as my first daughter Layla always called me, become a sledge dog.

Arved, bigger and stockier, had it easier with the weight of his sledge. For the time being he made good progress. It was laborious for us both. Even in the first hour's march I was reminded of Amundsen. No crevasses and this heat whilst moving!

The glaciers seemed as if they were very old and completely motionless, nowhere were new crevasse formations to be seen . . . in this hilly terrain we could not endure it in our polar outfits.

Arved and I took off our windproofs. We were in a hurry.

The technology upon which we wanted to depend as little as possible, had brought us into dramatic need of time. Thus our project had become more difficult than originally thought.

'We must do almost 30 kilometres per day if we want to be on the other side before winter returns', Arved had explained.

After the start we continued for three hours. Then Arved wanted to camp. He was the experienced one, so I agreed. 'Tentatively', he suggested, 'we can increase slowly'. On the first day we had done only 7 kilometres.

The ice desert turned out to be different from my dreams. As the nightly background to my fears, it had seemed hostile to me. A destructive power in its radiation of loneliness. Now it seemed peaceful to me. Yes, it had a quietening effect on me. Just as much as at home I had frightened myself about it, so it pleased me now.

The quarrel with ANI was forgotten. Now we had other worries than that which we had shared on the approach journey. Also, other rules of living together. Other things of importance. Now there were just the two of us who must get on together. We were two. I knew that breaking rules is only possible on solo trips and yet no one had to subordinate himself to another. We had agreed on a democratic expedition; either two voices for or one against the other.

Three hours we had marched today. Three hours in a never-ending, regular snow plain. There were no smells, no noise. Only you and your partner. The sun remained the same height in the sky. Shadows moved slowly. It was so hot with the sledge load that we sweated. On setting off, Arved had given me the compass and direction of march. I went ahead for the whole stretch. It was all a matter of course and I

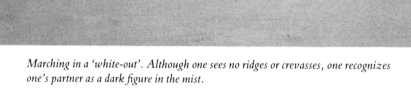

Marching in a 'white-out'. Although one sees no ridges or crevasses, one recognizes one's partner as a dark figure in the mist.

was puzzled when Arved wanted to camp. 'Another hour yet!' Arved was against it. The inexperienced one yielded.

We had trouble putting up the tent, often getting in each other's way. The arrangement, the grips were all still unaccustomed. But then in the tent, as Arved began to cook, I felt good. It was comfortable. Arved radiated calm and that gave me back my self-confidence. It was as if I had often camped with him somewhere on the ice.

With real, practical everyday life in the ice wilderness all my fears had fallen away. I no longer yearned to be back at Juval or in the mountains. I was here, on the move, and I knew this expedition would succeed.

During the first night I slept badly. Inside the tent it remained bright. For hours I observed from the interior of the tent how the sun disappeared. Nonetheless it remained day. From 'midnight' the wind took up. In the morning we had 'white-out'. I had read a lot about this phenomenon but one can only describe it if one experiences it. In mist and cloudy sky one sees absolutely nothing. One fumbles with the feet on the uneven snow floor as if it were pitch-dark night. With white-out, it is bright: in the tent we could even read. With the morning walk I finally experienced what white-out means: the white night.

Arved lit the cooker. It took a good half-hour until the water was hot and Arved put in the coffee. We drank it, ate fat biscuits and lay down once more in our sleeping-bags to wait for better weather. This coffee for breakfast! A luxury in the Antarctic. Arved's idea was grandiose: daily morning coffee. It contributed to a congeniality which was to make tent life pleasant during the whole journey. Later we cooked again. Often I fetched lumps of hard snow which we had laid ready in brick-sized pieces in the tent entrance the previous evening.

Midday we began packing up. After dressing, we went outside: it was stormy and grey. At 2 p.m. we left the tent site. We tried to sail and, without exactly observing the direction, glided swiftly away. Arved was ahead. For a time, I had trouble following him. Often, when the wind tore me to the side, I fell down and had problems with the 'collapsed' sail. But I didn't give up.

The sailing took the monotony out of the white expanse. The sledges jolted over the ice humps and sometimes I could even make little jumps with my skis. It was fun, travelling so into infinity.

Although we were going more west than south, this first day of sailing was a good experiment. From the Pole, I knew now that we could be in McMurdo in a month with a strong southerly wind.

In the evening, by the light of the low, never-setting sun, we were confronted by a gigantic field of 'sastrugi'. A sea of frozen waves. Dazzling white waves of hard snow, only slowly to be crossed with the 80-kilo sledge loads. We could not see the end of it.

'Sastrugi', a word borrowed from Russian, describes icy humps and crests built up out of the snow surface. Often they are beautifully shaped. Sometimes these closely packed ice bulges are 20 centimetres high, sometimes more than a metre. They run in the direction of the winter wind. In the winter months the storm in the Antarctic is at its strongest and it is that which forms the ice. It gives the sastrugi their direction. We hoped they would soon leave off.

In the morning I lay in the tent with open eyes. Arved still slept. I listened as the wind beat against the tent wall. I felt my painful arm which I had banged the day before in a fall and decided to risk a look outside. I peeled myself out of my sleeping-bag and opened the entrance of the tent. For a few seconds I hoped to see a smooth surface outside but there was nothing but sastrugi. As far as the eye could see, nothing but a glaring, waving, bright grey snow-scape. Flat and full of grooves at the same time. A single, glittering expanse all around. Where the horizon ought to have been, it lost itself in unsubstantiality. The world, if we were on it, appeared to dissolve there. Nowhere a point to hold the eye. In the diffuse light we would have run around in a circle without the compass. Nowhere a markedly separate snow cone rising out of the frozen plain. Only thousands of sastrugi.

> I had a feeling as if in sleep I had fallen from the earth and come upon a no-man's land between the active regions and the galactic spaces, in a sphere without time or place.

The American Barry Lopez had described this mood exactly. And Robert Falcon Scott, who was the first to penetrate into the heart of Antarctica in 1902 and was to end his life there, had lamented:

> What could be more terrible than this dumb, wind-swept immensity?

Arved and I had read the reports of the pioneers. We had come here nevertheless. Voluntarily. To outsiders, our insights had to sound like the moanings of incorrigibles. 'You crawl out of the tent and feel, despite your thick things, abandoned in the huge expanse', said Arved on our first radio contact with Ulrich Jaeger, who was waiting in Patriot Hills for news of us. And further: 'In a winter storm at Cape Horn you can find a sheltered bay on the lee-side. At the North Pole there are ice barriers which are difficult to overcome but ward off the wind. Here there is nothing, nothing, nothing, behind which you can hide.'

Now, at the beginning of our journey, we were slow. Much too slow. As Arved had much more experience in ice travel, I followed his tactics. To start with at least.

With us it was now exactly the reverse of Amundsen in 1911 on his dog-sledge expedition to the South Pole:

We wanted to cover the distance from 80° South latitude in daily marches of 28 kilometres: we could well have doubled that performance but as there is more to actually succeeding than advancing as fast as possible, therefore we made short marches.

We too had to do 28 kilometres and not once did half this distance. My calculation was simple and yet miscalculated. At our starting speed we would not have got far past the Pole. We had just 100 days for the crossing and a travelling distance of 2,800 kilometres ahead of us: 12 kilometres × 100 days comes to only 1,200 kilometres. That was little more than the stage from the start to the South Pole. Often we tried to sail but without success. We were always driven westwards. We had learned how to sail quickly. Although we lacked the experience which would have made sailing an enjoyment, it was still much less strenuous than pulling. Generally, however, the wind blew in our faces.

In the tent it was pleasant from the beginning. We squatted around the warming cooker, melted lumps of hard snow, made quick brew tea and soup. In the 'evening' we ate bacon and hard bread as appetizers. Then a main meal with rice, potatoes or noodles, which was enriched with pemmican, olive oil, meat. This fatty hot-pot we sipped down hot. It tasted delicious. Often there were even desserts: banana or chocolate cream. Breakfast in the morning – coffee, biscuits, bacon and bread again, remains of the evening meal – lasted again two hours. Then we filled our Thermos flasks with vitamin and mineral drinks. We also stuck energy sweet-bars in our anorak pockets; muesli and hazelnut fruit slices with honey.

Then everything was packed up. With a few grips we dismantled the tent and stowed it on my sledge. Once ready to march, we buckled on our skis, and slipped on the nylon-webbing pulling harness. It consisted of a shoulder sling and a broad belt round the hips. At the pressure points it was padded with foam rubber. Bound into the harness at hip level were, left and right, 2-metre long, thin shafts. We were harnessed like horses pulling a one-horse carriage. We pulled a sledge which looked like a flat rowing-boat. It had two

111

Double rations for a day: only the bacon is missing. Fruit slices, biscuits, mineral and vitamin drinks, prepacked meals, pemmican sausage and oil capsules.

narrow skids in its belly. It contained, under the fastened cover, fuel for the cooker, provisions and the remaining equipment for thirty days. At the beginning and fully laden, each sledge weighed 80 kilos. Daily it got one and a half kilos lighter. Light it never became.

Before I started, I fixed the aluminium frame with the spherical compass on my chest and checked once more the bearing on which to march.

Masked against the scorchingly cold wind and with glacier spectacles against snow-blindness each grasped his ski-sticks. We strained against the load. In order to get the inert mass of the sledge in motion, we had to put our backs into it like donkeys. The drudgery began. The pulling of the sledges across the Antarctic. On our Trans-Antarctic journey it was not so much self-pulling as self-chastisement. Also not about an epic. It we wanted to manage with natural energy – wind and muscle power – we had to pull, always pull. The renunciation of a howling bunch of sledge dogs as consequence of a style. No motor vehicles for load transport out of ecological considerations.

With the provisions and the pieces of personal equipment – spare clothes, socks, sleeping-bags – the pots and a Magellan GPS navigation device were stowed on Arved's sledge. In mine, in addition, were stored radio, tool bag and medicine chest, in which Arved had packed as a precaution also a pair of forceps for pulling teeth.

The GPS replaced the sextant and in its regular function was as simple to use as a pocket calculator. Already after a week I could determine our position as well. Nevertheless, navigation remained Arved's task, even though I went ahead with the provisional compass setting and thus navigated in detail. In my sledge lay a GPS replacement for emergencies.

Again white-out. Although it was a bright day, we fumbled like blind men on the snow surface. Again wind from the south-east. We stayed in the tent. This confinement to the tent, not being able to do anything, depressed me a lot. I would have preferred to go on, as long as the storm and our strength permitted it. During these hours of inactivity, we developed inside the tent a division of work which was to be preserved during the whole expedition.

I awoke at the hour agreed the previous evening. After a long stretch and sigh, I sat up in my sleeping-bag and looked out at the weather. For that I had to open the zip fastener on the triangular entrance flap. At the same time I fetched inside the coffee pot which Arved had filled with snow the previous evening. When Arved had also peeled himself out of his sleeping-bag, we shoved the sleeping-bags behind our backs. Arved fetched the small wooden board from the foot end of his bed and placed it in the centre of the tent. I placed the cooker on the little plank and Arved lit it, after I had pumped it up. I placed the small pot on the flame. Only when the coffee was made did we eat. After breakfast we began dressing. Over our thin underwear we pulled on the thick polar fleece jackets and trousers. With socks we had different methods. Arved followed a system tested at the North Pole: thin socks, vapour-barrier sock liners – thick socks – inner boots – outer boots. I stuck with my experience on the eight-thousanders: next to the skin a firm thin-meshed sock, over that inner boots and then outer boots. At last we pulled on overtrousers and corresponding jacket, both windproof naturally. We did up the zips in the tent. Finally we put on our caps and goggles, having already

smeared our faces with sun-cream. Then we clapped on our gloves and went outside.

The sledges were tugging at the tent entrance. The covers were undone. At once we packed our sledges. Each his own. The personal items of equipment were already stowed in a bag. Sleeping-bags and bags with apparatus we had placed by the tent door so that they could be taken from outside. Once outside we were constantly in motion, so as not to cool down. We packed the pieces of equipment in the sledges so that in the evening we could fetch them out again in the right order. At the bottom food, fuel and the heavy things, all so distributed so that the sledge was lighter in front. Over that the sleeping-bag, then the mats. Last of all we took down the tent. The anchorages, skis and ski-sticks had to be pulled out of the snow. We shook it so that all the ice and condensed snow fell out and laid it lengthwise on my sledge. Like a dead man. Before I fastened up the sledge, I placed the Thermos flask and my Leica on top. Then we harnessed ourselves and set off. Every 'morning' the same. We kept to this start the whole expedition.

If the snow conditions were good, we ran with narrow telemark skis and Eskimo boots. For sastrugi we took the heavy touring skis which we combined with our double boots. In really bad conditions – bare ice or especially icy sastrugi – we went with boots alone. The simple crampons, called Grödel, we buckled on for the first time two months later.

After a few days' running-in period, we decided on a running time of five hours per day. In these five hours we covered 20 kilometres maximum. These 20 kilometres which, because of the detours, did not bring us 20 kilometres nearer the Pole, were decidedly too little. I knew that my plan of reaching the Pole this year could not prove right.

Nevertheless, I felt well to begin with. Whilst moving my thoughts ran too. The going would have been much more strenuous if I had not been able to dream and fantasize. Often I awoke in the morning and what I had dreamed was still with me. My dreams were personified as

Arved Fuchs clothed for the march: wind-proof, face mask, double boots. As far as the Pole we often switched between touring and telemark skis.

usual. Genuine known faces. In the daytime, during the march, these shreds of dreams developed further. The ideas ramified in my brain time and again, wholly without my help. The continuation of the dream during the march was like something that spread out in me. Often there were people from the first third of my life who accompanied me. I could see them clearer than ever before, likewise my relationship to them.

My thoughts were much more radical and at the same time more distinct than at home. Erotic fantasies, for example, above all during the first few weeks.

The shadows fell much sharper. The sun stood always above me and, sharp as the shadows fell, so sharp were the outlines and contours of my thoughts.

After a week of acclimatizing I felt more secure as an ice traveller. I was explosively strong. Similar to the time when I, from the narrow climbing world of a small circle of climbing friends, first met with the famous mountaineers of the sixties and saw that my 'heroes' also climbed only with hands and feet, I knew now that in ice travel unperceived possibilities were open to me. As by my switch from the Alps to the Himalaya, new greater strengths accrued to me with the new higher goals.

Peter Scholz and Felix Kuen, for example had had not only the advantage of experience over me on our expedition to the Rupal face of Nanga Parbat in 1970, they had been mountaineers on whom I had modelled myself. To climb with them had been my honour and spur. After a few weeks I had learned everything from them. I knew spontaneously: high altitude mountaineering was capable of further development.

Arved told me about the Arctic. I admired his performances in Greenland and at the North Pole. At the same time I developed plans for adventure without his ability.

An adventurer who occupied my thoughts day after day was Sir Ernest Shackleton. In 1908 he had got to within 175 kilometres of the South Pole before he and his three friends had had to give up on account of lack of time and food:

27 December. If a great snow plain, rising every 7 miles in a steep ridge, can be called a plateau, then we are on it at last, with an altitude above the sea of 9,820 feet. We started at 7 a.m. and marched till noon, encountering at 11 a.m. a steep snow ridge which pretty well cooked us, but we got the sledge up by noon and camped. We are pulling 150 pounds per man. In the afternoon we had good going till 5 p.m. and then another ridge as difficult as the previous one, so that our backs and legs were in a bad way when we reached the top at 6 p.m., having done 14 miles 930 yards for the day. But it has been a fine day, with little wind. The temperature is minus 9° Fahrenheit. This surface is most peculiar, showing layers of snow with little sastrugi all pointing south-south-east. Short food makes us think of plum puddings, and hard half-cooked maize gives us indigestion, but we are getting south. The latitude is 86°19′ south tonight. Our thoughts are with the people at home a great deal.

How similar were Shackleton's experiences to our own. If I had models in ice travel, they were him and Nansen.

2 January, 1909. Terribly hard work today. We started at 6.45 a.m. with a fairly good surface, which soon became very soft. We were sinking in over our ankles, and our broken sledge, by running sideways, added to the drag. We have been going uphill all day, and tonight are 11,034 feet above sea-level. It has taken us all day to do 10 miles 450 yards, though the weights are fairly light, a cold wind, with a temperature of minus 14° Fahrenheit, goes right through us now, as we are weakening from want of food, and the high altitude makes every movement an effort, especially if we stumble on the march. My head is giving me trouble all the time. Wild seems the most fit of us. God knows we are doing all we can, but the outlook is serious if this surface continues and the plateau gets higher, for we are not travelling fast enough to make our food spin out and get back to our depot in time. I cannot think of failure yet. I must look at the matter sensibly and consider the lives of those who are with me. I feel that if we go on too far it will be impossible to get back

To march for three months across a flat snow landscape is more exciting than I had imagined; for example, the texture of the snow crust!

over this surface, and then all the results will be lost to the world. We can now definitely locate the South Pole on the highest plateau in the world, and our geological work and meteorology will be of the greatest use to science; but all this is not the Pole. Man can only do his best, and we have arrayed against us the strongest forces of nature. This cutting south wind with drift plays the mischief with us, and after ten hours of struggling against it one pannikin of food with two biscuits and a cup of cocoa does not warm one up much. I must think over the situation carefully tomorrow, for time is going on and food is going also.

What had we still ahead of us? Would I have gone on if I had known that also my sledge would break under the load? Would hunger plague us too? I am certain, had we perceived before setting out all the drudgery and danger, we would have stayed at home. Moreover, I was familiar with Shackleton's report and Scott's diary. In my sub-conscious, however, I hoped things would go better with us.

4 January. The end is in sight. We can only go for three more days at the most, for we are weakening rapidly. Short food and a blizzard wind from the south, with driving drift, at a temperature of 47° of frost have plainly told us today that we are reaching our limit, for we were so done up at noon with cold that the clinical thermometer failed to register the temperature of three of us at 94°. We started at 7.40 a.m., leaving a depot on this great wide plateau, a risk that only this case justified, and one that my comrades agreed to, as they have to every one so far, with the same cheerfulness and regardlessness of self that have been the means of our getting as far as we have done so far. Pathetically small looked the bamboo, one of the tent poles, with a bit of bag sewn on as a flag, to mark our stock of provisions, which has to take us back to our depot 150 miles north. We lost sight of it in half an hour, and are now trusting our footprints in the snow to guide us back to each bamboo until we pick up the depot again. I trust that the weather will keep clear. Today we have done 12½ geographical miles, and with only 70 pounds per man to pull it is as hard, even harder, work

The Shackleton expedition on their way south. Sails could be rigged on the sledges. The kilometre wheel served (with sextant and compass) for navigation.

than the 100 odd pounds was yesterday, and far harder than the 250 pounds were three weeks ago, when we were climbing the glacier. This, I consider, is a clear indication of our failing strength. The main thing against us is the altitude of 11,200 feet, and the biting wind. Our faces are cut, and our feet and hands are always on the verge of frostbite. Our fingers, indeed, often go, but we get them round more or less . . . I am of the opinion that to sledge even in the height of summer on this plateau, we should have at least 40 ounces of food a day per man, and we are on short rations of the ordinary allowance of 32 ounces. We depoted our extra underclothing to save weight about three weeks ago, and are now in the same clothes night and day. One suit of underclothing, shirt and guernsey, and our thin Burberries, now all patched. When we get up in the morning, out of the wet bag, our Burberries become like a coat of mail at once, and our heads and beards get iced-up with the moisture when breathing on the march. There is half a gale blowing dead in our teeth all the time. We hope to reach within 100 geographical miles of the Pole; under the circumstances we can expect to do very little more. I am confident that the Pole lies on the great plateau we have discovered, miles and miles from any outstanding land. The temperature tonight is minus 24° Fahrenheit.

5 January. Today head wind and drift again, with 50° of frost, and a terrible surface. We have been marching through 8 inches of snow, covering sharp sastrugi, which plays hell with our feet.

I didn't see myself as a hero as I pulled my sledge over the sastrugi. Laughable as it was to endure this drudgery, I wanted to come through. We must get to the Pole and across the other side! Only because we had undertaken it. All logical arguments were no longer valid. Unbelievable, how 'Shack' drove his men on eighty years before, although there was no chance of reaching the South Pole.

6 January. This must be our last outward march with the sledge and camp equipment. Tomorrow we must leave camp with some food, and push as far south as possible, and then plant the flag.

Our hopes were high. Despite all our delay and the slow speed of march. I did not want to hoist a flag, rather to endure, to come through like Shackleton.

7 January. A blinding, shrieking blizzard all day, with the temperature ranging from 60° to 70° of frost. It has been impossible to leave the tent, which is snowed up on the lee side. We have been lying in our bags all day, only warm at food time, with fine snow making through the walls of the worn tent and covering our bags.

Wild, Marshall, Adams and Shackleton got to within 90 miles of the Pole. Their 'record' signified nothing to me. But the experience that was bound up with that I would have shared gladly. Despite everything.

We were so dead tired that we only did two hours' march in the afternoon and camped at 5.30 p.m. The temperature was minus 19° Fahrenheit. Fortunately for us, our tracks were not obliterated by the blizzard; indeed, they stood up, making a trail easily followed. Homeward bound at last. Whatever regrets may be, we have done our best.

The return march is one of the most exciting Antarctic adventures. 'Shack' and his team arrived at McMurdo at the last possible moment – his ship had already put to sea. Scott was to lose his life four years later on the same return march. After Scott, no one had attempted the route from the South Pole to McMurdo Sound. We were the next ones. With similar technique, with self-drawn food sledges and sail help we wanted to try this return route, the whole stretch of which had been done by no one. Moreover, for Arved and me, there were no preconstructed food dumps like Shackleton had laid up for the return march.

10 January. We started at 7.30 a.m. with a fair wind, and marched all day, with a stop of one hour for lunch, doing over 18½ geographical miles to the north. It has, indeed, been fortunate for us that we have been able to follow our outward tracks, for the force of the gale had torn the flags from the staffs. We will be all right when we pick up our depot. It has been a big risk leaving our food on the great white plain, with only our sledge tracks to guide us back. Tonight we are all tired out, but we have put a good march behind us. The temperature is minus 9° Fahrenheit.

11 January. A good day. We have done nearly 17 geographical miles. We have picked up our depot and now are following the sledge tracks to the north. The temperature has been minus 15° Fahrenheit. There has been tremendous wind here, and the sastrugi are enormous.

12 January. We did 14 miles 100 yards today with little wind to help us. The surface was very heavy and we found enormous sastrugi. The wind is getting up tonight. I hope for a good breeze behind us tomorrow.

Never before had man penetrated so far south as Shackleton, Wild, Marshall and Adams in the 1908/09 Antarctic summer.

Shackleton and his men marched fast. Nevertheless they were too slow.

25 February. We turned out at 4 a.m. for an early start, as we are in danger of being left if we do not push ahead rapidly and reach the ship. On going into the tent for breakfast I found Marshall suffering from paralysis of the stomach and renewed dysentery, and while we were eating a blizzard came up. We secured everything as the Bluff showed masses of ragged cloud, and I was of the opinion that it was going to blow hard. I did not think Marshall fit to travel through the blizzard. During the afternoon, as we were lying in the bags, the weather cleared somewhat, though it still blew hard. If Marshall is not better tonight, I must leave him with Adams and push on, for time is going on, and the ship may leave on 1 March, according to orders, if the Sound is not clear of ice. I went over through the blizzard to Marshall's tent. He is in a bad way still, but thinks that he could travel tomorrow.

What an overwintering would have meant after all these exertions is scarcely to be imagined and thus understandable were the forced marches to which 'Shack' drove his people.

> *27 February* (1 a.m.) . . . We did 24 miles. Marshall suffered greatly, but stuck to the march. He never complains.

When Adams and Marshall could no longer go on, Shackleton went ahead with Wild. The failure shortly before the Pole was forgotten. The lost group was still on its way, back to the ship, back to safety. Survival alone mattered. On the first day of February 1909 their fate was decided.

> We reached the top of Ski Slope at 7.45 p.m., and from there we could see the hut and the bay. There was no sign of the ship, and no smoke or other evidence of life at the hut. We hurried on to the hut, our minds busy with gloomy possibilities, and found not a man there. There was a letter stating that the Northern Party had reached the Magnetic Pole and that all the parties had been picked up except ours. The letter added that the ship would be sheltering under Glacier Tongue until 26 February. It was now 28 February, and it was with very keen anxiety in our minds that we proceeded to search for food. If the ship was gone, our plight, and that of the two men left out on the Barrier, was a very serious one.
>
> We improvised a cooking vessel, found oil and a Primus lamp, and had a good feed of biscuit, onions and plum pudding, which were amongst the stores left at the hut. We were utterly weary, but we had no sleeping gear, our bags having been left with the sledge, and the temperature was very low. We found a piece of roofing felt, which we wrapped round us, and then we sat up all night, the darkness being relieved only when we occasionally lighted the lamp in order to secure a little warmth. We tried to burn the magnetic hut in the hope of attracting attention from the ship, but we were not able to get it alight. We tried, too, to tie the Union Jack to Vince's cross, on the hill, but we were so played out that our cold fingers could not manage

the knots. It was a bad night for us, and we were glad indeed when the light came again. Then we managed to get a little warmer, and at 9 a.m. we got the magnetic hut alight and put up the flag. All our fears vanished when in the distance we saw the ship. We signalled with the heliograph, and at 11 a.m. on 1 March we were on board the *Nimrod* and once more safe amongst friends. I will not attempt to describe our feelings. Every one was glad to see us, and keen to know what we had done. They had given us up for lost, and a search-party had been going to start that day in the hope of finding some trace of us. I found that every member of the expedition was well, that the plans had worked out satisfactorily, and that the work laid down had been carried out. The ship had brought nothing but good news from the outside world. It seemed as though a great load had been lifted from my shoulders.

The first thing was to bring in Adams and Marshall, and I ordered out a relief party at once. I had a good feed of bacon and fried bread, and started at 2.30 p.m. from the Barrier edge with Mackay, Mawson and McGillan, leaving Wild on the *Nimrod*. We marched until 10 p.m., had dinner and turned in for a short sleep. We were up again at 2 a.m. the next morning (2 March), and travelled until 1 p.m., when we reached the camp where I had left the two men. Marshall was better, the rest having done him a lot of good, and he was able to march and pull. After lunch we started back again, and marched until 8 p.m. in fine weather. We were under way again at 4 a.m. the next morning, had lunch at noon, and reached the ice-edge at 3 p.m. There was no sign of the ship, and the sea was freezing over. We waited until 5 p.m., and then found that it was possible to strike land at Pram Point. The weather was coming on bad, clouding up from the south-east and Marshall was suffering from renewed dysentery, the result of the heavy marching. We therefore abandoned one tent and one sledge at the ice-edge, taking on only the sleeping-bags and the specimens. We climbed up by Crater Hill, leaving everything but the sleeping-bags, for the weather was getting worse, and at 9.35 p.m. commenced to slide down towards Hut Point. We reached the winter quarters at 9.50 p.m., and Marshall was put to bed. Mackay and I lighted a carbide flare on the hill by Vince's cross, and after dinner all hands turned in except Mackay and myself. A short time after Mackay saw the ship appear. It was now blowing a hard blizzard, but Mackintosh had seen our flare from a distance of 9 miles. Adams and I went on board the *Nimrod*, and Adams, after surviving all the dangers of the interior of the Antarctic continent, was nearly lost within sight of safety. He slipped at the ice-edge, owing to the fact that he was wearing new finnesko, and he only just saved himself from going over. He managed to hang on until he was rescued by a party from the ship.

A boat went back for Marshall and the others, and we were all safe on board at 1 a.m. on 4 March.

Arved and I were delayed in arriving in the Antarctic. How would we get on? Although I feared that we too could get into trouble like Shackleton in his time, if we did not increase our daily distance marched, to begin with I had fallen in with Arved's proposals. He had crossed Greenland with dog sledges. His additional experience was for me grounds for listening to him.

However, when we came upon ever worse fields of sastrugi and our speed dwindled, I became uneasy. Now I ran faster and always ahead, whereas Arved got slower after the fourth hour. More and more I had to wait for him at the rest stops.

To begin with we had rested after each full hour. Over the days we had agreed on a compromise: six hours' running daily, divided thus: two full hours in the morning; then fifteen minutes' stop; then four times one hour with respectively fifteen minutes' rest in between. I could not be satisfied with that. I wanted only one thing – that we increase our march performance to 7 or 8 hours per day. I wanted to be at the Pole in good time, in order to have at least a chance of making the Antarctic traverse.

It was not that I went ahead from choice. I saw myself compelled to it. I had to do it if we wanted to do at least 12 miles in the day. As I had the greater speed, I reckoned the hours run by my watch. Arved needed decidedly longer for the same stretch. That was no problem unless I got too cooled down in the rest stops. Naturally, it would have been better to run equally fast. But it didn't work. Had we run at Arved's speed from the beginning, we would certainly have reached the Pole but not been able to do the crossing.

To the Thiel Mountains it was 500 kilometres. I wanted to use this first stage to learn from Arved, to gather experience, to get to know the Antarctic. At the start I had subordinated myself to Arved's standard. Except for his running speed. The daily shortfall would have become irretrievable. Reckoned at ninety days maximum, we would have been 400 or 500 kilometres short. How often I pondered how we could improve our tactics!

At this time the first critical newspaper articles about our adventure appeared in Europe. On 18 November there appeared in a 'daily':

Reinhold Messner . . . now precipitates himself upon the poor Antarctic. Together with Arved Fuchs, who is already unpleasantly conspicuous through a twilight [sic!] North Pole action. The new adventure is called 'Antarktis-Transversale'. They will travel some 3,500 kilometres across Antarctica. Naturally, not only the uninhabited ice desert entices them, rather they want also to draw attention to the danger of the ozone hole and to fight for a 'World Park Antarctica'. The six-man group 'Trans-Antarctica' have the same aim. These people, financed by a French insurance company and a dog food manufacturer, want to cover 8,000 kilometres with dog sledges. With their expedition, the 'last great land expedition before the start of the third millenium', they want, naturally, 'to direct the attention of world publicity towards the Antarctic'. Naturally, US television carries it live.

I accepted the scepticism. Although we had undertaken to leave no rubbish behind on the ice, mistakes happened. Already in the early days, when putting up the tent, the storm had ripped one of my two ground mats out of my hand. They were foam rubber mats and, although I had tried to catch it, it vanished into the distance, never to be seen again. In great bounds it leaped across the ice. There were no rocks, no crevasses, no bushes where the mat could have got caught up. A few days later I lost the kilometre wheel off the sledge. In sailing

On the other side of Antarctica lay the ship Barken. *If we arrived at McMurdo Sound at the right time (mid-February), it would pick us up.*

over the sastrugi the mounting had broken. Arved, who was travelling behind me, didn't find it. As our GPS system functioned faultlessly, we were not dependent on the wheel but it was civilization rubbish left behind. The 'daily' was right again. Our good intentions had been only lip-service:

> We know it sounds all right on paper but in an ecosystem in which the human species does not exist, any human activity is a problem. Exemplary as the recommendations and environmental protection regulations of the Antarctic Treaty are, nations offend against it already. Yet there is no central authority, and offences are still not discussed at the biennial consultative meetings.

Sure, our environmental sins were infinitely small in relation to the damage caused by each ship which cruised in Antarctic waters, to say nothing of the bases. Nonetheless, we took it seriously. When I thought I had lost my Thermos flask, I was doubly frightened. I wanted to be careful. Nothing, but nothing at all, more did I want to lose. After I had found it again on the sledge, I put it inside the tent. In the evening before going to sleep, I refilled it and talked to it as one does with a child. What would I have done without my flask!

Arved and I were travellers, not tourists. At least not here. Whatever befell tourism in the Antarctic, I pleaded that first it be restricted and secondly that it might take place only on foot. No one was to 'subdue' the ice continent with any sort of machine, which is the beginning of the ruin of any landscape.

Antarctica was proof that the world originally was paradise. Only when man began to work it and divide it up, had he invented 'hell'. It is an achievement of his culture. In the course of thousands of years then he has muddled up his 'hell' with his 'heaven'. Through technology, machines, atomic power stations, the strive after heaven became again a hell. In the interior of the Antarctic the primitive state ruled. Heaven and hell were one here. I set off in the morning; it was a fantastic day. Clear sky. After ten minutes a snowstorm broke out. The hell was real. Inside a few hours I had experienced heaven and hell.

The world, like man, conceals heaven and hell in itself. When man tries to separate the two his paradise is lost. In the Antarctic, nature determines whether heaven or hell reigns. And between these two worlds, the threatening and the blessed, there is a mythological gateway to the world. This possibility of amassing experiences is a hundred thousand and more years old. Before there were art and science, man knew what lightning meant, without knowing that it concerned a discharge of electricity. This possibility of experience is lost to us. And this is one of the most essential reasons why something like the Antarctic must be preserved. If the Antarctic is developed, divided up, exploited, there is no more space where man can experience nature so directly. We must not parcel out, build on and wire up the 'useless' landscapes such as, for example, the Antarctic or Mount Everest. Man will starve spiritually if he can no longer think wilderness, which is undisturbed nature. This dimension in him is a power, which many primitive races have defined as divinity: nature mysticism. Through it man can perceive himself, yes, in the Antarctic

I felt myself stronger because there was nothing which distracted me. I went and I knew: you have come a long way, have a long way to go and in between you are somewhere. Statements of kilometres become meaningless. You know you go eternally and it lasts eternally until you arrive. Man is no more the measure of all things. Simultaneously, you give the Antarctic your human dimension with each step. Truth becomes relative and it becomes separable. Every perception, mine or whosoever's is always true here.

Arved and I marched through a manless world. Each with his sensations and thoughts. The rules of living together had reduced themselves to a few necessities: tolerance and readiness to help.

I no longer needed a world without people for my thoughts to play with, to experiment with. The past was here because no people were here. Here behaviour patterns were, for once, real rather than hypothetical. This march through a piece of truth, which once had filled the whole world, gave rise to another image of the world. The evaluations, right or wrong, good or bad, heaven and hell were not to be found in it.

Nature existed without these concepts. It was not even beautiful. I was here, saw, heard, moved. From ethic and aesthetic I was more and more removed. The plain was always the same. I was neither scientist nor theologian, nor romantic, nevertheless I knew. The realizations went right through me, without me trying to formulate or analyse them. The experience of existing came to me. What we now did and perceived, reached us as world. For all outsiders it appeared as a perception which they could not sympathize with.

How long ago was it that I had read the *Divine Comedy*? Twenty-five, thirty years? Why did Dante's images affect me so here?

> For visual strength, refining more and more,
> Bare me into the ray authentical
> Of sovran light. Thenceforward what I saw,
> Was not for words to speak, nor memory's self
> To stand against such outrage on her skill.
> As one, who from a dream awaken'd, straight,
> All he hath seen forgets; yet still retains
> Impression of the feeling in his dream;

It was as if the Antarctic were the paradise which Dante describes. Without knowing of the existence of this ice continent, some 700 years ago the poet had described those moods which we experience here in good weather. And only here.

> . . . give my tongue
> Power, but to leave one sparkle of Thy glory,
> Unto the race to come . . .

I was running easily now. In an ecstasy of thought chains, the hours passed quickly although the sledge was heavy. My sense of time shrank to the single day. And success depended on the sum of this single day. Yesterday was unimportant, tomorrow far away. Now is what counted.

Naturally, it cost an effort to get up at the right time each morning, to cook, to creep outside, to dismantle the tent and march away. Frequently the sledges stuck between the sastrugi. And when drift snow lay in the hollows, it was heavy as sand. We were fitter meanwhile, although the exertion was, on that account, no less great. My circling thoughts however, made me generally forget it.

In the first two hours of the morning I ran mostly without any feeling of tiredness. I enjoyed this running by myself. When once I was warm, I would have liked not to interrupt the rhythm again. Nevertheless, time and again I looked back to see whether Arved was following, particularly when the weather was bad. In mist or when we marched in white-out, we had to remain in visual contact. Also in powder snow, although my sledge track remained recognizable as waymark. There was never any danger of losing ourselves. In white-out I went slower. But I was compelled to stop time and again.

The going in fine weather was something else. As far as I could see then, so far could I think too. Often I ran kilometres ahead. Nothing held me back.

The blisters which had bothered me in the early days were healed. I had no pains. Feet and joints recovered during the hours of sleep. It was quite otherwise with Arved. His feet became worse day by day. Running was a torment for him.

131

Compass on my chest, I pressed on, thinking away to myself. Generally, on awakening in the 'morning', I took the tip of a dream with me as a thought trigger on the ice. The corresponding fantasies pursued me the whole 'day'. The chains of thought branched out like a great tree. The further I went, the longer I went, that much clearer became the details. My mental pictures were precise. Frequently I was on my estate at Juval. During the march, in thought I arranged rooms anew. I became conscious of breaches of style. Architecture as thought game. I saw the room proportions clearly before me. My ability to remember coincided completely with reality. I was distracted by nothing. No music. No telephone. No street. Nothing. Another day during the march the idea for a museum of graphic buildings developed. A fantastic place in South Tyrol served me as a real reference. The place is called Lichtenberg and it is a ruin. The hill on which the empty walls stand, has a special light. All the roofs which no longer exist, in fancy I built anew. Out of glass and steel. Roofs like crystal: amethyst, cairngorms, mountain crystal. From outside, my dream museum looked like an illuminated mountain. A glass castle. The visitors were to pass through and understand what mountains meant for people. I reflected on symbols which every one understands, and about that mountain of light which we would all like to climb in order to descend enlightened. Lichtenberg as a key to the orientation of the soul.

This running gladdened me. I enjoyed it. I am conscious that many dismiss my lust for running as sickness. Specialists call it dromomania. I did not believe in an erotically motivated roving spirit but my travelling is compulsive. A life at the office desk, I could not have endured. Rather I moved through the ice desert like a pubescent, as the psychoanalyst Magnus Hirschfeld explained this running mania.

All explorers, amongst whom, however, I did not count myself, are thought to have suffered from dromomania: Marco Polo, Sven Hedin, Roald Amundsen. The ancient Greek adventurer Odysseus was reputedly the father of all eccentrics who had become slaves to this 'delusion', which had suggested the theory to the psychologist Ludwig Märzbacher. Adventuring was also morbid. Don't make me laugh! Given that man is a pedestrian and, other things being equal, wants to travel all his life, many stay-at-homes understandably react aggressively. To make amends for their own inactivity, they impute to us wanderers, next to inner unrest, also the inability for sexual union. As simple as that!

After we had run for a week across the ice. I had resigned myself to the sastrugi. The journey was now more enjoyment than sorrow. For me a new slice of life had begun. It was as if I had always been an ice traveller. There was only one burden, one doubt: our slow progress. Yet I hoped Arved would get faster by and by and that his blisters would heal. As yet I did not perceive that the delay was to become a permanent misfortune, that for three long months we would run behind schedule.

6   Sastrugi, nothing but Sastrugi

For days we had been going through fields of sastrugi. In stormy weather I could see exactly how these snow waves were formed. There, where there was a hard place in the snow surface the wind caught hold. First it dug a hole in the 'head' of a growing sastrugi. Behind it, often a dozen or more metres, a long drawn-out body developed, which was scraped out of the surface like a narrow, giant-size fish. From above, the landscape here would look like a freshly ploughed field. The ground still climbed evenly. We did not pull the sledges, we tugged them across the heavy snow and tore them free when they jammed between sastrugi. Thus we went on day after day across the ice.

In giant waves it 'flowed' northwards. The landscape here was similar to the snow surfaces described by Vivian Fuchs on his 1957–58 Trans-Antarctic expedition. The dip and ridges were only distinguishable by the differing lighting. The valleys were bright, the wave ridges darker, about 8 kilometres apart.

It was spring, according to the calendar. But spring had never got this far. This snow was not thawing. On the other side of the globe it was now autumn. When we returned, it would be spring again there. What did spring look like? Or autumn? Without bubbling springs, without damp ground, without plants? Between a stormy winter and a summer with minus 40°C, spring and autumn look alike. Nothing but snow and ice all around. We knew now how the summer would be, although it was still ahead of us. Here there were only winter and summer. Twenty-four hours of night or twenty-four hours of daylight. Now was always evening or morning. Long shadows fell and moved around us. We marched for more than six hours while the sun described a third of a circle. I went ahead so as to maintain a regular speed. Whilst moving now, I experienced a feeling of vitality and self-confidence. I did not suffer from the strain of sledge pulling, only

134

from the fact that we were limping along behind our schedule. If we were to be at the Thiel Mountains in fifteen days, we had to march at least six hours per day. We were doing about 2 miles an hour now. Arved was up to it despite his pain. Each step a torment. His feet were sore or bloodshot on heels and balls.

It remained important that Arved did not lose his enthusiasm and self-confidence. I had to urge him on without hurting and thereby weakening him. We understood each other, although we said little, and the relationship between us remained unproblematical.

In the 'evening' in the tent, we recovered quickly. Cooking had become a routine. Arved operated the GPS set and determined our exact position. The wind slowly died down. In the tent it smelt of cake and damp clothes. It was more pleasant than I had pictured it to myself at home. Our conversation remained confined to practical questions. We never asked ourselves whether this march made any sense. We were just going to our next supply dump. In the morning, while packing the sledges, sometimes many of our survival aids seemed to me so unnecessary. I would have loved to throw them away. The weight of the sledges was our drag. It held us back. It gave rise to blisters and made our tendons swell. In the last analysis, all our troubles stemmed from it. It was as if we were constantly pulling a cart out of the mud. Nevertheless, we reckoned to be at the Thiel depot by 5 December. If no depot had been set up there, our expedition was again in doubt and our survival not ensured. I didn't want to think about that. Often it was as if I were crossing a stream bed of white marble which a torrent had modelled out of the ground over thousands of years, so rumpled was the glittering snow surface. And in the 'evening' it was accordingly difficult to find a level camp site. Still more difficult was to make radio contact with Ulrich Jaeger who was still stationed at Patriot Hills: to make our sledge load as bearable as possible, we had taken the smallest possible radio set with us.

The little Spillsbury Radio – made in Canada – which we had with us weighed only 3½ kilos. Indeed, its output was only 10 watts. On the first contact, the set had worked without snags. Came the next arranged time – no contact, so we tried it again on the following 'evening'. Contact was established. 'Polar Cross, Polar Cross, do you copy?' called Ulrich Jaeger on his set at Patriot Hills. In the short wave ether of the southern hemisphere regular contact took place less frequently the further we distanced ourselves from the camp. On the three frequencies (4,441, 5,583, 8,980) which our expedition radio received, often we heard only indefinable noises and Jaeger, at the other end, a rustling vacuum. We wanted to establish radio contact only twice a week, but even that did not succeed. I had been afraid that the batteries would run down quickly in the cold: then we would not have been able to radio in emergency. In order to be able to transmit, each time we had to lay out 16 metres of aerial. Ulrich Jaeger had it easier. His radio set, type Yaegu, stood in a 20-square-metre head-high tent, with a long table, a propane gas stove and a petrol oven. The team tent was the community centre of Patriot Hills Camp. It smelled of matted hair and bubbling spaghetti sauce: a jumble of howling wind and English chatter.

At last we were ready. The radio set was in the tent and warmed up, the aerials outside, one hanging to the left of the tent, one to the right. The wires were stretched between a ski in the middle and the tops of two sastrugi.

'Romeo Bravo, Romeo Bravo, do you copy?', called Arved.

'Romeo Bravo to Polar Cross. Yes, I hear you. Do you read? Over.' That was Jaeger.

Each time there followed a long conversation. Jaeger wanted to know exactly how we were progressing. For the time being the sastrugi were always our main obstacle and I wisecracked about it: 'We guess that "sastrugi" comes from "sastrugo" and means something like disaster.'

'What's your daily routine?'

'Dismantling the tent takes forty-five minutes. Then we set off, run two hours. Then a rest for fifteen minutes, with a drink from our Thermos flasks. Then we go on for another hour, have another stop and so on, until the six hours' run are done. Then I look for a place for the tent. The tent is laid out and fixed to the ice-axe on the windward side. We get the equipment, then ourselves into the tent. Once inside, we de-ice our faces and strip off down to our underwear. Everything damp and icy we hang up in the roof. After fifteen minutes it is warm in the tent. The evening cooking lasts at least two hours. The food tastes good. We sleep more than eight hours.'

Sastrugi 'head'. Often I could make out figures in the sastrugi: a dragon, a fish; also familiar human faces.

'Any frost-bite?'

'Our noses are a bit swollen, our cheeks have thickened.'

'Do you alternate the leading?'

'No. We set off together. I go ahead and run by compass. Arved, meanwhile, checks the bearing from behind to see if I am on course. Besides, the sastrugi set the course as well as a compass. On a bearing we cross them all the time at a predetermined angle. We meet up again mostly after each hour.'

'Is it easier for Arved, who weighs more, to pull the sledge?'

'It's not easier for Arved to pull the sledge.'

'Are the sastrugi the reason for your slow progress?'

'Not entirely, although the sledge often sticks. Then it moves jerkily and bangs against your hips! If Arved had no blisters, we could do 30 kilometres per day.'

'Does the wind hold you up?'

'There is a great difference going against the wind compared with no wind.'

'Do you believe you would have got through on the original route?'

'Had we set off at the right time and gone from the Filchner Shelf Ice, at all events we would be further on today. We would have been able to sail much more often. Here we have encountered unfavourable terrain. I think we have clicked for the worst possible stretch.'

'What do sastrugi look like? There aren't any here in Patriot Hills.'

'Sastrugi are hard, angular and on average a metre high. It is especially bad when visibility is bad. Then we stumble along like drunks.'

'Can things get any faster?'

'With an ideal wind, sailing and no sastrugi we could cover 40 to 45 miles per day.'

'How is the sailing?'

'Sailing is the ideal means of locomotion. It exerts only legs and arms. Your fingers get cold because your hands are raised all the time. So far we have had unfavourable winds, always head or side. The sails would be a tremendous help if we could use them properly. They are also what give us hope. From the Pole to McMurdo we could be much faster – assuming we reach the Pole at the beginning of the New Year at the latest. The stretch down from the Pole should not be so full of sastrugi.'

'Any injuries, other than Arved's feet?'

'We both had cracked lips, from wind and sun which we attended to carefully. They have cleared up.'

'Reinhold, is it easier or harder than you had imagined?'

'Harder. When I developed the idea, I worked on different ground conditions, that is soft snow, no sastrugi.'

'A question for Arved. Put him on, please.'

I gave Arved the microphone.

'Yes, receiving.'

'Arved, how are your feet?'

'On the balls I have deep blisters and my heels are rubbed raw.'

'Is it different from the North Pole?'

'At the North Pole it was certainly rougher but there are no sastrugi there.'

'And in Greenland?'

'In Greenland the surface is soft. This year it seems to be especially bad in the Antarctic. I had imagined the top surface to be softer.'

138

'Are you too slow because of it?'

'If we could run directly southwards and no longer have to cross the sastrugi, we would be fast enough. Running over sastrugi is like crossing a gigantic sheet of corrugated iron. For the time being we want to stick at six or seven hours' march daily. We estimate that we can be at the Pole at the beginning of January.'

'Describe the sastrugi for me as well.'

'Sastrugi are the result of erosion. It is like on the beach or in sandstone mountains. The wind carves bizzare forms out of the hard snow.'

'Can you recover during the stops?'

'At the North Pole the stops were more pleasant. You could tuck yourself behind an ice block and enjoy the rest. That's not possible here. Here you are always exposed to the wind and you cool down after a short while.'

'And the scenery. What's the scenery like?'

'The dimensions one has to cope with here are different from anything in Greenland. It's like a ship on the open sea. Day after day. Never the feeling of getting anywhere.'

'A few more questions for Reinhold. How are you coping with everyday life?'

'For me the expedition is not unpleasant. I had expected more tent boredom. Only our speed worries me. Living in a sleeping-bag, having to cook, are not to my taste but more pleasant than in the mountains. As a climber, I am used to having Sherpas cook for me. And at home I am pampered by women. Nevertheless, I am enjoying life in the tent. Arved makes it congenial.'

'Is it cold?'

'In the sleeping-bag it is so warm that we can sleep in our underwear.'

'How are you sleeping?'

'Good in comparison with sleeping high on a mountain. There it is much more difficult to find a campsite. There you sit through storms always scared stiff of being swept off the ledge on which the tent stands in the night. I don't have this anxiety here. Nevertheless, to begin with it was difficult to sleep during storms. Meanwhile we have confidence in our tent.'

'And the exertion? I mean the effort to progress compared with mountaineering?'

'The going with the sledge is more strenuous than I thought. We are pulling a heavy load behind us. Time and again the sledge sticks. You are continually waiting for a bump from behind.'

'Do you see a real chance of making it?'

'I think we can and must increase our daily performance from seven to eight hours. More is wellnigh impossible without risking injury.'

'When do you hope to be at the Pole?'

'I am still confident that, God willing, we can still reach the Pole at the beginning of the New Year or even on the last day of this year.'

'Do you regret the decision to set off?'

'I am now as before glad that I have attempted this march. Once more in my life I have opened up another dimension of adventure. A world which, previously, was strange to me.'

'Your trek is being criticized in Europe.'

'I have to smile at that. Time and again in my life I have had to battle against critics and there were always know-alls who warned me against something. On none of my previous expeditions have there been so many calls, letters, warnings as on this one. They all wanted to have me unconditionally restrained.'

'Aren't they right, your critics? Isn't the trip too hard?'

'It's a part of life, like I experienced on Mount Everest or K2. Only here it all lasts much longer. Much, much longer. We are even more dependent on ourselves alone.'

'But without any reference point, without goal.'

'We are going to the Pole. We have a goal. It is not entirely different from a mountain.'

'So you're not thinking about giving up?'

'No. At the moment I see our chances as positive.'

Ulrich Jaeger wished us all the best.

'Roger, Roger.'

We had understood. After these words we confirmed the next radio time: 'Next Sunday, 9 p.m. Roger, and Out.'

Jaeger agreed. 'Ciao, Ciao.'

That was on the tenth day of the journey – Thursday, 23 November. On the following Sunday, 26 November, we were to wait in vain.

Arved and I had played down our situation with journalist Jaeger. We were slow. Things couldn't be worse. Our situation was hopeless. I did not ask myself about the sense of this journey but for days I knew that what we were doing was ludicrous; yet I still wanted to do it. We had covered less than 200 kilometres. We had run uninterruptedly through fields of sastrugi. How could we hope that these snow waves would cease? How might we be faster? Navigation was no problem, life in the tent restful. Only with our speed of march was there something wrong.

With the GPS set we had a good feeling all the time. We could do without the sextant. Although a mountaineer, I had not done any surveying. I trusted Arved's positional data. And I saw our movements on the aeronautical chart. No, I had neither a mountain nor a nunatak or a crevasse as orientation mark in front of me. Holding the course with the compass was strenuous, no more.

We were not only slow because Arved was suffering from foot problems and lack of training. Again and again we lost time or ground; in each storm, in each white-out. Once we had such bad visibility that we could scarcely see our ski tips and groped along as if it were dark. That cost energy and time. I was conscious that we were not the first to be plagued with initial difficulties on this continent of storms. All Antarctic expeditions since Scott and Shackleton have found it hard to get started. That was a comfort and a spur not to give up. We hoped for better terrain and better weather in December and January. We must, however, soon increase our performance to 28 kilometres per day. Only then had we a chance of being at McMurdo by 15 February before winter returned.

For the time being it looked as if we would not make it. Even with good visibility I believed we were only marking time. Marching gave me energy and hope, however. My gaze lost itself in the boundless ice waste and I forced the pace. Then metre-high snow waves again.

On this first stage, where no one had ever been before, often we had no choice but to unbuckle our skis and to lug the sledges over the sastrugi step by step. Also, here a flat surface is uneven in detail. Wind grooves and dents everywhere, in which grainy drift snow collected. With each wind it was newly filled and blown around. As our bath-tub

Mostly the British party under Scott's leadership had pulled their sledges. Generally speaking, our method of locomotion was comparable with theirs.

sledges slid over such drift-snow fields, they slowed down, as if they had got into dry sand. A jerk. You stop. Redoubling your effort, you lay into the harness in order to get going again. Only when the sledge kept moving did it glide well. When it stuck it was as if a brake had been applied. The young 'Birdie' Bowers, who, as a member of Captain Scott's Pole expedition lost his life with his chief, had called this sledge pulling 'the worst bone-shaking I have ever come across'.

Despite all, running was the most beautiful, at least for me. How I enjoyed this movement! How widely my thoughts digressed! Arved experienced it otherwise. He suffered. And he was cross about my speed. He hated me off and on for my hurrying ahead, for my heartlessness. I noticed his anger but could not help him. I was running indeed with the same load as he, but the drudgery of pulling sapped me less than him. I ran constantly below my performance limit. Accustomed to hard work from childhood and, through climbing, familiar with the sport of suffering over three decades, this ice travel was for me a timeless walking along. I could have gone a life long thus. Movement as a pastime; movement as the rhythm of thought; movement as meditation.

In bad weather, in storms from the south, it was otherwise. The wind in my face checked and disturbed my thoughts. Often then I lost my footing on the sastrugi. Then there was the new snow. Alternately hard and soft underfoot. Otherwise, the route led easily uphill all the time. Sometime we must arrive on top. We could go upwards for weeks without ever arriving!

When once we were sailing, I forgot everything. The snow surface ran away under me. Vapour and drift snow, however, made sky and earth quickly blur into a white soup. You became blind; sailing was impossible. Therefore all you could do was run, run, run, with no recognizable sign that you were going forward. In storms we could only leave the tent in the 'morning' to relieve nature. With 90kph wind and 20° frost no one wanted to go outside. If the piss-pot were full, in the morning we each did 'the relief run': a freezing shock.

These days of storm were not entirely lost days. Arved could cure his feet. We rested. The hope that, without pain, Arved would be able to run faster was like a narcotic for me.

Arved has big feet – size thirteen – and he attributed his foot problems to his boots. We wore the same boots but with him the leverage was longer. Our boots were made of leather. That gave us both problems. The tongue in the middle got out of place and pressed on the inside of the ankle. Socks got out of place. After six hours of marching this produced blood blisters. Each swelling was hellishly painful and the pain was debilitating. Our feet were constantly exposed to excess pressure: body weight plus brake load/horsepower of the sledge plus wind resistance. Under the balls of his feet – in fact under the thick horny skin – Arved formed blood blisters. They could be pricked open but they did not want to heal. Often in bad weather we sat in the tent and doctored Arved's feet. With a sewing needle, which he had sterilized in the flame of the cooker, he pierced the blisters and drew threads through them. These threads remained between flesh and horny skin and were to dry out the blisters. Part of the time Arved had up to four threads in one foot. The fluid oozed out but, nonetheless, fresh blisters formed, more blood.

Rest days – voluntary or otherwise – lasted up to twenty-four hours. Then we had to carry on. That was painful. When you climbed into your boots in the 'morning', it started to hurt and continued to do so until you took them off again in the 'evening'. The cramping through the pain and the loading led to inflammation of the tendon sheath. With the sledge behind us came a double pressure on the front foot, on the balls, on the heel. Man is not built to pull a sledge load. After a while each bone hurts you. I was in pain too, even though I have smaller feet, thus less leverage and less pressure. After Nanga Parbat in 1970, most of my toes were partially amputated. My much shorter feet were an advantage, here at least. Not only his feet, but also his bindings suffered under Arved's bigger pressure. He managed to bust two ski bindings which I had been assured could not break.

During the first three weeks, Arved's feet got worse daily. He complained each 'evening' that they pained him. An end to his pain was as little in sight as the end of our route. The distance was unreal. We could only calculate how far it was. And we were too slow. When, in the 'evening', I multiplied our day's performance by the days at our disposal, I knew that we would not make it. Arved knew it too.

For what miracle were we waiting? For wind, sound feet and lighter sledges. Each on the other. Thus all calculation remained only theoretical. Somehow we would get through. Arved was for the time being not fit to and not ready to march more than six hours per day. Plus the fact that, in bad weather, we stayed in the tent or gave up after a few hours' march. Each week we lost many hours of marching time.

Often as I lay in my sleeping-bag in the 'evening', eyes closed, the day's snow surface ran away under me. It was like being in the cinema. I saw the many rugosities, the sastrugi which I had seen daily emerge and vanish under my skis. Although I had consciously registered nothing, it remained stored up. Snow pictures frozen in my memory. My nightly dreams were more vivid than my reveries during the day. Often I woke up. Lying awake in the tent, endless memory chains combined into a dream picture of my life. Suddenly it would occur to me that we needed something in the Thiel depot. I noted it for the next radio contact:

144

For Thiel: one pocket knife, fingerless gloves. Mail, *Der Spiegel*. Radio set U/S.

Because I was already sitting there and writing in my diary with clammy fingers, I recorded an equipment suggestion which had occupied me the day before:

Markill Thermos flask: very good, stays hot a long time. Drawbacks: cup too small; must have flat bottom. Screw fastening needs better grip. Colour the flask red. Only white available! Easily left behind in snow.

I lay down again. Hoar-frost crumbled from the inner wall of the tent. Outside the sleeping-bag, bare shoulders and arms were cold.

Outside it was always bright. Always cold. In the tent the temperature sank to minus 10°–20°, depending on how cold it was outside. 'Day' and 'night' were not only the same in the brightness. Also in my sensations I could not distinguish dreams from thoughts. My observations had shrunk to a minimum. There was no tree, no bush, no mountains. Only the forms of the sastrugi were always different. Now and then they looked like animals, then like sculptures. Often I recognized people in the 'heads' of the snow waves. Otherwise only white surfaces. Around us the oval, grey horizon.

There were no sounds other than those we produced ourselves. And the wind, naturally. As we skied across the rough top surface, the snow crunched, as it did each time a ski stick was inserted. The sledges behind us created an irregular rumbling. The storm crashed, above all; when we were sitting in the tent. When a blizzard swept over the tent walls, it was so loud that we could not make ourselves heard in the tent, although we were only a few feet apart.

We had now our own rules for living together. No one had written them down and yet we lived by them. Our relationship was born of necessity and tolerance. The rules, which the civilized community had laid down, were ours no longer. We stood outside civilization. And on that account other laws served here. We were not rude to each other. On the contrary, we took pains to be nice to one another. Only with. mutual respect could we remain strong. Our self-confidence

Sastrugi field. When Arved was 2 or 3 kilometres behind, I could scarcely make him out. He was indistinguishable from the shadows of the sastrugi.

must never be jeopardized. Nevertheless, sometimes there were fierce discussions. Each knew what was necessary to carry this expedition to a conclusion. And more we did not want. Each had to remain capable of playing his part. Alone neither the one nor the other of us would have come through. The Antarctic was too big for experiments.

Some rules, some noises and no smells. Throughout the day there were no smells. Our own body odours were not noticeable by the time we had dressed, done up the zips and gone outside into the open. Only in the evening, when we came into the tent and thawed out, could we smell ourselves. When the tent zip fasteners were closed, we began at once to undress. Each smelled the other and himself. To begin with I had thought of this musk under our wind-proofs as stench. Now I thought of it as comfortable warmth. Cooking cancelled out all body odours. The tent was really pleasant; it smelled of food, fat, damp clothes; it smelled of humanity.

How could we go on day after day with so much hopelessness! We knew we mutually motivated each other – Arved through his quietness, his self-confidence; I through a cheery word in the 'morning'. I might not reproach him for his lack of condition. I was sure he would soon be fitter, and if his feet healed, we were saved.

The most important thing now was an exact time division. After we had agreed to run six hours per day, these six hours had to be filled out. When the weather allowed it, I went exactly six hours to the minute, always equally fast. That meant that the gap between us during the hours on the move became bigger and bigger. Each minute that we lost, we would need at the other end.

Some days before we were to have reached the Thiel Mountains, suddenly they appeared somewhere to the south, at first as mirages, then real. As narrow, glimmering lines they stood on the horizon. Often they disappeared again. Day after day I would not have been able to say whether the dark streaks in front of us were real mountains or only an optical illusion. We did not know whether our dump had already been set up. For ten days now we had been without radio contact with Patriot Hills. Just before the Thiel Mountains, Arved made contact with the Steger group.

It was Monday evening, 4 December. The six members of the

dog-sledge expedition were camping, surrounded by their huskies, half-way between the 'Thiels' and the South Pole. They had made good progress. Arved said we could not get through to Patriot Hills over the radio and asked Jean-Louis Etienne to pass some news to the camp: 'Fuchs and Messner will be at the Thiels in two days. They expect dump.' 'Trans-Antarctica' too had had no radio contact with the outside world for a week. Our dump was to be situated to the right of Kings Peak. 'We hope it's there!' Arved said that in such a tone that I began to wonder which he preferred: the dump, thus the chance to go on; or no dump and the necessity to give up.

For the first time that night, bourgeois dreams again. It was odd to wake up thinking about appointments and obligations. For a long time I was unable to get to sleep again. Finally I saw myself at home at Juval with 'Trans-Antarctica'. For the rest I had indigestion.

On Tuesday, 5 December, Jaeger was once again able to get through on the radio. Evening after evening he had waited in vain at Patriot Hills for a signal from us. 'No joy.' The miserable atmospheric conditions, to which much stronger radios than ours had capitulated, were at last past. We were in the vicinity of the 'Thiels', 530 kilometres as the crow flies away from the South Pole.

'Tomorrow we shall be at the Thiel dump.'

'Understood.'

'Where exactly is our dump?'

'There is no dump yet!'

We were shocked. A 90-kilo food dump was to be ready for us. Of course, Brydon, pilot of the Twin-Otter, had been instructed to fly to the Thiel Mountains with provisions and letters from home on 6 December, but who knew whether wind and visibility would permit the flight?

'We have fuel for a week. Not much more food. A full day's ration and reserves. We are doing well. We are in the best of health. Position: 85°11' south.'

In jargon, I passed on all the news. At the same time, we seemed to lose contact once more.

'Until tomorrow then, hope it works out with the dump.'

Now we knew that all the others knew that we expected our depot at the Thiels, that is our sponsors, ANI, the pilots. Previously, we

The pilot Brydon Knibbs (right) had a lot of Arctic flying experience. A quiet, conscientious man. He had been flying for ANI in the Antarctic since 1988.

could only hope that the radio link via 'Trans-Antarctica' had confirmed to Ulrich Jaeger, Wilhelm Bittorf and Jürgen Bolz that we were still alive.

Yes, we were alive. I felt strong. My old instincts had come alive again. I was always lying in wait, like a wild animal. Not only when marching during the day; but also on awakening or 'nights' when I slept superficially, I was ready. Ready to react, ready to resist. Against the wind, against futility, against tiredness.

The marching did not sap me as I went without sense of time or place through the emptiness. I did not think about how far it still was. I kept to the schedule. Had I not been able to meditate, hour after hour, on a recollection, an idea, a plan, I would have become tired more quickly.

Arved complained not only about his feet. It was to him as if the Antarctic trip were a continuation of his march to the North Pole. Often nothing more occurred to him whilst marching. Moving

149

without day-dreams is brutish. Would he recover at the Thiels? Arved's feet were still raw, his toes bloody, suppurating stumps, lacking nails. With such feet, standing was a torment, sledge-pulling unbearable. At each step his body transferred the sledge load to the soles of his feet, and these were one big blister, with water and blood under the thick horny skin. What ought we to do? We both suffered from it. The Antarctic ice, however, was indifferent.

7   The Thiel Mountains

How swiftly the vastness around us shrank when clouds and mist closed in. In no time the white infinity became a bright nothing. We scarcely saw the skis under our feet. Nevertheless, I would have been able to keep going hour after hour on this 6 December. It was a misty day. In the 'morning' we tried to sail. Then we marched across sastrugi in the direction of the Thiel Mountains. After some hours I could discern the bottom of the steeply towering rocks.

Arved had wanted to stop twice. If the depot were not there, we were running in vain in any case. Suddenly – it was on the fourth rest – I noticed a coloured speck under the mountains. I was not sure whether it really was a coloured dot on the ice. I sensed it was. As the mountains were orientation marks for me, I ran easier. I directed myself more to the ridges and gullies far ahead than to the compass, which I had carried for three weeks slung on my chest. When Arved arrived, I asked him for the binoculars. He gave them to me. I focused them on the mountains and looked at the coloured speck. It was the aircraft! Unbelievably, it was standing there. 'Odd we didn't hear it!' So our depot was there.

I was convinced we would be there in ten to fifteen minutes for, through the binoculars, the aircraft had seemed so near. I ran on at once: half an hour, an hour, two hours. The aircraft was no longer visible. Arved was far behind me. We continued over ridges and mighty hollows.

Suddenly the mist cleared and the world became glistening bright. I thought of Amundsen, as he discovered the mountains for the first time on his march to the Pole seventy-eight years before:

On 11 November we could distinguish the mountain chain. Mighty pinnacles, each one higher and wilder than the other rose to a height of 5,000 metres. What struck us all immediately were the cold faces which these mountains presented. We had expected to find them covered with much more snow. The Fridtjof Nansen Peak looked quite blue-black, only far above was it covered with a mighty mantel of ice.

This world seemed to me now unreal, repelling mankind. If the aircraft had not been there . . . but it had vanished. No more to be seen. Thus I began to doubt whether I really had seen the aeroplane. I wanted to make sure. Arved, however, had the binoculars and was far behind. I did not want to wait for him. The ground was icy, the sastrugi occasionally a metre high and more. It was windy and cold. It couldn't have been anything else but the aircraft! Across enormous ground waves I dragged my sledge towards it. Always towards the one point. Now and then it disappeared. It seemed to me now further away than the moment when I had discovered the coloured spot for the first time. On this blue-grey ice surface nothing else was red. No, I did not believe I had seen a phantom mirage. In the mountains that was possible. At great altitude the lack of oxygen is so great that it conjures up mirages; hallucinations. The higher you go, the greater the exertion, so the greater the feeling of loneliness. The results are hallucinations. In the Antarctic there are no hallucinations. That I sensed. There were mirages. Mountain ranges which I saw although I could not see them geographically. As I approached these mountains, so I saw them for real. Close to them, they appeared often further away than the previously corresponding mirages, a known phenomenon that had often been described. But not hallucinations.

After more than two hours I was standing in front of the tail fin of the aircraft which suddenly rose up above a ground wave. The red-white aircraft was standing in a hollow: like a foreign body.

As I approached, two men got out, Brydon Knibbs and Eric Stephens. They waved to me. They had been trying to put up their tent and went at it again, without success. The wind tore it out of their hands. I drew my tent out of the sledge, together we erected it. All three of us crawled inside and waited for Arved.

'It was a difficult flight', remarked Brydon, 'Bad visibility. Around 3.15 p.m. we flew low past the Thiel Mountains. We flew a leg to the north-east to let you know we were around. Then we landed on

The Thiel Mountains depot. The Twin-Otter, our tent, container with provisions on a snow island in front of the Thiel Mountains. Half-way to the Pole.

the blue ice above the depot site. The rock nose over there is so recognizable.'

Three hours Knibbs and Stephens had waited in the red-white Twin-Otter while we struggled towards the co-ordinates of the depot, 85°17′ south and 88° west. The 'Thiels', as the Canadians call the mountains, look from the air like a dark herd in the endless snow plain, a mountain range as big as the Dolomites. The individual peaks are less marked. The highest reaches to 2,800 metres but the ice cover which surrounds it is almost the same height.

The blonde-haired Brydon Knibbs looked grave. The flight from Patriot Hills to the Thiels had been right on the limit of the possible. He repeated, 'Completely flat visibility'.

Our dump had been arranged at the last moment, yet at the right time. For that we had to thank Wilhelm Bittorf, who had pressed in Punta Arenas, and Brydon who, despite the light being against him, had flown out there. 'The visibility was so bad as we flew south that we would have had to turn back', related Eric, his mechanic. 'Before the Thiel Mountains we made a pass in the hope of discovering you somewhere, but nothing.'

'And the landing?'

'We landed under the mountains, as you see, and not on the face.' We all laughed. 'It was all three hours ago.'

'The mist lifted at the right moment.'

'Luckily!'

'When do you want to go back?'

'We have to go on.'

The pair were not waiting for our arrival, they were waiting for better visibility. They wanted to fly to the Pole where they had to unload dog food, equipment and provisions for the 'Trans-Antarctica' expedition.

After twenty-three days in the icy waste these taciturn fliers seemed to me like an exciting change. They sensed my curiosity. 'Isn't it boring', asked Brydon, 'always the same ice under your skis?'

'The micro landscapes under your feet are here more manifold than anywhere on earth.'

Eric laughed. 'And otherwise?'

'Not a woman for miles!'

Now they both laughed. Meanwhile Arved had arrived with his sledge. He came into the tent and got the cooker going. His face taut with pain, he took off his boots. The two airmen saw how raw Arved's feet were; from the balls of his feet to his heels. With Brydon, I went over to the Twin-Otter, to speak with Ulrich Jaeger at Patriot Hills over the radio – Arved stayed behind in the tent.

Contact was good. The conversation at once came round to our speed. 'Do you want to carry on regardless?'

'Yes.'

'And if you don't get any quicker?'

'Sorry for our delay.'

Jaeger, Bittorf and Bolz needed information. For thirteen days we had been without proper radio contact.

'The Spillsbury is no good, I'm sending it back.'

In the aircraft behind the windscreen it was warm. The radio contact with Patriot Hills remained outstanding. I sensed, without

Argos (left) and GPS, the two satellite devices which gave our position. The first transmitted information to the outside world; the second told us where we were.

Jaeger saying so, that our helpers were thinking about our progress. Jaeger was not disappointed, he suffered with us. At this rate of progress we must fail! I tried to make him believe, what I myself had believed for days: 'It can only get better'. I invented no excuses and explained that Arved's feet looked bad. 'The blisters! With such pain, he can't go any faster.'

'I understand but what can you do about it?'

'We'll rest here a couple of days and continue on 9 December at the earliest.'

'Do you believe his blisters will heal that quickly?'

'I hope Arved's feet will improve and his condition is such that he must be strong enough to go 30 kilometres per day. After the difficult acclimatization I am completely fit. If I were alone, I could go twice as far in a day. This evening I would go on with the freshly laden sledge instead of stopping here two days.'

Brydon and Eric pressed me to sign off.

'When do you want to be at the Pole?'

155

'Over New Year.'

'And you really don't want the radio any more?'

'No, there's no sense in lugging 4 kilos when neither you nor we get anything from it.'

'Take the Argos with you so that we at least have your position, seeing as the radio doesn't work.'

Arved operated our GPS navigation instrument, a high-tech device, no bigger than a walkie-talkie. It took bearings on satellites in space and showed its operator his position exact to 150 metres. That had sufficed for us. With the Argos apparatus we could announce our position to the outside world but nothing more.

'But supposing you don't make it?'

'We shall increase the rate of march', I said.

'Perhaps Arved only wants to get as far as the Pole?'

'I don't know.'

'When will you know.'

'In the first week of the New Year. Then we shall all know more.'

'If you want to give up at the Pole, we must know now.'

'I shall certainly go on.'

We were in a hopeless plight. The news of the opening of the Berlin Wall, mentioned by Ulrich Jaeger as an afterthought in this so pertinent radio conversation, seemed to me as unimportant as the height of the mountains on the moon. Here there were fields of sastrugi, European politics only a memory. How far away all that was! And how unimportant it was to us! Jaeger asked for detailed information about the days on which we had not been able to make radio contact with one another. Spontaneously, I offered him my diary. How else could Wilhelm Bittorf in Punta Arenas have described our march. I promised to ask Arved if he would lend Bittorf his diary but he refused to hand it over. I understood his objections. Our contract with *Der Spiegel* did not call for delivery of a diary. If Arved wanted to make full use of his diary exclusively in a book, it was no use giving it away in *Der Spiegel*. Nevertheless, it would have been better if Bittorf could have looked at both diaries. The coverage would have been less one-sided. Arved's diary notes were so different from mine that readers would have had to believe that our journey was not a two-man undertaking, rather about two different journeys.

156

On that account it was so important that Wilhelm Bittorf, who had to report on our progress from 3,000 kilometres away in Punta Arenas, had read both diaries. Both Arved and I were interested in an accurate coverage. We had the best possible medium, the best possible writer as spokesman to the outside world. So we guaranteed that, as well as our progress or failure, also environmental questions, historical and geographical associations were to be included in the publicity. Now, as we no longer had a radio, Wilhelm Bittorf was dependent solely on our daily Argos position, his knowledge and our notes. I tried to make Arved understand that. Nonetheless, he kept his diary to himself.

I had decided to go as far as the South Pole with Arved. If he gritted his teeth as previously, we had a chance of putting behind us the 530 bee-line kilometres to 90° south in three weeks. I calculated a maximum of twenty-four days' travel. That left us time, just time it is true, with a following wind, to get to the other side of the ice continent before winter came.

Originally, I had wanted to spend only one day resting at the Thiel camp. Pack the sledges and get on was my proposal. Arved insisted on two rest days. I gave in. The second rest day was a beautiful day with hardly any wind. We read, talked, sorted the provisions. When Brydon returned from the Pole, we had even packed the sledges. He landed, took on board all the rubbish which had accumulated meanwhile and talked about the South Pole. A fuel dump for further Pole flights was being constructed. Brydon and Eric got into their machine after a bit and flew north, back to Patriot Hills. The weather was fantastic all the time. Clear visibility. An ideal day for marching. The Twin-Otter disappeared over the horizon.

Next morning mist. Nonetheless, we set out.

Under the firmly secured cover of my sledge now lay the round, black Argos apparatus. It looked like a tube with an aerial. This Argos device sends out a signal on a constant frequency. At an altitude of more than 800 kilometres, this signal is received by satellites and passed on. With a trick called 'Doppler shifting' the satellite could locate the transmitter which we intended to operate each evening in our tent. The ensuing data would be conveyed at once to the computer centre of the French space travel authority CNES in

Toulouse. Supplied with these co-ordinates, Bittorf could follow our advance from the Thiel Mountains in the direction of the Pole. The French had developed this ingenious system with the American space authority NASA. With it, not only could solitary ice travellers like us be followed via space, rather any object to which one could attach an Argos transmitter. Every other day the CNES in Toulouse forwarded our position to Punta Arenas over the teleprinter.

Arved had assured me before departure that he would go to the Pole, regardless of his feet. Each day six hours' actual running time. That corresponded to 12 miles. I also stood by this travel schedule, not simply as a concession to Arved's feet, rather also to husband our reserves of strength. We could not afford to expend ourselves too early. Also I was afraid of injuries brought on by going too fast.

After the two rest days, we made good progress on 9 December despite the windy weather. Soon, however, snow drifts prevailed again, then white-out. Nil visibility and distinctly heavier sledges as well. Fresh snow had fallen during the night. It was relatively warm, so warm that I could do without gloves. We marched for the first time with instep crampons on our feet. Both pairs of skis were buckled on the sledges. We traversed along at the foot of the rocks, overcame a smooth glacier. Then we climbed over a moraine. It was not easy forcing the sledges between the stones. Over several steps, partly ice, partly snow, we climbed to a pass to the right of King Peak. I could recognize only the foot of the mountains. Over there lay thick mist. The saddle in the 'Thiels', across which we wanted to get to the high plateau, I only sensed. It became a strenuous day. We were now navigating with a detailed map. With sufficient visibility we would have had no problem. In mist, however, with 100 metres visibility at best, I was often not sure whether we were on the best route. Our first attempt to reach the saddle direct over a steep slope failed. I crossed the slope. With my hand I gave Arved, who was behind me, a signal. He was to stay in the valley hollow and ascend the slope where it was flatter. After a laborious crossing I too reached the flat section. There were crevasses. The slopes were steep; accordingly, it was strenuous getting out of 'holes' again.

When we had reached the top of the pass, the ground continued upwards; at least that was my impression. We were going across a

Moraines at the foot of the Thiel Mountains. Carefully, I towed the sledge between the stones and patches of gravel. Arved followed my track.

high plateau which we couldn't see. The fully laden sledges generated more friction than in the previous week. Over many ground waves and soft snow we proceeded directly southwards.

We did not see the highest points of the Thiel Mountains. In good weather we would have recognized nunataks and mountain chains, the better to be able to orientate ourselves visually. In this weather we saw nothing at all. It was snowing and the snow was rather heavy. We advanced slowly. Once we crossed the track of 'Trans-Antarctica' who had passed through here three weeks before.

Arved had difficulties despite the two rest days. He was pulling a lighter sledge than I, but needed per 'hour's running' on average a quarter of an hour longer. So my stops became too long. When I was sweating from climbing, I froze that much more whilst waiting. That was our main problem.

Our mood was good otherwise. We had left camp with many hopes. It was now naturally depressing to go across the passes and between these mountains without being able to see them.

'If we had set out a day earlier, we would have had lovely weather.' This statement was not meant as a reproach. 'We would have seen the mountains, experienced another mood.' 'I never thought it would be bad again', replied Arved. 'You can't see your hand in front of your face!'

These difficulties were also the result of our optimism. The weather would hold, we had thought, and now this lousy weather! We bore it and didn't complain. We went on. The first six hours in the mist were full of tension. Beyond the 'Thiels', the slope went on even further and not downwards as expected; at least, with my full sledge I always had the feeling it was going upwards. Even when the terrain was pot level.

Again I would have preferred to run faster. 'Each day we save getting to the Pole', I said, 'is a reserve day on the other side'. The South Pole had never been my goal. This imaginary point at 90° south was indeed a kind of high point in this traverse but not more. Arved again argued about signs of bodily wear and tear.

'With too long daily stages we risk having to give up even before the Pole!'

'At our present speed we have no chance of crossing the Antarctic.'

'Better at least to reach the South Pole, than to fail earlier at your desired speed.'

We argued more and more in a stop-go style. The speed which resulted was for both of us a compromise. That it was eventually to lead to success, we could not divine. Almost daily we discussed tactics in the tent. On 10 December I dictated for the first time my anger on tape. I had to get rid of it:

I pressed time and again. I tried to enthuse Arved for longer stages. He wouldn't listen to reason. He pushed it all aside and thinks we shall get wind. The terrain will get better. Antarctica is not to be crossed with these tactics. I am of the opinion that Arved is physically too weak to make such a hard trip. He can't do more than six hours marching per day with this weight of sledge. I'm sorry. I can take only a part of his weight as I have done in the first stretches already. I'll offer to do so tomorrow. With one lighter and one heavier sledge our speed is somewhat evened out. Nevertheless, even that doesn't do much good. The actual running speed must be higher. No problem for me. These quarter hours, which per hour I run faster than Arved, could add up to 500 kilometres by the end.

Apart from these discussions about marching tactics, Arved and I complemented each other well. We were a team and I never had the feeling that we could really get into danger. If we made an error, it would be our joint error. Sure, we could both have died. There was sometimes a momentary fear but never a feeling of being lost. On the one hand, it was good that Arved applied the brakes. We made progress, yet did not exhaust ourselves. In the Antarctic, slowness is as important as speed in the mountains. Here success was decided over the course of months, not a few days, as in the mountains. Perhaps Scott had lost his life also on that account, because he led his people to the Pole too fast and had pressed on with the return march. We had to arrive fresh at the Pole if we wanted to continue.

Whilst moving I felt fine. In the tent I forgot my surroundings. The 2 × 2 metres became 'home' to me. Whether the Antarctic were outside, or something else, did not concern me inside; there I felt as if I were in a cosy farm parlour in winter. It was warm and pleasant.

Marching was something else. It allowed you to think.

Nothing could be more exciting than the continual moving over the ice. I discovered no new lands and yet each sastrugi, each cloud aroused my imagination. With the visible my memory combined an imaginary world in me.

Now there were big depressions, holes such as we had not met with so far. They looked like craters. Frequently we could not get round them; also, the crevasses increased. Nevertheless, we went unroped. We made for a last nunatak which soared out of the ice like a pyramid. These rock pinnacles looked like the orienteering points of a lost age. The Eskimos had named them thousands of years ago.

Also on the second day in the Thiels, we were no faster. Although we marched as on other days, on account of the many detours and the steep ascents, our hourly performance was distinctly less. We moved southwards more slowly than our scheduled target. Then things improved. Beyond the last nunatak, the world became a plain again. It

The Thiel Mountains. Just as they had emerged over the horizon – like tiny, black triangles – so they vanished again as we ran southwards.

was still strenuous, finding the most direct way possible amongst big ground waves and sastrugi, but we progressed somewhat faster.

In the tent I made Arved the proposal: 'We could', so my idea went, 'even up our speed if I took some of your weight.' Arved hesitated. 'Since you need about a quarter hour longer to cover the stretch between rest stops, our speed would be the same and we could add the extra quarter hour which you take.' Arved said nothing. Presumably he agreed. 'If we are the same speed and do seven hours march per day, we shall be at the Pole before New Year's Eve.' Arved agreed. Next morning I took about 10 kilos out of Arved's sledge, mostly fuel.

We were now decidedly faster. In the morning we marched two hours without rest as before. As I went out ahead, my speed determined the stretch which we thereby put behind us. After a short pause, while I waited for Arved, we ran another four lots of one and a quarter hours, with short stops in between. Thus we worked up to

seven hours marching. As I went as fast as the previous day, despite the extra weight, we made nearly 30 kilometres per day. Arved was surprised at my speed. But he kept up. Suddenly confidence recovered again. I was convinced that the continental crossing could still be done.

Arved was tougher than I had thought. If he had only wanted to go to the Pole, now he saw a chance to get further. And this hope gave him strength.

We never became really fast. Of course, we moved also in white-out, in storm and mist, but never more than 30 kilometres per day. We could not lose any time.

When the sun broke through, the Thiel Mountains were only recognizable as black silhouettes in the north, between mist and cumulus clouds. Ahead of us again the expanse which from the middle of the first stage was familiar to us. To the right curved a long drawn-out, fairy-like, shimmering mountain ridge. It was furrowed with crevasses and looked like a gigantic fish skeleton. Behind me the Lewis Nunatak, the last rock pyramid which we were to see on the journey to the Pole.

Again I was far ahead. In the first two hours, a constant up and

163

down, I had tried to go exactly in a southerly direction. But it wouldn't work. I came to smooth ice slabs and had to detour. Always sastrugi. Not the pointed type, rather flat and broad. The landscape looked like a tossed up sea of fast waves. Again we could not go with the sastrugi and we crossed them at an angle of 60°. The most frequent wind direction was south-west and we had to go south. Always I hoped that after the last nunatak the conditions would improve. After the white mountain chains the ground must be 'quieter'. That was no hope – it was like a promise.

We had been going four and a half hours. Arved was recognizable as a small black dot on the horizon. He approached over sastrugi which time and again swallowed him up. I was lightly dressed again. In previous days I had had too many clothes on and had suffered as a result. If you have too much on, you sweat. By evening everything is wet and clothes were difficult to dry. So I froze.

On the move I followed a single idea as far as it went. It became an endless chain. Now new ice-travel ideas came to me. The Antarctic expedition was the beginning of a series of adventures in snow and ice. I was capricious. This third change in my life – rock-climbing, high altitude mountaineering, ice travelling – constituted an idea and energy supply. And again it was bound up with joyful anguish. As at age fifteen under the most extreme rock routes in the Dolomites. At twenty-five on Nanga Parbat. At thirty-five on my Everest solo ascent. Now I was forty-five and still like a lad when it came to venturing something 'crazy'.

The snow, especially on the big sastrugi, looked as if it had annual rings. Many hundreds of annual rings. Then again the ground looked as if thousands of tractors or tracked vehicles had turned on it. All appearances of erosion. There, where the wind came down from the mountain, it seized hold of everything. Anything movable was ripped away. Only the hard, icy blocks remained behind, built up by snow-drifts.

In the west fine mist developed, with fringes as if it had been combed out. As Arved approached, he looked ghostly: the glittering ice surfaces in the foreground, in the background this mist, over there the blue sky. It was unreal, that people were on the move here. I was bewildered. What was unreal? The Antarctic or us? Man did not belong here! Nevertheless, onward. I had to go on. I would gladly have gone on 14 miles. The sastrugi which Etienne had told us about, on that radio conversation we had had with him shortly before the Thiel Mountains, were still there. Since we marched seven hours daily, we were crossing one degree of latitude every four days. All the problems with Arved were solved thereby. I was calmer. His habits did not disturb me. He had shown much comradeship and had hesitated a long time before giving me weight from his sledge. It was more strenuous running with the heavier sledge but I didn't have injured feet. Also, unlike Arved, I hadn't been to the North Pole, which had sapped him. For me this ice travel was new, full of excitement. It was something that I had never done, something which absorbed me.

At last the Thiel Mountains were behind us. This to and fro, up and down trudging between the mountains, was worse than the mulish plodding on the inland ice had been.

Certainly, we both stank but I smelled it no longer.

During these days I experienced the most peaceful weeks of the expedition. Confidently, full of enthusiasm I marched southwards. In good weather, full of joy at moving. Always the same rhythm: I ran ahead and determined the course with the compass. Seven hours of marching per day. In the evening we met up again in front of the tent. All was habit: unloading the sledge, erecting the tent. First the foam rubber mats went into the tent, then the sleeping-bags. Our personal belongings we placed round the edge. Arved left side, I right side. Arved filled the cooking pots with snow. Cooker, fuel bottle and wooden plank, to keep the cooker stable, were placed at the bottom end. Melting snow took a long time. We enjoyed our food.

We did everything to an exact routine. The 'Argos', which we had taken over on the Thiel Mountains, I switched off before going to sleep. Wilhelm Bittorf must know by now where we were. Despite the sterile and incomprehensible technology, this form of communication was like a conversation with him.

We didn't miss the radio. What use to us would a radio have been if we had been able to use it only once a month? On the contrary, it would have been, for those who maintained contact with us, more of an uncertainty. They would have had to assume the worst if once we had not made contact.

With Jaeger, I had evolved a code in case we were in danger of losing our lives and needed help. But we never came in danger of losing our lives. Meanwhile I had accustomed myself to the storms. There was no giving up. The enjoyment surpassed the drudgery.

Arved was a pleasant partner. He didn't complain, he could be good company. Above all, he had a taste for practical things. Nothing could disturb his placidity.

Certainly, it was not easy to be the driving force. Always rousing, saying 'We must get on!', 'We must go further'. Now and then a yell of 'Let's go' from Arved would have done me good.

The sledge braked, the wind burned my face. When Arved was 4 kilometres behind I could scarcely make him out. Between the shadows of the sastrugi a dark stripe bounded here and there. I played a children's game, 'It is he – it is not he'. Everything moved the longer I looked back. So onwards. 'He will be following.' The horizon before me was a grey, curved line. It didn't fool you, because you long knew that it shifted without you noticing it. You resign yourself to this white infinity. The storm holds you back and you press against it, although you scarcely move from the spot.

8 Where is the Pole?

I was moving really easily. The longer I wandered across the snow desert, the more all horizons lost themselves. The free play of my fantasies became greater. Perhaps the wild natural landscape of the Antarctic was only important for humanity because it stimulated one to dreaming. Not all our dreams had to be realized. With this thought I astonished myself. How I had let myself be dragged along by my enthusiasm for crossing the ice continent! How free was now the dammed-up energy of my dreams!

If later on I no longer developed ideas, I would be dead. Is it not so that this continent can also inspire those who do not come here? Through its vastness, its quiet, its not being occupied.

My generation, we post-war children in central Europe, were brought up by our parents to be practical people. There was little room for dreams. But today many adolescents seek other qualities of life over and above material well-being. Was it not for that, specifically important to guard the interior of Antarctica as *terra incognita*? A land which stimulates dreams is worth defending – even if man himself should never come there. Voluntary abstinence must be part of the culture of technological humanity. Only man's self-control can contribute to his survival. Renunciation must become for that reason part of our self-understanding. Renunciation of the exploitation of natural resources, renunciation of occupation of certain regions, renunciation of always wanting to have more. If we do not want to lose assets like wilderness, infinity, quietness, we must know what it is. In the ice of the Antarctic these values, which the consumer society had driven out of their 'paradise', were preserved: stillness, peacefulness, unoccupied space. These virtues were here, sealed and frozen in like the land.

The first good day after leaving the depot was 12 December. The weather was fantastic, the air relatively mild, the wind blowing from the south-west. In our dark clothing it was pleasantly warm. As black dots we attracted the sun's rays. In the morning we had set out half an hour earlier than usual. I tried to extract a seven-hour march in the hope of doing 15 miles.

Around midday we came on the tracks of the Steger expedition which were easily recognizable: running tracks of sledges and dogs. I saw distinctly how the dogs had dug their claws into the snow when it was a matter of pulling the sledges across sastrugi. Between the snow waves they had trotted regularly. Should we stay on this track? It snaked along, not so direct as ours. With the compass I could stay exactly on the ideal line. Nevertheless for a while we stuck to the dog trail. Thus I didn't have to navigate. Later we would take to our own track again and go exactly in a southerly direction to the Pole. The snow surfaces were always irregular. Once hard, then soft snow, fewer sastrugi. Over wide stretches, a *firn* crust covered the terrain, toothed with small sastrugi. Our rhythm tallied. We were on our feet about eight hours a day, plus a half-hour dismantling the tent in the morning and a half-hour putting it up again in the evening. We cooked for two and a half hours in the morning and the same in the evening. Ten hours remained for rest and sleep. It worked well like this. We had accustomed ourselves to it. What was never easy was the getting up in the morning, and going out into the cold, grey air. It took me a half-hour of marching to get warmed up. How the surfaces glittered!

In the north-west a mountain ridge. We had crossed the 2,000-metre mark and it made itself felt. The thin air increased the exertion of sledge pulling and our acclimatization was slow at first. In the north-east some small clouds, as if painted in the sky. Otherwise it was shining cold. Arved had recovered. Now he was running faster. Perhaps also because his sledge was lighter.

During the day the horizon was the orientation line towards which I ran, with the bearing on the compass. That apart, I was free for all the thoughts which went through my head. Generally, it was a single connected chain of thought which occupied me. From 'morning' to 'evening'. On starting, some memory or other out of my dreams nestled in my thoughts and haunted them all day.

I myself perceived this world as relatively small. I don't mean the part which we saw in front of us and that which we knew behind us. It was this feeling of being on my own.

And yet no outsider can picture our situation: two people dependent upon one another and yet each running for himself across the endless ice desert. In the tent I forgot the surroundings in which it stood.

What were space and time in which actions and impressions repeated themselves thousandfold every day? How often I sat there and waited for Arved. The first two hours of marching were done. Sitting on the sledge for ten minutes was pleasant. Resting. But then it became unpleasant. The cold penetrated my hands and legs. I wanted to get on but waited another ten minutes, until Arved had had a drink and something to eat. Then we could go on, with Arved scarcely rested and I cooled down. The snow was heavy, drifted granular snow which braked the sledge and our skis.

The ground was more even. Seldom now sastrugi. No comparison to that which we had experienced on the first stage.

We had left the Steger trail again, for it ran further to the west. We didn't know whether we would ever cross it again.

Every time we started the day's stage together but soon the gap between us was measured in kilometres. We were unable to go at a common speed. When Arved was 4 kilometres behind, I could scarcely make him out amongst the shadows of the sastrugi. We couldn't lose ourselves but the rest stops lasted longer for me the faster I went. Not always was the sun warm. I didn't want to go slower. If I had run slower I would have lost energy and we would not have put 15 miles behind us in seven hours' marching. For me there was nothing to do but run ahead and freeze during the stops. In the wind the waiting was deadly. In good visibility, now I no longer waited in the second half of the day's stage until Arved closed up. He had often invited me to go ahead regardless and I did. With the compass on my chest I ran to the end of the time which we had arranged. In order to find shelter at last, I erected the tent, a trick I had soon learned; necessity is the mother of invention. The tent had not to be allowed to fly away, otherwise we would have been condemned to death. In wind I anchored it with the ice-axe, then laid it out and fixed one arch. With the second I raised the envelope.

Once the tent was up, I crept inside and lit the cooker. When Arved arrived it was already warm in the tent. Despite my anger at waiting I was glad when he was there. In unexpected mist he could see the track of my skis and sledge runners etched in the snow. When it was generally misty I stayed within visual range. A long waiting time. I was amazed at the fortitude with which Arved bore his pain. He struggled through with great will-power. After he had invited me to go on ahead in the 'afternoon', without waiting for him during the rest stops, we both felt better.

For two weeks things had been going well. We progressed swiftly, just as I had imagined it. We made just 30 kilometres in one day. We put in rest days only when the wind compelled us to wait.

From the middle of December the weather got worse again. Clouds out of the east swept over us and piled up in the west. We had left the 87° latitude behind us. Arved broke another binding and exchanged his touring skis for telemarks. In twelve days, I calculated, we should be at the Pole.

As I marched across the ice desert, sometimes I felt like a giant on gigantic skis marching across an ever-changing landscape. The Thiel Mountains alone cover an area of more than 2,000 square kilometres. In three days we had crossed them. We were now at an altitude of 2,200 metres. It had got colder. Luckily, it was not windy. Arved's nose had frozen again.

I sat there and rested. Thereby I noticed that we were going through a hollow. Like a gigantic egg-shell. The ground seemed to climb on all sides. Up above a line, an oval line – that was the horizon. Above the horizon, a bright blue line which changed to a steely blue. The sky was flecked, covered with low clouds. The sun was still clear, shining now on my back and I felt its strength through my dark clothes.

Christmas Eve. When I opened up the tent, the sun shone in. No wind. On going outside, after the initial shiver, a feeling of spring in the air. This spring air was −25°C. It was a peaceful, white Christmas, like at home. Such cosiness in the tent. It was only possible because for hours we forgot where it stood. Our 'home' – 2.20 × 2.20 × 1.20 metres – was spacious, warm and dry. It smelled of us. The hoar-frost stuck to the inner tent, of course, but evaporated with the cooking.

We wanted to spend Christmas Day resting. We sat in the tent, read. Each dealt with his jobs: fetching snow, cooking, diary-writing.

We slept a lot. The cake which I had baked out of muesli and chocolate was sticky and tasted delicious with a drop of whisky.

Not only on 24 December, but also whenever we had crossed a degree of latitude, we allowed ourselves a ration of whisky in the 'evening'. That had become a custom. Generally, we drank it 'on the rocks' with pieces of ice and for days looked forward to this moment.

North wind at last! We had crossed latitude 88° south. Unfortunately, the ground was so heavy that, despite help from the sails, we progressed only at *langlauf* (long-distance skiing) pace. Nevertheless, it was quicker than otherwise. I invented all sorts of games with the sail. If I swung the canopy in front of me – up and down, to and fro – I got on better.

Suddenly, after going for three hours, the wind increased. For the first time we sailed in the right direction: southwards. Time passed without having to march as well, which felt like flying. The most satisfying experience of the whole expedition! Although I could not estimate how fast we were going, I knew suddenly that we would pull through.

We were now faster than sledge dogs. Weather and visibility were not good. Mock suns stood in the grey sky. This marvel of light in the Antarctic sky! Behind a veil of vapour hung five suns. A whirl of mirages. The sky gave me the impression of another firmament. Or was I travelling with my sledge across another planet?

It had got colder. The wind, which was ever stronger, enticed me further. I wanted to wait for Arved in the tent. How far ahead was sailing still possible? As I travelled on with stiff legs, I calculated how far we could get daily with this technique.

I could no longer see Arved and I knew that my sailing ahead was dangerous. The track of my sledge was, of course, distinctly recognizable in the snow, but what if he lost it? Soon it would be 'midnight'. Misty. Cold. I didn't want to stop, not yet. With each hour that we travelled now we saved three or four hours' march. In the next three days it would become less strenuous.

Suddenly, with a powerful side wind, I lost control of sail and skis,

Our method of sailing was different from Nansen's technique. The sails – fixed to our bodies – were manoeuvrable. An ideal means of locomotion.

and fell head over heels between two sastrugi, cracking my right elbow. How easily you can break a leg, an ankle, an arm in this way! I looked back hopefully. Could Arved have hurt himself? Despite this anxiety I kept putting off the final halt. Not until far past 'midnight' did I erect the tent. In the protection of the tent I waited, often looking out, anxious that Arved might have got tired. Perhaps he could no longer sail. At last he arrived. For the first time he was annoyed about me going ahead, about his icy hands and feet. Nevertheless, he was glad to have done such a long stretch. We had sailed for many hours. Ought we to go out once more and sail on? We stayed. Bided the 'night' and, hoping next day to be able to sail again, we slept deeply.

Next morning the wind changed. It was strong but now came from the north-east. When sailing we would be driven to the west. It was hardly worthwhile.

'I was right', I said during a rest stop. 'We ought to have used the sailing wind yesterday. We ought to have travelled further.' Arved nodded. Being right didn't help now. Now only our own legs helped.

Again I was in doubt. How were we, with our different speeds, ever to get to the other side of Antarctica? Not even with sailing could Arved maintain my speed. The stretch from the Pole to McMurdo Sound was longer than the route which we had thus far accomplished. That worried me! Certainly, we progressed twice as fast when sailing but the waiting was worse. In order to warm up freezing hands and feet you must go, move yourself. The cooled down body soon becomes clumsy and irresolute. On this first good sailing day we had put 57 kilometres behind us. That was an enormous distance but, contrary to my hope, the sail had not helped to equalize Arved's speed to mine. In fact, I had frozen more than usual. Had I not been able to erect the tent alone in the storm, I would have frozen solid.

For three days now this mock sun hung under the sun. The scene was uncanny. Two discs vertically above the horizon. Grey veils of mist round about. Especially in the south, towards the Pole, the sky was gloomy. In the 'evening' mist sprang up. Luckily, I had already set up the tent when the sun finally disappeared.

Navigation had become harder. We trusted our Magellan GPS–NAV–1000 set absolutely. In the daytime we marched fixedly southwards by compass. In the evening Arved took the readings off this navigational device which took the bearings of the satellites installed in space specially for that purpose. When at least three satellites were in position, the operator could ascertain the position he found himself in as exactly as it would have been possible to do with a sextant. Often we were astounded at the readings on the set. We were running more directly than we thought and with an almost machine-like constancy. That helped us to a feeling for distances and directions. Nevertheless, without fixing our position, we would have been lost. Like in space. Without feeling for space and time.

When the Magellan apparatus had calculated our position, I multiplied the marching speed by the days still remaining to the middle of February. If we were able to sail a lot, the crossing were possible – on paper, at least.

Often during this night I woke up. Storm gusts passed over the tent. It was gloomy, so no sun shone. The entrance was blocked by a pile of snow. Drift snow. Inside, the tent was scarcely iced up, the piss-pot not frozen. It was relatively warm.

About eight o'clock in the morning Arved was still snoring, so I let him sleep. At half past eight we agreed to wait a while. In the sleeping-bag it was warm. Perhaps the wind would slacken. It was so pleasant to let oneself doze. While the wind outside drove the snow grains through the icy air, I fell asleep again. Arved stuck the Magellan set in his sleeping-bag to warm it up. Just before 10 a.m. I peeled myself out of my bag and put on pile jacket and trousers which had served me as pillow. With my bare feet still in the sleeping-bag, I pulled on socks and down boots. Then I rolled up the sleeping-bag and stowed it in the corner behind my back. While Arved dressed himself, I shuffled forward to the tent entrance and banged the snow from the surfaces so that a layer several centimetres thick slid off the outside, whilst from the inner side the hoar-frost crumbled and fell on the foot end of our sleeping mats. At once everything felt damp, cold and unpleasant. Carefully, I opened one of the three zip-fasteners which, in the shape of an upturned 'T', made the opening and shutting of the tent possible. A small snow avalanche poured in! The wind threw snow grains after it. I tried to close the tent entrance again but the zip was iced up. It stuck and more snow slid inside the tent.

I filled the water pot with this hard-packed drift snow, up to the top. Then I peered through the open slit: snow streamers, mist, sky overcast! In this visibility we would not find the South Pole! Of course, we could navigate exactly with the Magellan device, but how were we to rely on the degree of longitude data in the vicinity of the Pole? There all lines of longitude ran to a point. Moreover our satellite navigation worked only a few hours a day.

While I pumped up the cooker and got it going, Arved tried to determine our position. It had been too late the previous 'evening', for when we had set up camp, the GPS had located only two satellites. We knew that at 10 a.m. three satellites would be available again.

The snow in the coffee pot began to melt. The storm increased. As Arved dictated our position – 89°44.94′ south and 113°09.39′ west – we knew that we had travelled 13 miles southwards the day before, as well as being too far west. Without visibility the Pole was not to be found. What ought we to do?

We breakfasted. Each of us came back from our morning toilet outside looking like snowmen, so that now snow lay inside the tent.

Socks and gloves, which we had hung up to dry in the tent roof, were clammy. We waited. We needed good visibility if we were not to run around the South Pole in a circle. In this vastness, patience was just as important as strength and endurance. In this infinity you could in the long run and in stormy conditions only impose slowness. Anything else would have been certain death.

We still had five rations of food, including bacon and hard South Tyrolean farm bread. The fuel would suffice for ten days. In 1912, on his way home from the legendary race to the South Pole, Scott starved only 11 miles from his last big dump. We had 15 miles more to go to the South Pole.

Naturally, we wanted to get there as quickly as possible but nothing could be forced. We must wash ourselves, relax. Our next dump was to be at the South Pole. In any case, there we would find a big US station in which, in summer, more than 100 people lived. We were looking forward to seeing other people. After nearly fifty days on the ice, I would have been ready to run for eight or nine hours to reach our destination. The South Pole was the first real goal of this journey.

The snowstorm continued through midday. Clouds. Mist. Ought we not, nevertheless, to march on a bit? The cooker was still burning as we pulled on socks, overtrousers and boots. Finally, anorak and gloves. Once outside the tent I put on my storm goggles. Firmly wrapped up and still warm, one can endure the storm. I tugged my sledge out of the drifted snow. Then I banged it off and began to load the sledge. First the cooker, the fuel bottle, the remains of the food. Then I placed the bag with my spare clothes in the rear section. Right up front I stacked the 'Argos' machine, and photo-and-writing bag. The sleeping-bag I spread over the top. It lay loose in the sledge. Once more over that the mats. Then we dismantled the tent. Firstly, we loosened all the anchors, except for the ice-axe. Then I lifted the back high and Arved tidied up the entrance. With two grips we folded the tent up into a sausage and pushed it like a dead man over my mat in the sledge. We pulled the zips over the sledge load, tugged everything together. Then we harnessed ourselves and were off.

Cloud banks in the south. In between rays of sun, time and again an extreme change of light. Visibility was miserable. I had corrected the previous day's direction of march by 15 degrees and hoped to run

Although Scott, on his 1911/12 expedition to the South Pole, had laid in depots for the return march, he perished with his polar team.

directly towards the Pole. The more we approached the Pole, the worse became the weather, with visibility less than 200 metres! Snowstorm. White-out. That cost strength. Across a rough, heavy snow surface I marched into the mist. Time and again, a ghostly atmosphere whenever sunbeams pierced the banks of clouds. The light changed fast.

In the 'evening' of this 29 December we believed ourselves to be somewhere in the vicinity of the Pole. I asked Arved for the binoculars. We had put up the tent and wanted to slip inside straightaway. Briefly, I looked around. Then, after yet another break in the weather, there was something! To the right of the direction where I had supposed the Pole to be I recognized elevations, black specks, a gigantic aerial. The Pole!

'There's the Pole!' I shouted excitedly. Arved confirmed it. We were completely beside ourselves with joy. 'The Pole!' Despite the mist, we had found it. 'The Pole.' The tent was already up. Enticing as it was, to run on immediately, we stayed where we were. We were in agreement: 'Tomorrow we go to the Pole whether it storms or snows!'

176

The British at the South Pole. When Scott and his four companions arrived at the South Pole, the Norwegians led by Amundsen had been there already.

'Take its bearings', Arved advised me. 'Perhaps everything will be closed in again tomorrow.' Before I went into the tent, I took an exact bearing. '90° south', I said to myself and knew that for the time being we were saved.

Unlike us, Amundsen and Scott had not been able to see the Pole from a distance. Amundsen first had to search for it and determine his position; Scott was to find the Norwegian flag there.

How well I can imagine that! The feeling at that time! Amundsen approaching the Pole. I believe that for Scott the tragedy began when, a month later, he came upon the tent which Amundsen had left behind. At the moment when the British realized that all their struggles had been in vain, that they had not reached the Pole first, their powers of resistance crumbled. Only as 'victors' could they have survived the return march.

It was quite different for Arved and me. The fact that 'Trans-Antarctica' had reached the Pole before us did not trouble us; no depression on that score. We had not been in competition with Steger and his expedition. On the contrary, we were pleased for them. If only they made it through to the other side. We had not wanted to be first at the Pole. Getting through was what mattered.

In the tent I tried to change Arved's mind. I would have been madly pleased to have run as far as the Pole that same day. I estimated the distance at two or three hours' march. However, Arved insisted on only going on next day. I gave in.

Next day we got away early. For us it was 'morning' but we had a vague idea that at the Pole it would be 'night'. Again no visibility, again white-out. Often the feeling that we had been deceived by the sighting of the polar station. No buildings, no aerial – nothing. Only in the third hour could I make out the first elevations in the mist. A dark speck first, then aerials. An unreal world and yet fiercely longed for. At last we could see the station which had been frequently rebuilt over the past fifty years. As we approached the Pole, we ascertained that nowhere were people to be seen. No movement, no smoke – nothing. It had got brighter. For the Pole's garrison, nevertheless it was 'night'. At a distance of a kilometre we spotted two tents and assumed that it was the Adventure Network camp where we wanted to wait for 'morning'. In the hope of meeting either Bolz or Jaeger there, we pushed on directly towards the tents and as we neared the camp, we recognized our cameraman's aluminium boxes. We knew that our helpers and reporters were there. Stopping in front of the tents, we woke the men with shouts. The pair were not a little astonished to greet us in the middle of the 'night'. Jürgen Bolz filmed, Ulrich Jaeger photographed, talked. He was as excited as if he had done the stretch with us.

We chatted for a long time in a tent which looked like a kitchen/living-room. Meanwhile, it had livened up in the polar station. Jaeger and Bolz went ahead. Arved and I harnessed ourselves to the sledges and marched the last kilometres to the most southerly point on earth. A couple of dozen people greeted us there, both men and women. The South Pole was marked by a metal pole which year by year had to be moved a few metres in the ice. The ice-cap wandered here also. Amongst so many people and so much technology; I had already forgotten where we were. The South Pole was a complete contrast to the ice desert, instead of being its culmination.

Arved Fuchs and I approaching the geographical South Pole. In the mist one can see the flags which mark the US landing strip.

On my mountaineering trips, the summit had never been the culminating point of all exertions, and yet each summit was an especial goal. All desires were focused on it. So, like a marksman has his target in his sights, as if he were one with it, thus the mountaineer identifies himself with the summit which he wants to climb. All my instincts, energies and longings converged, when climbing, on this one point in which visibly all flanks, ridges and edges run together.

The Pole, on the other hand, was only an imaginary mathematical point in this endless expanse, invented by people by the decision to superimpose a network of co-ordinates over the earth. Ninety degrees south could have been anywhere on this regularly flat snow landscape. If no aerials and domes had stood here the Pole would not have been tangible or visible. Ninety degrees south is an absolutely imaginary point. This consciousness must have given an irrational dimension to the heroic journeys of Shackleton, Amundsen and Scott.

No, for Amundsen and his men certainly, it had been no disappointment to experience the Pole as a white nothing. Just the

Technology at the South Pole. Winter quarters. The dome on the right is a gigantic cupola, containing living and work accommodation.

opposite. They had sought, found and 'conquered' it. For all practical purposes, however, afterwards everything remained as before. The only thing which the men altered after the Pole was their direction of march; and their motivation. There was a before and an afterwards. Today, however, you go 1,000 kilometres and more through the stillness, through an inestimable vastness and suddenly there stand domes, cubes and masts. What I saw at the Pole was futuristic. It appeared to me as an inversion of all forms and perceptions which belonged to this landscape.

A black tent – pointed, tattered – ought to stand at the Pole, nothing else. Amundsen yes, the rest was a symbol of human megalomania. What else?

One experience richer, I stood at the geographical South Pole. Arved and I hugged each other. I liked this man. He had given me much. He was, despite everything, the ideal partner. We would also make the second half.

'Summer camp' at the South Pole. On the right, ANI's Twin-Otter which had flown in our supplies. A few weeks later some tents in the camp were to burn down.

The reception at the Pole was heartfelt. Many technicians, manual workers and radio operators stood around to shake us by the hand. Even some scientists had come to congratulate us, although adventurers like us were not officially welcome in the US station. We sensed appreciation, readiness to help, sincerity. There was no feeling of ingratiation between the people of the Pole and us. We all felt what we were: a few dozen people at the edge of the world.

We were offered quarters in Barracks J–5. One meal after another. Near the extended military tent in which we lived in the summer camp, John showed us the shower. We could use it any time. There was even a table. We could sit there, write, relax. What a contrast! After the many days in the white snowscape and our restricted tent everything was strange at first: bed, table, the many people. The barracks in which we lived was overheated. The strangely futuristic steel, glass and sheet-metal buildings outside blocked out the sky. Nevertheless, it was pleasant in J–5.

Arved and I changed our clothes. We emptied the sledges. For

Today the South Pole is marked exactly. Here is the international time and date line. In good weather the buildings at the Pole can be seen from 10 miles away.

hours we sat in the simple kitchen in the summer camp, eating and drinking wine, talking. There was a good mood there. 'Another beer?' 'Yes, thanks.' Occasionally, I looked at the television which was uninterruptedly fed with videos, we talked with the men who do the manual work at the Pole: joiners, electricians, electronics engineers, blacksmiths, radio operators. For the time being I did not think about what lay ahead.

In writing up my diary I had noticed that we had lost a day. According to our calendar we had arrived at the Pole on 30 December. Now, still on the same day, it was 31 December. We were on the International Date Line. Twelve hours' time difference. The rhythm built up over four weeks – day – night; go – sleep – had got me lost.

Ahead of us lay another 1,500-kilometre stretch, the route on which Captain Scott and his fellow travellers had lost their lives in 1912. We had needed forty-eight days to reach the Pole. From the Pole onwards the sledges would be heavier, the stretch longer. No depot. We would have no chance of reaching McMurdo in forty-five days if we continued at our previous speed. We must increase it to 35 kilometres per day. That was only possible with sailing. Not once had Amundsen and his dogs achieved such a speed. We banked on the wind which was now to blow helpfully on our backs. No more having to fight against what Scott called the 'piercing' wind, which blew on the polar plateau, was like hoping in Purgatory for Heaven. It was late before we got under the shower.

For the first time for two months, to stand under a shower again and wash our hair, was for me the greatest pleasure at the Pole. It took an hour to wash all the dirt from my body, which for weeks I had been oblivious of. Arved and I had taken tablets along the way which cleansed the skin. Thus we had no boils. Freshly washed, composed and informed about events in the outside world, I felt myself strong again. I would have loved to run on immediately. My enthusiasm for ice travel was greater than ever. I did not doubt that we would make it to the other side of the continent.

It was a timeless hour between 30 and 31 December as we lay on our mattress beds, washed, freshly clothed and satisfied.

9   New Year's Eve at the South Pole

We were living now in another world, in another time. I felt myself behaving as if it were night-time and yet was wide awake. The room in which we sat was dirty, simultaneously kitchen and living-room of the summer camp. A prefabricated structure. But it was all there: oil furnace, sink, cooker. People were ready to help and were friendly towards us. We were served shrimps, wine, beer. We were pampered by everyone. Our time on the ice was forgotten. The television in the kitchen/living-room led us to believe in a fictitious world beyond this ice desert: a fairy-tale world. Constantly, new videos were playing. People came and went. Each one interrogated us, wished us luck. It was a long time before Arved and I got back to Barracks J–5. Ought we to take another shower? For weeks we had looked forward to the shower more than anything else. Now it was no longer so important. I promised myself to use the sauna before departure. In the tent, between the little folding table and sleeping-bags, I read the first issue of the report by *Der Spiegel*. Bittorf recounted our journey as exactly as if he had been there. And yet the cold had not been so fierce. There was talk of strain and suffering which now seemed to me exaggerated.

Through the luxurious life in the South Pole station everything became at once played down: the vastness outside, the Antarctic, its history, our daily cares. The Antarctic travellers of the turn of the century had called this land 'the ladyless South'. 'The Antarctic is the most peaceful place in the world because there aren't any women there', the American polar flier Richard Byrd had fulminated. One had to be able to envisage that. South Pole travellers were compelled at that time to go for two or three long years without the opposite sex. Amundsen and Scott would not have been able to foresee what we were to experience at the South Pole.

Olav Bjaaland at the South Pole. For Amundsen and his men the Pole had been a running and reckoning exercise. They needed three days to determine their precise position.

'We have the Pole in sight and I can hear the axis of the earth squeaking', Olav Bjaaland had noted in 1911; he was one of the four Norwegians who first came here with Roald Amundsen and their dog sledges on 14 December. Otherwise, no sound. They had the Pole in sight, but where was it? There was at that time nothing to see apart from an immense plain. Everything flat. The dogs were so hungry that they ate their own excreta.

When we had reached 90° south, we had also abandoned the ice continent. There was not only a bronze pole, thick as an arm, stuck in the ice, rearing up several metres above the snow crust. Above that was a plaque: 'GEOGRAPHIC SOUTH POLE (Altitude 2,835 metres. Ice thickness more than 2,743 metres)'. There it was swarming with people, machines, impressions. Directly by the Pole sign stood a tent. A few young Americans, members of the US polar station, had decided to camp on the ice, so as not to miss our arrival. The tent still stood there. It reminded me of Amundsen and his expedition. At Bay of Whales, on 20 October 1911, men and sledges had been ready for departure:

We harnessed our draught animals – thirteen dogs to each of four sledges – and set out. Pestrud filmed us all as we descended

Amundsen with dogs and team on the way to the South Pole: only by using the tactics of successively killing huskies ('dog eat dog') could he travel so fast.

to the ice slab. A few seals with new born pups lay around. He 'shot' us again as we climbed the barrier on the other side of the bay. When we had covered a small part of the barrier, the weather worsened. H.H. [Helmer Hanssen] led and steered by compass. For some reason or other we got too far east on unknown terrain full of crevasses. I kept with Wisting. His sledge was the last. Suddenly a large piece of the ice surface vanished and near the sledge there opened up a yawning abyss, big enough to swallow up all of us. Luckily, we were a bit to one side so that we got away with it.

Thus, factually, Amundsen describes the start. He and his Norwegian companions made swift and regular progress with the dog sledges, which their 'competitors', the British, had not held possible. Amundsen's dogs – 'they are really true, true even to death' – were to be killed for their pains. Killing off the weaker dogs was part of Amundsen's tactics: on the Axel Heiberg Glacier it was certainly a terrible event

when the dogs were shot. The men named the place 'the butcher's shop'. The remaining dogs got to eat the flesh of their dead comrades, which gave them new energy and saved the life of the expedition.

On 14 December 1911, fifty-seven days after setting out from Framheim, Oskar Wisting, Olav Bjaaland, Sverre Hassel, Helmer Hanssen and Roald Amundsen reached the South Pole.

> It was 3 p.m. when it happened . . . we arrived here with three sledges and seventeen dogs. Immediately on arrival, Helmer shot one of them; Helgi was totally exhausted. Tomorrow we shall march away in three directions to circle the Pole. We have consumed our celebratory meal – a small piece of seal meat each.

Helmer Hanssen, who with his dog team had been ahead all the time, experienced this 'sublime moment' differently from Amundsen.

> Amundsen thought as always of his companions and as we hoisted the Norwegian flag at the South Pole, he let us all grasp the bamboo pole with the flag after it had been made fast in the

snow . . . For my part I had no feeling of triumph at this moment – as perhaps one would have expected. I was relieved to know that from now on I had no longer to stare at the compass in the biting wind which continually blew in our faces as we marched southwards. From now on we would have the wind on our backs.

Amundsen and his men went out at 'midnight' in order to 'shoot' the sun. The calculations showed that they were at about 89°56' south. Thus something over 6 kilometres away from the Pole. Bjaaland, Wisting and Hassel marched away on skis, to circle round the Pole. Bjaaland went north-east by north, Hassel north-west by west and Wisting south-east by east.

> They were to cover a stretch of around 19 kilometres. Each of them had a stake (spare sledge runner) with a black pennant on it. To each stake a small bag with information about the exact position of 'Polheimen' was attached. The weather was magnificent, windless but a little gloomy . . . By 10 a.m. they were all back again.

As Amundsen noted in his diary, it was a rigorous job to determine the position of the Pole exactly. But they had reached the goal first and gladly undertook this task. The most marvellous thing was that no Union Jack fluttered at the Pole, although if they had been second they would have found it faster. Time and again, Amundsen had to line up the mirror image of the sun on his sextant with the horizon. At the geographical South Pole he could see that, day and night, the sun stood at the same height in the sky. His camp was not standing at this point. Two days after the calculation, Amundsen shifted it 9 kilometres further to the spot which he had determined as the point of the Pole. There once more he took hourly measurements for a day and a night. The dogs lay full-fed and outstretched in the 'warm sun'.

17 December. The Norwegians quitted the Pole. The tent, which they had taken with them for emergencies, they left behind to mark the spot.

The British at the South Pole. In the middle (standing) Scott. The fact that the Norwegians had been there already was a shock.

The Norwegian flag and the pennant from the 'Fram' fluttered at the top of the tent pole. I left behind various things in the tent. . . . In a bag I left a letter for the King and a short message to Scott who I assumed would be the first after us to visit the Pole.

A month and a day later it was so. The British reached the Pole and found the tent. Scott, disappointed and faint-hearted, wrote in his diary:

18 January. Decided after summing up all observations that we were 3.5 miles away from the Pole . . . More or less in this direction Bowers saw a cairn or tent.

We have just arrived at this tent . . . about 1½ miles from the Pole. In the tent we find a record of five Norwegians having been here . . . [on] 16 December.

The tent is fine – a small compact affair supported by a single bamboo. A note from Amundsen, which I keep, asks me to forward a letter to King Haakon! . . .

Nansen's Fram *in Bay of Whales. Although Nansen himself had dreamed of a trip to the South Pole, he lent the ice-worthy ship to the young Amundsen.*

Left a note to say I had visited the tent with companions. . . . sights at lunch gave us half to three-quarter of a mile from the Pole, so we called it the Pole Camp. We built a cairn, put up our poor slighted Union Jack and photographed ourselves – mighty cold work all of it – less than half a mile south we saw stuck up an old underrunner of a sledge. This we commandeered as a yard for a floorcloth sail. I imagine it was intended to mark the exact spot of the Pole as near as the Norwegians could fix it . . . I think the Pole is about 9,500 feet in height; this is remarkable, considering that in latitude 88° we were about 10,500 feet . . .

Well, we have turned our back now on the goal of our ambition and must face our 800 miles of solid dragging – and good-bye to most of the day-dreams!

The British had not only arrived too late, they were broken men. The return march had to turn into tragedy.

Some days later, on 26 January, the Norwegian polar team was back at its starting point, at Bay of Whales! Amundsen wrote:

Before we rightly knew it we were back at our place of departure. 'Framheim' was bathed in the light of the morning sun and looked exactly as when we had left it. We did not take long to cross the bay and at 4 a.m. we were again in our snug little hut.

The Norwegians' sledge journey had lasted ninety-nine days, an eternally long ski tour with sledge dogs for transporting loads. It would be completely wrong to compare the two journeys with each other. When Captain Scott and his four companions reached the southern end of the world with their self-drawn provisions sledges, they had not only lost the 'race' for the South Pole, they had sacrificed themselves, expended themselves, tortured themselves. What a mission for the sake of the Union Jack!

> Great God! This is an awful place and terrible enough for us to have laboured to it without the reward of priority . . . It will be a wearisome return.

It seems to me that Scott foresaw the coming tragedy. Unlike that bold planner Amundsen, he could not rely on the speed and strength of the huskies to get him back to his ship. Moreover, the Norwegians had the joy of success on their side. As on the last stage of the march to the Pole, the British had to drag their provisions sledges on the return march themselves. It would be pointless to lament that they had neither ponies nor dogs or snow vehicles to help them on the return from the Pole. Only the fact of having been the first could have saved them. The British were second, the losers. 'Doomed to death', also because the news which they had to bring back was not that wished for. Perhaps Amundsen and his team, if they had been second, would have foundered too – disappeared into one of the ice-falls, which on the ascent he had named the 'Devil's dancing floor'. Only with much luck had he got through there. Certainly, there were a hundred reasons why the British had been slower. The worst part was that Scott was too late for the return march. Moreover, he and his men were badly nourished. Nevertheless, I venture to maintain that success would have saved them.

Hard (dried) rye bread and bacon (smoked and dried for a long time) have been for hundreds of years the staple food of the South Tyrolean peasants, when they are 'on the mountain'.

Joyful Anticipation

In 1980 I first thought in concrete terms about a crossing of Antarctica. Only ten years later the idea was to be realized. For this my mountain experience was an advantage. Already as a schoolboy I was a good long-distance skier and I spent many winters with the mountain peasants. Who could imagine, for example that, for an expedition on the ice continent, bacon and hard bread would suffice as basic foodstuffs?

My joy of anticipation was great and it increased when Wilhelm Bittorf promised me his participation. Bittorf is a profound student of Arctic and Antarctic literature, as well as a committed protector of the environment. As I too wanted to recruit for a 'World Park Antarctica' by my journey, so Dr Wilson had indirectly also done with his paintings. Bittorf was the ideal manager and reporter for us. From his announcement of the expedition (summer 1989): 'Reinhold Messner and Arved Fuchs intend to apply Messner's climbing principle "by fair means" in Antarctica too and manage with a minimum of technical assistance. They will not disturb the frozen stillness of the ice continent with the noisy vehicles of the motor age or poison the crystal air with exhaust fumes. Their journey will also not be dominated by the turmoil and hunger of a pack of sledge dogs; for to provide for dogs the expedition would have to be supplied at great expense by aircraft. Instead Fuchs and Messner will each pull their food, tent and fuel for their cooker on sledges. Relying on neither motors nor dogs, rather trusting to their own powers is what counts for both men. From the first, their journey will be throughout an adventure again, a challenge to their own abilities, a new thrust to the limits of human experience.'

192

II. The Journey in Colour Pictures

Oswald Oelz on top of Mount Vinson (Antarctica). My life as a mountaineer was not over with the ascent of the highest peak in the Antarctic. I knew I would have to go to the mountains again, but I dreamed now, above all, of Arctic travels and a crossing of Antarctica on skis.

From Mount Vinson we skied down to base camp which lay behind the pointed nunatak to the right of the ascent ridge. There, with practice runs, I tested, for the firs time with a heavy sledge load, my long-distance speed under Antarctic conditions.

(Overleaf)   For forty years I had been climbing mountains. Nevertheless, in the Antarctic a new world of experience opened up for me: ice travel. When 'Ramuner-Franz' of Villnöss had taught me long-distance skiing, I was not yet ten years old. In 1989–90 I was able to employ my mountaineering abilities and my decades of endurance training, to survive the longest 'ski tour' of my life.

With Arved Fuchs at Patriot Hills. As I alone had financed the expedition across the Antarctic continent, I was obliged to wear the sponsors' logos. Arved advertised for sponsors who in part had also financed the 'Ice walk' expedition (leader: Robert Swan) to the North Pole, in which Arved had participated.

(Overleaf)   Departure of the Trans-Antarctica Expedition from Patriot Hills. In 213 days Will Steger (45, USA), Jean-Louis Etienne (44, France), Victor Boyarsky (39, USSR), who mostly ran ahead of the dogs, Geoff Somers (40, UK), Keizo Funatsu (34, Japan) and Quin Dahe (43, China) were to traverse Antarctica by the longest possible route (about 6,400 kilometres), with three dog teams which were supplied by air. Expenditure: about DM20,000,000.

The camp of the Canadian organization ANI at Patriot Hills. Here we had a stop-over after a two-week delay in starting from Punta Arenas (southern Chile). Before we were flown in a Twin-Otter to the starting point of our 'Würth-Antarktis-Transversale', on the edge of the mainland, we had to alter our plans.

Navigating with the compass. Whilst I ran ahead on an exact bearing (after allowing for the magnetic variation) on the spherical compass, fixed to an aluminium frame in front of my chest, our satellite navigation device, which Arved Fuchs attended to, ascertained our position almost daily. With this method of navigation we could not lose ourselves in the white infinity.

(Overleaf) Crevasses and sastrugi were the main obstacles on our journey. It is horribly strenuous dragging a sledge weighing more than 100 kilos across sastrugi fields. It is more dangerous to run over glacier crevasses. We had to overcome more than a thousand kilometres of sastrugi and to cross more than 6,000 crevasses to get from one side of the ice continent to the other.

Arved Fuchs navigating. The battery driven device (GPS) showed our position at certain times of the day to within 150 metres, when three satellites were available. If four satellites were 'up', we could also get a digital reading to the exact height of our position above sea-level. We were the first to employ the GPS system for ice travel in the Antarctic.

Tent life: when the tent was up we got inside, shut the entrance and put the cooker on. Then we undressed (down to our underwear), hung cap, gloves and jacket in the roof to dry off and began to cook. Arved had already filled the three pots (coffee, food, water) with snow. We put them over the flame in turns.

(Overleaf)   Arved resting on a field of sastrugi. These hard snow-drifts develop during storms in the direction of the wind and grow up to a metre high. When the sledge slid into a groove, frequently we had to unbuckle our skis and release our pulling harness in order to get the load free again. Big sastrugi fields made our route longer.

Campsite. Our tent, a special construction with sewn-in poles was carried on my sledge. Its dome form could be put up with few grips. The skis and ice-axe served as anchors for the guy ropes. The entrance was turned away from the wind, with a snow wall or the sledges as wind protection. Thus we erected the tent day after day.

Arved Fuchs in front of our camp at the 'Thiels'. Behind is ANI's Twin-Otter which had flown in our depot and which took our rubbish away. In the background, a portion of the Thiel Mountains (King Peak) which are just 3,000 metres high. From here, freshly provisioned, we skied without another dump to the Pole.

(Overleaf)   Arved Fuchs sailing. Before the South Pole we could employ our sails for only half a day to real effect as the wind blew mostly out of the south. After the Pole we set our hopes on this natural form of propulsion. When my track remained visible (almost always) we could not lose each other.

Rest on the sledge and view back towards the Thiel Mountains, which have almost disappeared below the horizon. Generally, I waited five to fifteen minutes until Arved caught up; but in the late hours of the 'afternoon' often only until he emerged as a tiny point on the horizon. Then I skied on, already rather cooled down, in order to erect the tent at the end of the day.

At the South Pole on 31 December 1989. Thus Arved Fuchs (right) became the first man to reach the North and South Pole inside one year. At the Pole we had to switch time and date and reload our sledges. No further dump was to lighten the march to McMurdo. After three rest days we set off again on 3 January 1990.

Tent site on the high plateau. (A mock sun under the sun.) Arved fixes the tent. The sledge behind the tent serves as a wind-break. We are more than 3,000 metres above sea-level and notice the thin air. It is dry and cold (down to −40°C). After three days' sailing, we lost a lot of time here through hesitation and head wind.

(Overleaf)
Measuring pole on the Mill Glacier. Charles Swithinbank, a British glaciologist, who had measured this spot a year before, asked me to measure the poles again. He had recommended us to cross this ice stream down to the Beardmore Glacier. So we had to run 150 kilometres over rough, bare ice.

Arved Fuchs crossing a glacier crevasse. The crevasses were between 20 centimetres and 20 metres wide and often bottomless. The bridges of hard packed snow, however, were stable. We were always able to find a safe route even if it often required detours. So we moved almost all the time unroped, for a 20-metre length of rope generally would not have sufficed for an impeccable belay.

(Overleaf) Arrival at Ross Island. Scott Base (Ross Sea beyond). In the background White (left) and Black Island (far right). Across the saddle in between (the mountain ridge Minna Bluff is recognizable in outline) we had returned to civilization. It was now 'autumn', winter approaching. 'Evening' and 'morning' were once more distinguishable.

Rest on the Beardmore Glacier. In the background the 'Cloudmaker', a mountain which heralded the weather. The ice is rough and fractured. Our four-toothed crampons were worn out, my sledge scrap iron. Only a rubber strap held it roughly together. There were still 700 kilometres to go to the end of the journey.

Arved Fuchs on the ship Barken, *which was to take us from Terra Nova Bay (Italian Antarctic Station) to Christchurch in New Zealand. Although Arved and I had no serious quarrel on the entire land journey, discord now arose. On 20 February 1990, while we were on the high seas, a picture paper carried the following headline: 'After the Antarctic the feathers fly'. I was able to read (faxed to the ship) how Arved was to take part in fifty linked TV shows and interviews. At the South Pole Arved had spoken of his role as brakesman in front of video cameras, journalists and the Pole garrison. Now, evidently, the press relations officer of the Hamburg environmental organization 'Icewalk' had concocted a presentation which did not correspond with the facts and which was to end in my character assassination. Yet I hoped that, once at home, Arved would distance himself from these defamations. But no. On the ship he refused to speak with Wilhelm Bittorf who radioed us. The game of hide-and-seek had begun.*

(Bottom) The last members of the official Italian Antarctic expedition come aboard the Barken. *A few days earlier we had been flown in a helicopter from Scott Base to Terra Nova Bay. On the ship we were pampered.*

„Südpol-Expedition" nur ein Werbe-Gag

Hamburger Umweltschützer: Messner mißbraucht das Abenteuer

Während sich Star-Bergsteiger Reinhold Messner und der Polarexperte Arved Fuchs aus Bad Bramstedt noch durch die endlose Eiswüste der Antarktis quälen, gibt es hinter den Kulissen Krach. Holger Hansen von der Hamburger Umweltschutz-Organisation „Icewalk": „Die ganze Aktion gerät zum reinen PR-Spektakel für Reinhold Messner. Von Umweltschutz spricht niemand mehr."

vor Ort, berichtete Messner beim Zwischenstopp am Südpol, daß er immer öfter auf Fuchs warten müsse: „Für mich sind diese Rastpausen das Schlimmste, weil ich dabei schier erfriere."

Hansen: „Völliger Blödsinn. Wenn Messner wirklich kilometerweit vorauslaufen würde, wäre das lebensgefährlicher Leichtsinn. So etwa Arved nicht mitm~ das gan~

dition zum Nordpol, ist damit der erste Mensch, der innerhalb eines Jahres beide Pole erreicht hat – und das zu Fuß!

„Das Herausstellen von Messners Leistung ist unseriös", sagt Hansen, „im übrigen finde ich es mehr als merkwürdig, daß Messner gegen die Umweltzerstörung am ~ gerechnet mit~

With this newspaper article (Hamburg Morning Post, 11 January 1990), and through no fault of ours, a quarrel had broken out which would for ever affect relations between Arved and me. The headline reads 'South Pole expedition only a publicity stunt'.

Aftermath

On our return to Europe we had a joint press conference with journalists. Subsequently, Arved adopted more and more the 'Icewalk' version, as if one could bend the facts somewhat. After he let himself appear as the quiet hero of the quarrel which had been provoked by others, Arved suppressed the facts more and more. It pleased him evidently to play the role of the 'oppressed'. Whilst still in New Zealand, he had described himself as the 'brakeman' of the expedition and in point of fact, from the Pole to McMurdo, he had travelled in front perhaps 5 kilometres out of 1,450 kilometres. I had made the speed and track in order to save the expedition. Now suddenly, all that had been Arved's deliberate tactics.

Was I supposed to be the 'fall guy' twice? First used, then slandered? Was Fuchs so sly? The quarrel with Arved Fuchs made me ill and sleepless. I was as hurt as after a broken love affair. The breach of trust gave me so much pain at first that I needed a long time to recover. This argument was not the first disappointment with my touring partners. Time and again I had been publicly slandered by 'comrades', always after the relevant expedition, always only after a great success. Thus one or another managed to come out from 'my shadow' on the title page of magazines or daily papers.

The Stern utilized the 'media lust' of some of my 'quiet, oppressed' climbing partners shamelessly, in order to concoct a story out of falsehoods, half-truths and distortions, which I was able to expose in a live ZDF interview ('Sportstudio') as deliberate character assassination. Nevertheless, some of it stuck with the readers, above all because Arved Fuchs knew how to disguise the facts. In half a dozen TV appearances and many lectures. Arved dodged all critical questions so adroitly that I still stood branded as

Lost in the white infinity. Arved follows. This picture comes back to haunt me a thousand times.

a liar. I distanced myself from him. I had not thought him capable of such a selfish representation. That the environmental organization 'Icewalk', which had been behind this quarrel, now deplored th[e] it reflected badly on the environmental case, was the high point of this character assassination campaig[n] What did I do to counter it? I went my own way. I spoke with the Italian President about the renewa[l] Antarctic Treaty, strengthened the Foreign Minister in his intention to enforce the 'World Park' idea. Before the European Parliament and at lectures I advanced my conviction that the ice wilderness of the Antarctic must be a 'World Park' for mankind. I did not want to subordinate my commitment to the environment and my convictions to a quarrel which only served sensational make-believe.
For two decades I have known that success can end abruptly in gloating and disarray. Arved and I we[re] not unaware of that. We had furnished the media with suppositions: a drama on the ice without eyewitnesses. The conflict was quickly fabricated. Clearly, by this trip Arved had been able to increas[e] enormously his celebrity without investing money. These things did not bother me. Only his falsehoo[d] upset me: that he concealed having run behind almost the whole way. In a commentary, the Wiesbade[n] business journalist Stefan Baron summed up his view of the 'Messner-Fuchs-Media Quarrel':

> It is a tragedy: two men battle for months and thousands of kilometres across an uninhabited ice desert, survive the murderous cold and annihilating storms, in short, accomplish a performance such as no one before them has accomplished – and what sticks in the minds of most television viewers, newspaper and magazine readers? That the pair have quarrelled.
> Naturally, Reinhold Messner and Arved Fuchs have quarrelled. If you have to sleep for

194

Photos like this one and countless video shots prove that the facts are irrefutable.

ninety-two nights in a confined tent next to a person, whom beforehand you scarcely knew, you wouldn't be able to stand him. And not only because he himself – just like you – hasn't washed properly for weeks.

Judged by that, Messner and Fuchs got on surprisingly well with each other. Even his friends have their problems with Reinhold. The South Tyrolean is an ego-maniac. Preferably, he does everything himself because only he satisfies his demands for perfection. One must well be so to get as far as he has done. Messner's carefulness, discipline and performance will seek their like. The man is singular – and he knows it. That makes him easily intolerant of others, slower people, weaker people. That Messner has quarrelled with his partner Fuchs is not to be wondered at in the slightest. In several issues, Der Spiegel described graphically and sympathetically what an extraordinary performance Messner and Fuchs achieved together. The unavoidable quarrelling between the pair played only a side role.

The quarrel first developed in the Stern which saw in them a chance still to get in on the act. Cribbing from Fuchs' PR manager, a former colleague, the Stern took up the cause of the weaker party. Henceforth, less was said and written about the performance of the two men who had crossed Antarctica than about their personal arguments. Such are now the laws of our media world.

I can live with that.

What is success? What did it mean here? Success is a measure of effort and yet it can be as wrong as a court verdict. Success gives power also to him who is in the wrong. Success guarantees a return flow of energy that is indispensable where survival on an adventure at the limit is concerned.

Compared with my Himalayan tours, this Antarctic trip was by far the most expensive undertaking. In order to judge our costs, one must compare them, for example with those of the parallel 'Trans-Antarctica' dog-sledge expedition. Our just DM1,000,000 against a total of US$11,000,000. 'Trans-Antarctica' had meanwhile covered a stretch of 4,000 kilometres. Their enormous cash expenditure would not have achieved success, nonetheless, without US and USSR assistance. USSR transport aircraft had brought dogs and equipment to the starting point at the edge of the Antarctic. At the Pole the NSF (National Science Foundation) placed 30 tons of fuel at their disposal. All because a Russian, Victor Boyarsky, was with them. The USSR was officially prepared to fly fuel to the Pole, so that 'Trans-Antarctica' could get further. Like us at the start, the six members of the dog-sledge expedition were dependent after the Pole on the help of ANI. And ANI had not been able to supply the promised fuel dump. At once the US intervened and supported likewise the 'Russian Antarctic expedition', as 'Trans-Antarctica' had to be called in the polar station. Steger's route was long but the expedition had ten times as many depots at their disposal as we did and the route had been professionally surveyed. I don't want to make a bagatelle of our 'commercialism' but, measured against the expense, for the dogs of 'Trans-Antarctica' alone, we travelled modestly. Tired huskies were flown out to southern Chile to recover. We were not sure whether, in emergency, anyone could have come to fetch us.

Arved and I had never wanted to measure ourselves against 'Trans-Antarctica'. The two means of travel were as different as those of Scott and Amundsen. And we were living, luckily, no longer in the age of 'conquest'. Scott and Amundsen would have used aircraft in 1911 to get to the Pole first had they been available. Any means that guaranteed success would have been right for them. We had voluntarily renounced all such help, which had not been available to Scott. We

In this old dark tent I spent two nights at the South Pole. It had been erected by our fans in the polar station. Here they had awaited us.

marched according to his method for the sake of adventure and Antarctica.

I had forgotten the world which we had been in yesterday. Now we were sitting at the Pole and recovering for the longest stage of our journey. I was not especially curious about the high-tech buildings outside near the summer camp. Also, the arriving and departing aircraft – Hercules machines – did not interest me. After a few hours I had lost my feeling for the mysterious world outside. To me it had been clear that the South Pole is inhabited by Americans and furnished with the comforts of civilization, and yet I was now distracted. At first by the appearance of the station. Then by the many people. I had not really expected Amundsen's black tent at the South Pole, yet I would have been glad if in Antarctica, the 'last wilderness', only pedestrians were permitted. The stations armoured with technology should be scrapped. Perhaps I enjoyed the hospitality less on that account than I had expected whilst still outside on the ice. In the overheated Barracks

197

J–5 I could not sleep. What would this place be without the cupola, which everybody called the 'dome', without the landing strip, without the containers on stilts which might just as well be on the moon? The Pole was flat like the rest of the Antarctic. It is not apparent that all lines of longitude meet here. For thirty years now the Pole has been constantly inhabited. The Americans call their station 'Amundsen-Scott-Base'. The fluttering flags and the plaque with the inscription 'Geographical South Pole' nearby do not make this point any more interesting. On the contrary, the constant presence of people here has taken away the mystery that had inspired Amundsen to journey here.

I felt myself peculiarly unwell. It was unaccustomedly warm and much too noisy. After so many quiet days the buzz oppressed me. When the Norwegians and the British had reached this point eighty years before, they were further away from civilization than ever before in their lives. In the same place we were in a high-tech centre of civilization.

Arved and I ate the whole day. Bits of our equipment had to be mended: skis, bindings and my broken spoon. Then we sat on our beds amongst the curtained-off cubicles in J–5 and read. I wrote up my diary. Certainly, the station here was important to science. The hole in the ozone layer could be examined nowhere better. Also for observation of the stars and for many other scientific tasks, this location was suitable. But how was the sewage problem solved? How was the fuel stored? How many poisonous substances seeped daily into the ice? The Antarctic was pure, one assured us. Yet for how long? The wreck of the Argentine supply ship *Bahia Paraiso* near the north point of the Antarctic peninsula in January 1989 – a few weeks after the Exxon tanker accident in Alaska – made one shockingly conscious of the danger which threatens the seventh continent. Over 800,000 litres of diesel oil leaked from the sunken freighter. The oil pollution had cost tens of thousands of penguins their lives. No one knew the number of annihilated whales and seals. Damage limitation was impossible. Biologists reckon that it will be a hundred years before the micro-organisms – first link in a delicate food chain – are re-established in the Bismarck Strait.

This environmental catastrophe in the Antarctic should be a beacon, as at sixty research stations, the technical expenditure constantly increases. And with it also the stress on the environment. Many of these stations have at their disposal their own harbour, their own aircraft and helicopter landing sites. Along the coast, where the stations are, lie abandoned vehicles, ruined buildings, empty oil tanks – like paper cartons on a rubbish tip. In the dry, cold air of Antarctica nothing decays. The rubbish heaps grow constantly bigger. Engine oil and sewage from the shipping traffic pollute the sea offshore.

It is not true to say that the bases are intentionally poisoning the environment. The environmental sins in the hard polar climate are also the consequence of the high costs of rubbish removal. Big support teams do more damage than small ones and the number of back-up personnel in the Antarctic exceeds that of the scientists. By a long way. Infrastructure and logistics consume 90 per cent of the present budgets.

Only about 4,000 people live in the Antarctic during the short summer months. Nevertheless, the human presence is noticeable. On the narrow strip of the 500-kilometre ice-free coast, human activities disturb the fragile balance of wild animals and plants severely.

Certainly, the consequences of tourism show too but most of the curious visitors understand the environment. It is not they, rather the burning rubbish heaps, helicopters, dynamite and bulldozers that have soiled the cleanest place in the world. The almost two dozen nations, which have established themselves in the Antarctic since the end of the 1950s, are the invaders who have made Amundsen's fear come true that cupidity could destroy the Antarctic.

A grotesque game of Monopoly has begun. There is speculation about raw materials and national territorial claims. Above all, on the Antarctic peninsula, Argentine women bear children there. The Chileans underline Chilean sovereignty in the Antarctic with their airforce.

All honour to serious science but that part of polar research which investigates the damage originated by other parts of science, advocates a protected world park which people should be allowed to visit only under strict conditions. The wilderness must remain wilderness.

For a day now we had no longer lived in the wilderness and

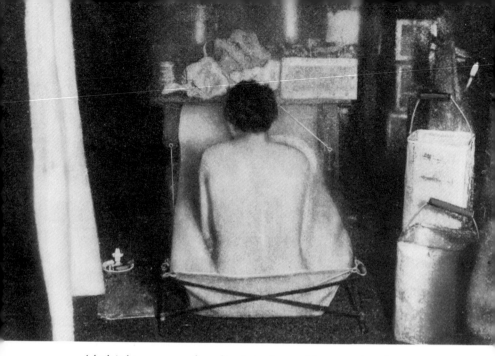

A bath in base camp was for earlier Antarctic expeditions an awkward process. We showered at the South Pole. Once in 100 days.

everything was different: time, date, rhythm of life. Everything was unusual. Also, my waterworks were all muddled up. Every half-hour I had to go to the lavatory to pass water because I was no longer exerting myself. I felt lack of sleep, hunger, hope, wholly different from the previous weeks.

So ready to help were the Americans at the Pole, so forthcomingly they attended to us, yet I felt myself unwell. Everything seemed to me unpleasant, useless, narrow and less beautiful than life in our tent.

In the evening there was to be a New Year's party in the 'dome', the big cupola in the centre of the polar station in which the scientific and radio cabins stood. Until now, I had only seen this building from the outside. Would we be invited? I was curious. 'Welcome to the South Pole' stood over a gigantic entrance doorway. What was hidden behind it?

We had arrived at the US polar base on New Year's Day. Without looking around further, we had spent the day in J–5 and the kitchen.

When three young women in fancy dress invited us to accompany them in the evening, Arved and I were more than astonished. Were we really welcome? No one had invited us officially to the party! Our companions led us into the big aluminium cupola. Blaring music mixed with the humming of the diesel generators. In the cafeteria section, now the party locale, a milling crowd of people: sixteen women and seventy men. This change of scene after 1,000 kilometres of loneliness was a shock for me. I had not felt deprived until then, nevertheless these 'wild' New Year's night women pleased me.

The people, above all, the girls, were dressed like space invaders: post-punk-era. Chains around the neck and leg-irons. Some looked as if they had come from Mars or from a planet where the living conditions were humanly degrading. Many were fooling around, dancing. Some women also invited us to dance; it was all very platonic. Arved and I enjoyed the few hours. We played at forgetting. Also, when a huge fellow offered me marihuana and time and again urged me to smoke a 'joint' with him, I did not feel tempted. I don't like any drug, above all not now after this long march. The 'descent' to McMurdo surfaced for a few minutes again in my consciousness.

The ordinary folk who had invited us were contravening local regulations. No private adventurer could expect help from the base. Our hosts didn't bother themselves about that. It was these same manual workers, joiners, hydraulic engineers, who had given up their sleeping places for us, so that we could sleep properly once.

In the late 'evening' of this 31 December 1989 we were still at the New Year's party in the dome. After a luxurious evening meal I ventured a dance. I was somewhat stiff after the many days on the ice, perhaps also awkward. Also I couldn't shake off the notion that I still smelled strongly. Once more I was offered marihuana. When I refused the 'joint' again, because I am generally against drugs, my 'friend' laughed approvingly.

Arved and I got to bed late. Despite tiredness and ample intake of alcohol, I did not fall asleep. I remembered the tent that I had seen in front of the barracks. A green military tent that resembled the one that Amundsen had used on his polar journey. With my sleeping-bag under my arm, I went outside and crept into the tent. At once I fell into a deep sleep and awoke wonderfully refreshed.

On 3 January we wanted to move on. It was time to reflect on the problems which had slowed us down on the way from the Thiel Mountains to the Pole. First of all, I asked a joiner to stick new skins on my skis. The aluminium spoon which had broken on me on the first part of the journey was mended. The readiness to help was great.

When I had confirmed that Steger had got 30 tons of fuel at the Pole for his 'Trans-Antarctica', so that ANI could set up his dumps as far as the Russian station Vostok, for my part I asked for a little help. I wanted to radio the Italian station 'Terra Nova' to let them know we wanted to be at Scott Base by mid-February. My request was refused. Now I experienced the hidden facts. Steger was not only supported because the NSF saw themselves compelled to intervene. After Adventure Network had once again not been capable of redeeming promises – in this case bringing sufficient fuel to the South Pole – the USSR had declared itself ready to fly the fuel for the Steger expedition to the South Pole. But before they tolerated a Russian machine at the South Pole, the Americans gave in and themselves helped. I expected therefore that at least I could briefly radio 'Terra Nova' – it would have been a great help and relief to us. Nothing. The chiefs of NSF stuck to their policy of isolation. Officially, as far as the Americans were concerned, we were not there. The head of the South Pole base neither welcomed us on arrival nor visited us in our quarters. Friendly as the ordinary people were, a radio contact with 'Terra Nova' would have been too risky without permission. It could have cost the radio operator his job.

In mid-February, Arved and I wanted to travel to New Zealand in the official Italian expedition ship. While still in Europe I had promised to call from the South Pole. But I got no chance. On the first day of the year I was tired and short of sleep despite the refreshing night.

The Canadian pilot's Twin-Otter had brought fresh provisions for us and so we could go on. We had not hesitated to use the polar station, certainly, but practical help we did not receive. Although we did not bother ourselves about the official policy of Washington's National Science Foundation, we could not get round it. According to their regulations, we would not once have been allowed to use the shower. For the NSF in Washington only officially promoted undertakings of

*Our depot at the South Pole. With provisions and fuel for forty-five days we set off
again. Also we renewed some pieces of equipment.*

the signatory nations to the Antarctic Treaty who were allowed to
exist on the ice continent. That the station management obstinately
refused me as an Italian citizen to speak over the US radio equipment
with the Italian Antarctic support point 'Terra Nova', was thus not
astonishing. In the Antarctic it was quite simple to defend claims.
They had only to refuse all help to undesirables. Thus the radio ban on
us. Vivian Fuchs had better luck in 1958. He led an official Antarctic
expedition and needed a great deal of public money:

> We decided to make a strong push for the Pole. For the next
> twenty hours we drove steadily on, rarely doing more than
> 3 miles an hour. Every six hours I shot the sun with my sextant
> and plotted a position line. By eight o'clock on 3 January, we
> had covered 60 miles and were straining our eyes for some
> glimpse of human occupation. We were just stopping to refuel
> when I suddenly noticed a blackish dot ahead. I swerved
> towards it and then realized it was a marker flag. In considerable

203

relief I waved to the others to stop and then switched off my motor. We were very tired and needed a sleep before pushing on.

Just before midday, on 4 January, we drove through the last few miles of soft snow into the American South Pole Station. It was very pleasant to be greeted by friendly faces and welcoming voices and to feel we could relax again. Our tractors had performed quite remarkably when one considered their limitations, but we weren't sorry to clamber out of their cold seats for the last time and to know that our 1,250-mile trip was over.

That was now more than thirty years ago – and from the mood which Scott had experienced at the South Pole, we were all an eternity away.

Tuesday, 16 January. The worst has happened, or nearly the worst. We marched well in the morning and covered 7½ miles . . . We started off in high spirits in the afternoon, feeling that tomorrow would see us at our destination. About the second hour of the march Bowers' sharp eyes detected what he thought was a cairn . . . Half an hour later he detected a black speck ahead. Soon we knew that this could not be a natural snow feature. We marched on, found that it was a black flag tied to a sledge bearer; nearby the remains of a camp; sledge tracks and ski tracks coming and going and the clear trace of dogs' paws – many dogs. This told us the whole story. The Norwegians have forestalled us and are first at the Pole. It is a terrible disappointment, and I am very sorry for my loyal companions . . . All the day dreams must go . . .

Wednesday, 17 January. The Pole. Yes, but under very different circumstances from those expected. We have had a horrible day – to add to our disappointment a head wind 4 to 5, with a temperature −22° . . .

We started at 7.30 a.m., none of us having slept much after the shock of our discovery. We followed the Norwegian sledge tracks for some way . . . In about 3 miles we passed two small cairns. Then the weather overcast, and the tracks . . . obviously going too far to the west, we decided to make straight for the

The drudgery and danger of falling into crevasses endured by Scott and his men is scarcely imaginable. With five of them straining at the sledges, they had reached the South Pole.

Pole according to our calculations. At 12.30 p.m. Evans had such cold hands we camped for lunch . . . We started out and did 6½ miles due south . . . We have been descending again, I think, but there looks to be a rise ahead; otherwise there is very little that is different from the awful monotony of past days. Great God! this is an awful place and terrible enough for us to have laboured to it without the reward of priority.

Also for us still a very long way to the McMurdo Bay/Ross Island terminus. The route, on which Robert Falcon Scott and his four companions had perished in 1912 on the gruelling return from the South Pole, still lay ahead of us. In two days we would have disappeared into the vastness of the polar plain, without connection with the outside world, almost without possibility of rescue. Nevertheless, I refused to take the Spillsbury radio set with me, which Brydon had brought to the Pole for us. On the first part of the journey, as far as the Thiel Mountains, it had seldom functioned. A more powerful set was out of the question on weight grounds.

We wanted to continue sending our present position with the high-tech positional system 'Argos'. The signals of the automatic transmitter were received by two orbiting satellites and passed on via the appropriate computer centre in France to Wilhelm Bittorf in Punta Arenas. Moreover, we knew that it functioned, Bittorf trusted the data. He was from now on our contact with the outside world with which we could not communicate.

On 2 January Arved and I loaded up our sledges. We had received a new tent and Arved a new pair of skis. We filled up the sledges with forty-five double rations, each of us taking half of them, as well as some bacon and hard bread. Our sledges were about the same weight. I had the tent.

Suddenly, in the evening, there was a radio message from Punta Arenas. Via Patriot Hills and the radio set in the Twin-Otter at the Pole, Wilhelm Bittorf was trying to contact me directly. Unfortunately, it became a one-sided conversation. I could understand Wilhelm, he could not hear me. Point by point I made a note of his instructions. Ulrich Jaeger was to fly back at once with the diaries, preferably from both of us, the films and his notes. I was to try, once more, to call up the Italians in 'Terra Nova'. I was to make a note of a short Argos code so that, in emergency, he would know what to do.

Once more I asked in the polar station for permission to speak with the Italian station. Nothing doing. With the radio set on the aircraft we couldn't transmit that far. Therefore I had to keep to a second instruction from Wilhelm: we must be at McMurdo by 15 February at the latest. 'Even the Italians cannot fetch you in time with their helicopters at Scott Base', he had explained. If we were not at their station by 16 February, the ship belonging to the Italian 1989–90 Antarctic expedition would leave without us. The last possible date for the departure of the *Barken* from Terra Nova Bay was 19 February and the helicopter flight there from McMurdo was only possible in fine weather, perhaps once a week. Between McMurdo Sound and Terra Nova Bay it was generally misty. If we wanted to be sure of leaving for New Zealand with the *Barken*, we had to arrive with a week in hand. In emergency I had envisaged a second possibility for getting home. I had made an arrangement with Giles Kershaw that, at the end of the expedition, he would fetch us from McMurdo in a small Cessna. However, this flight over the whole Antarctic – McMurdo, Patriot Hills, Punta Arenas – was expensive and risky. I had endless faith in Giles Kershaw, the most experienced polar pilot generally, but preferably I wanted to return by ship. Before our departure from Munich I had met the lively Giles and we had discussed the matter, considered all possible options, and negotiated a price. We had come to a handy arrangement. Nevertheless, I hoped now to be able to render this flying adventure superfluous by a fast crossing. We just had to arrive on time in Terra Nova Bay.

In 1957–58, the Fuchs expedition with their tracked vehicles had needed less than forty days for the second half of the crossing. However, Hillary had reconnoitred this route beforehand and installed supply depots. Hillary, who had arrived at the Pole earlier than Fuchs, feared that Fuchs would have no chance of making the entire crossing, on account of his lateness. There was a dispute between the pair of them, which at once went through the world press and was discussed publicly.

We knew too that our speed to the Pole had been too slow and that also our expedition was being publicly discussed. On the stage from the Thiel Mountains to the Pole we had progressed decidedly faster than in the first quarter of the journey. Could the speed be increased further? I was confident. Besides, we hoped for a following wind. With a constant wind behind us we could have reached McMurdo in thirty days; without such a wind, in sixty days. However, with a sledge load of 120 kilos this longest stretch would be murderously strenuous. Perhaps even impossible.

At the Pole there was a pile of letters from stamp-collectors who all wanted to have a postal cover from the South Pole. We fulfilled the wish, with a grumble to be sure, but we did it. There was also a letter from Steger. He invited me to run the North-west Passage with him and his sledge dogs. To Jürgen Bolz, who was to remain alone at the South Pole, I repeated then the Argos code for a possible rescue. Finally, I went into the sauna. Then I lay down again in the old military tent that still stood outside J–5.

South Pole start. More than half of the Pole population has come to wave goodbye. Weak breeze from the south, so we run 'penguin' style.

The longer we were on the move in Antarctica, the greater became my respect for previous expeditions. Not only Shackleton, Amundsen and Scott, but also Steger and Etienne had my undivided esteem. And the Arctic travellers. Above all Fridtjof Nansen, Julius Payer and Wally Herbert.

Yes, we wanted to set off on 3 January. We had to. In half-sleep, time and again, a date went through my mind: 15 February. On 15 February at the latest we must arrive at McMurdo. This deadline was to test my relationship with Arved sorely on the route which lay ahead of us.

Next 'morning' Arved and I were invited to breakfast by the boss of the polar base, John Fay. We were presented to the chief. They entertained us and wished us luck. A scientist gave us statistical data about wind direction and speed between the South Pole and McMurdo. We knew it already but it was reassuring to see it once more printed in black and white. Everything pointed to the assumption that in the next six weeks we would have ideal wind for sailing and good weather.

At lunch-time on 3 January we quitted J–5. Two Americans lugged each heavy sledge to the landing strip on which normally the bellied Hercules machines floated in. Coming from McMurdo, they landed safely in the snow on their ski runners. Just now a longer flight interval had been announced.

Arved and I explained our sails and made them climb into the air. Jürgen Bolz rushed from one to the other to film. He was full of life. I could only wonder at the energy with which this man worked. Using a 16mm Arriflex on a tripod, tape recorder and video camera, he operated everything himself, often filming two things at once. Gloves in pocket, he ran behind us with white fingers, a cloud of vapour around his head.

We ran towards the south. There were no farewells. As we had arrived, so we disappeared again. The wind was not strong enough to blow us and the sledges across the plain. We ran with the sails in front of us, sledges behind us. Off into the endless polar plain which we had forsaken for three days. Already after a quarter of an hour I could no longer see anything of the polar base. In front of me the grey snow surface and the darker horizon. Above me a milky blue sky, across which more and more streaks were drawing.

10 The Sails are Set

The hospitality at the Pole was pleasant and yet I would have preferred it if we had found only a depot there with our provisions.

On 3 January, we departed with relief. The 'White Mama', as the Americans call the glittering vastness all around, was again our only world. We had the wind behind us. From now on we would let ourselves and our sledges be pulled by the parachute sails.

At first the breeze was moderate so we marched more than we were blown. Like rectangular spinnakers, the sails bellied out in front of us. In the white vastness of the polar plateau they looked like coloured kites. Just 3,000 metres above the coast towards which we were travelling and more than 1,400 kilometres away from it, we travelled northwards. Ahead of us now lay 500 kilometres of high plateau, then 200 kilometres of glacier through the Trans-Antarctic Mountains; finally, 700 kilometres across the Ross Shelf Ice.

We had developed three sorts of locomotion, as I noted in the margin of my diary:

1. 'Donkey', i.e. pulling the sledge in the conventional way. (Speed: 2mph max.)
2. 'Swallow', i.e. sailing, standing on our skis and being pulled along by the sail/wind together with the sledges. (Speed: 5–8?mph.)
3. 'Penguin', i.e. skiing with outstretched sail, as if we were trying to sail (fly) but couldn't. (Speed: 3–4mph.)

During the rest stops, the sail was lowered, then raised again on re-starting. As the wind began to fill it, it wriggled, rustling across the frozen snow. Then it rose 6, 8 metres in the air, and was away. The sail was secured to a seat harness, separate from the pulling harness to which the sledge was attached. In a good wind the sail pulled man and

Taking in the sail. During our rest stops the sails lay on the snow. After use they were stowed in their own sack and carried on the sledges.

sledge over the snow crust. That was some sensation! Often I gave a shout at the start or as I travelled over the plain, a triumphant yodel, even though I am not really a yodeller. However, when I sensed the power of the wind in the sail, I could not help myself.

Scott too had sailed in 1912 on his way back but the sails had been mounted on the sledge, not attached to the men.

Friday, 19 January. Came along well this afternoon for three hours, then a rather dreary finish for the last one and a half. Weather very curious, snow clouds, looking very dense and spoiling the light, passing overhead from the south, dropping very minute crystals; between showers the sun shows and the wind changes to the south-west . . . Our old tracks are drifted up, deep in places, and toothed sastrugi have formed over them. It looks as though this sandy snow was drifted about like sand from place to place. How to account for the present state of our three-day-old tracks and the month-old ones of the Norwegians? It is warmer and pleasanter marching with the wind, but I'm not sure we don't feel the cold more when we stop and camp than we did on the outward march. We pick up our cairns easily, . . . but, of course, one will be a bit anxious till the Three Degree Depot is reached (still over 150 miles away).

How similar our situation was. The same snow, the same wind direction, the same weather. Only we had no tracks to follow and for us there was no supply dump the whole of the way to McMurdo. Progress was slow. Despite the sail, marching was strenuous. With the extended kite above me and the deep snow under my skis, I was compelled to adopt an unrhythmical pace. Time and again the strength of a wind gust tore me to one side. Often, when the wind varied, I lost balance. Slowly, I accustomed myself to this sort of 'penguin' sailing. Really and truly we ran like penguins; just as if we were always trying to fly without being able to.

After each hour of sailing, in the rest stops. Arved and I moved around stiff-legged. This kind of locomotion was especially hard on the thighs. On the first day we made about 30 miles. That was more than we had thought. On the second day we started late. It was a stormy morning with white-out. Only in the afternoon, about 3 p.m., could we set out. The wind was good. Despite the bad visibility we covered more ground than the previous day. It was like a downhill race in mist. We were travelling over a hump-back piste, without seeing where it went. Only the compass gave me the direction. The difficulty consisted of not losing one's partner.

This gloomy, threatening atmosphere! Dark clouds, snow streamers just above the ground, and the sun as a bright circle behind everything. I felt I was floating in the universe. Often we crossed waves of heavy snow which broke like emery-paper. Constantly, I looked around. I must not lose Arved out of my circle of vision. Had we lost each other in the thick mist and had the one not found the track of the other, both of us would have been lost. As we sat in the tent after the second day of sailing, our confidence had grown. Despite the bad visibility, the bad snow and the few sailing hours we had come a long way. 'Had Scott had our sails, he would certainly have made it', I thought and discussed it with Arved.

212

On this evening we had problems with the GPS set for the first time. It read 'error'. We got no position. 'Perhaps someone's been tinkering about with the satellites', suggested Arved. It was important for us to know where we were and at the same time to know how fast we were. We must develop a new feeling of speed. Just as we had had with marching. Our Argos set was functioning but it didn't help us at all. It announced our position to the computer centre at the French space authority in Toulouse, allegedly to within 200 metres. Daily, it was passed on by telex to the *Der Spiegel* reporter in Punta Arenas in southern Chile. Just dry co-ordinates which marked our present position on the earth's surface. Nonetheless these numbers testified that, on the first two days out from the Pole, we had covered a distance of 100 kilometres.

That was a sensational speed which had never been achieved in the Antarctic without engine power. Not even the sledge dogs of the Steger/Etienne expedition could keep up with that.

In the evening in the tent everything was so peaceful, still, congenial. It dawned on me that yesterday had been Magdalena's second birthday and I tried to picture my child. When would I see her again? But, actually, I wanted only to think ahead one day at a time. To visualize the whole stretch at once, all 1,500 kilometres of it, that would have been too much. We had forty-five days' food and fuel with us. Plus emergency rations. We had to manage with that.

With each day our journey now became more similar to Scott's. Had I not known how tragically this had turned out, I would have indulged myself more in the euphoria of our initial progress. Despite the heavy drift snow, the cold, which we now felt *more* than at the beginning; despite the hidden crevasses.

Saturday, 20 January. At first we went along at a great rate with full sail; then we got on to an extraordinary surface, the drifting snow lying in heaps; it clung to the skis . . . The pulling was really awful, but we went steadily on and camped a short way beyond our cairn of the 14th. I'm afraid we are in for a bad pull again tomorrow; luckily, the wind holds. I shall be very glad when Bowers gets his skis; I'm afraid he must find these long marches very trying with short legs, but he is an undefeated little

Sabine with Magdalena. Before departure, Sabine had stuck this photograph in the first volume of my diary.

sportsman. I think Oates is feeling the cold and fatigue more than most of us . . . It is everything now to keep up a good marching pace; I trust we shall be able to do so and catch the ship. Total march, 18½ miles.

Sunday, 21 January. Awoke to a stiff blizzard; air very thick with snow and sun very dim. We decided not to march owing to likelihood of losing track; expected at least a day of lay-up, but whilst at lunch there was a sudden clearance and wind dropped to light breeze. We got ready to march, but gear was so iced up we did not get away till 3.45 p.m. Marched till 7.40 p.m. – a terribly weary four-hour drag; even with the helping wind we did only 5½ miles . . . Luckily, the cracks are fairly distinct, though we only see our cairns when less than a mile away; 45 miles to the next depot and six days' food in hand – then pick up seven days' food and 90 miles to go to the Three Degree Depot. Once there we ought to be safe.

At the Pole people had slipped so many sweets into our hands that we had trouble eating them up. But as we didn't want to drag them

214

along, we gulped them down. The sledges were already heavy enough. One hundred and twenty kilos is a load for a horse, not a human being.

On the third day it was overcast again in the morning. Ideal sailing wind once more. The snow became ever sandier. It blew across the plain. It was as if a silk scarf were fluttering just above the ground. We sailed for five and a half hours, despite pain in my knees and cold during the stops. My arms hurt. We had first of all to accustom ourselves to sailing. Our hips hurt from the tugging hither and thither of our sails. Two enormous haloes surrounded the sun, as if today it were making a special effort to warm things up. My hips were rubbed raw by the sledge harness. When the wind fell away, we hardly moved. A bad omen.

On this day again we got no fix; again 'error'. We guessed every possible reason except the right one. We thought that one of the satellites might be defective or perhaps one had been swopped for another. A few days later, after lengthy examination, Arved twigged that, at the Pole, he ought to have switched the set over from west to east. Evidently the computer couldn't do this itself. After it was switched over, the GPS set was functioning again.

On the morning of 6 January an aeroplane flew over our tent, confirmation that we were on the right route. It was beautiful sunny weather but there was no more sailing wind. It was 'warm', at least we had the feeling that it was warm. Nevertheless we stayed in the tent. After the first three days' sailing we were so certain of success that we wanted to wait for the time being. It would have been false tactics to expend ourselves in pulling and then to hang around tired in the tent when there was a sailing wind. We wanted to save our strength for the hours of sailing.

But the wind failed to materialize. I wanted to run on for a bit at least, Arved saw no sense in enduring the drudgery of sledge pulling if the wind could lighten the work. Tension arose again between us. It was an unaccustomed feeling, staying in the tent in beautiful, sunny weather. I was rattled. Perhaps Arved was right, perhaps it was the only correct decision, to wait, only to go with the wind. But what if the wind didn't come? We tried to run on a bit but didn't get far with the heavy sledges on the sticky ice. We believed we knew now that the wind was on our side. Arved refused to move in fine weather without wind. After the good start – 156 kilometres in three days – our difficulties recommenced. Without wind we progressed at a crawl. Why slave at a snail's pace when the wind would heave us forward at least twice as fast! Perhaps tomorrow. Patience was now the tactic – as previously mulish perseverance was.

The sledges were heavy, fields of sastrugi slowed us down. Our average speed dropped. After the first windless day, it looked alarming. At this speed we would need sixty days to reach the coast. With provisions for forty-five days and the Antarctic winter at the door, we would be desperately short of time.

In his attempt to reach the South Pole, in 1909, Shackleton had also got as far as here. Scarcely imaginable how tired, despairing and sad the four men must have been when they ascertained that neither time nor rations were sufficient for them to reach their goal.

Shackleton, like Scott, had supplied the return route with dumps. They had slaughtered their ponies and deposited the meat for the return march. For Arved and me there was no dump. The heavy snow, the thin air and the exertion, however, were the same as in years gone by.

When we, muffled up as we were, put up the tent after an hour's run, we were almost 3,200 metres above sea-level. Nowhere a sign of a mountain. An ice sea without shores. On the horizon, a fine vapour overall. As soon as the tent was anchored with the ice-axe, we grabbed the tent poles and pushed them diagonally together. The mini-dome was up. Not only by the navigation instruments, but also in our lungs, for several days we had noticed that we were nearly at the highest point of the crossing. The sun circled now on a flatter track but irregularly around the mighty polar plateau. Time seemed to stand still; like a fixed recollection.

We were camping right on top of this high plateau and noticed the lack of oxygen. Meanwhile the daily rhythm and manipulating the tent had become a ritual. Each movement a matter of course. From getting up in the morning to cooking in the evening. Each had his special tasks. Each did what he had always done and he was also to do tomorrow. Whilst marching, I let my imagination rove. I didn't think

Oates with 'his' ponies. These tough, Siberian horses performed the indescribable. Finally, they were slaughtered and the meat stored in depots for the return march.

so much as let myself be carried along by the river of thoughts. Thus I was often far away from the Antarctic.

At night my thoughts continued. Old stories, which I had not digested, troubled me. I woke up often. The gentle wind on the tent walls sounded like the music of Vangelis. The world here was still and yet full of tones.

Arved and I were travelling without any scientific pretension and yet we endeavoured to grasp this white infinity, to assess it, to find a relationship with it. For the time being it held us fast, nevertheless we were not yet fully conscious of its significance.

These weeks of living with unadulterated nature gave me again that self-confidence which earlier, before mankind and his technology had 'subjugated' the world, had fulfilled each living, feeling creature. It seemed to me as if I were restored to that time and that state when nature alone was 'God'. Our ecological problems stem from the rift which has occurred between man and nature. Where do the two meet still today, how and how often? Man was obliged to forget to

217

conserve nature when he tried to perceive it rationally, instead of emotionally and instinctively. I have nothing against science – but must all myths be sacrificed to it?

Already after two days spent more or less in the tent, I began to forget where we were. Despite the delay I was again confident about a successful outcome. How quickly this Antarctic melted in my mind's eye; another month and the green spring must also be here, I thought. During the day we read or cooked. In the tent it was always pleasant without storm.

Oppressive as I found the waiting, it was at present rational. I would have been able to bear failure through weakness, but not through stupidity. With these thoughts I comforted myself over the wasted day. In the evening a grey cloudiness drew over the sky. In the south, towards the Pole, stood a black curtain of mist. Still no wind!

In the morning we set off on the freshly calculated bearing. Through vapour banks, sunbeams, with again a mock sun hanging under the sun, which shone obliquely through the mist. These two small suns, called panhelions, arose through refraction of light on the ice crystals floating in the air. This spectacle was inspiring and alarming at the same time, like many phenomena in nature. As if megalomaniacs had constructed an anti-sun. The light and cloud play lent wings to the spirit of Antarctica, likewise my thoughts. To me it was again clear where we were. Lost in nothingness. I became nervous.

I couldn't stand much of this squatting around in the tent on this high plateau in good weaher. The knowledge that each hour which we waited now would be one less in the end made me frantic. As organizer of the expedition I was worried above all that the Italian ship would sail before we could arrive at Terra Nova Bay. I insisted that now even without wind, we must do at least a partial stretch daily. After we had made scarcely any headway for days, we discussed even the possibility of breaking off the expedition at Gateway, for I knew that our chances of getting to McMurdo were virtually nil if no wind blew. However, I did not want to gamble away this possibility from the outset.

'Unload the sledges and take only the most essential for the route as far as Gateway', suggested Arved.

'No!', I said. I didn't want that, although it sounded rational. At Gateway the true continental crossing would have been at an end but I wanted to safeguard the smallest chance of getting past Gateway. For that reason we had to continue to drag all our equipment. All the provisions, all the fuel.

Arved exerted himself further when he appeared to have arrived at the limit of his endurance. He was a reliable partner. He carried out his portion of the daily work with care and precision. He never complained. If I missed a quality in him, it was cheerfulness. An expression of joy of life in the 'morning' perhaps, if the sun were shining or wind got up. But even so Arved and I as ice travellers made a perfect team. The three types of moving – 'donkey', 'swallow' and 'penguin' – we both applied at the same time. Not only because the wind forced us to, also because there was a symbiosis between us.

There was only this one problem: our respective speeds. Our tactics were reduced to a mulish stop-go. One braked, the other drove; as if this were a tacit agreement.

Meanwhile, for me it had become a matter of course that I ran ahead. Naturally, it was strenuous, staring at the compass uninterruptedly and breaking trail when the snow was soft. But leading cost me less effort than the constant speed setting. Slave-driving doesn't suit me. I care nothing for performance pressure. My motto is performance will.

Our blatant speed problems crowded out my joy of movement from my diary. Often I waited for hours. Days passed without hope of reaching my goal. My despair grew. Nevertheless, we would succeed, that I knew; because I wanted success.

Our snail-like progress oppressed me, not only because we had heavy sledges and no wind but, above all, because we were at odds and undecided. On account of our democratic voting day by day – as to how many hours' running time – compromises were necessary and these compromises meant that we were too slow – with no chance if we had to go on without wind.

The constant driving had become, therefore, my task because Arved always wanted to wait. Driving was my duty, as it was Arved's task in the evening to fill the pots outside the tent with pieces of hard snow, with which we could cook.

My diary now functioned as father confessor for me. Although often I could only jot down facts instead of feelings, behind these few sentences lay a whole reservoir of emotions and thoughts. I didn't ask myself whether, once back home, I would be able to recall this reservoir from the relevant triggers. I wasn't just recording. With the making of notes I got rid of everything: my anger, my tiredness, my despondency. Whatever I didn't want to scream in Arved's face, so as not to hurt his feelings and thereby weaken him, I jotted down so as to unburden my soul.

It was not Arved's fault that we were too slow, it was simply a fact and it made me boiling mad. In the evening, after writing up my diary, I was then free of anger. Then new courage revived in me and I was again certain that we would make it to the other end of the ice continent.

11 The White Infinity

For days we had had no wind; and when a breeze did get up, it was a north wind which blew in our faces. In this week of torment across the high plateau we were also held up by the angular ice of the fields of sastrugi. Daily performances: 5.5km; 11km; 13km.

I was anxious and slept badly. Hour after hour I stared at the tent walls, registering each gentle movement of the taut cloth. At the same time I listened to the world outside. I could hear wind rising and in its finest nuances I sensed the strength and direction, just as I registered the mist which passed over the tent. Now, when we were dependent on wind and snow conditions, I could not resign myself to the realities. Arved too was alarmed. No longer did it seem so important to get the whole way to McMurdo. Now I too would have been satisfied with the edge of the continent. Success had receded into the background. Why, then, these hopes, doubts, fears? It was all a matter of survival. Making it to the coast was now only possible if wind and snow conditions improved.

We had studied wind diagrams at the Pole as well as back home. Two predecessor expeditions – Scott and Swan – had written up the daily wind directions and strengths and I knew that Scott too had complained in his diary about frequent headwind on the way back. Nevertheless, I had not held possible such a dead calm. Had the atmospheric conditions been as they had been described to us at the Pole, we would have got to the Mill Glacier quickly.

Complaining helped nothing; so we hoped. I was prepared to double the marches. If the wind helped us at least half the day, we would catch up on the backlog again.

As we stood in the dead calm, Arved also knew that we must march, march, march. For him it was so much more difficult to brace himself up to it, for not only were his injured feet a hindrance whilst moving, but also his previous North Pole trip played a part in it.

During this journey he had spoken English all the time because that had been the common language of the group. So now, in the Antarctic, as he laid into his harness, he began to think in English. That meant that the distance, the time-span which lay between North and South Pole, was as if it had never been. It seemed to him as if he were carrying on where he had left off at the North Pole. That was on the one hand an advantage, on the other a drawback. Always to march on, without tangible beginning, without hope of an end; that was too much for him. Arved lost his sense of time and space.

The days in the tent passed in domestic routine: breakfast, a stroll around the tent, reading, chit-chat, lunch, music, reading. In between a few minutes outside. We were camping in the middle of the most hostile desert on earth, without back-up, without dumps ahead of us. From time to time I read Friedell's *Cultural History of Modern Times* and, forgetting everything, lived in the past.

The strategy of waiting for the wind had not proved right. Too late, only as time ran out on us, did we stir ourselves to run regularly in dead calm.

What was happening at home at this time – the fall of the Berlin Wall, the many Trabant cars in the west, the revolutions in eastern Europe – occupied us only peripherally. Naturally, we discussed them. At the Pole we had read newspapers and accepted the political changes as fact. Like news from another planet. The relevance of our expedition in such a politically turbulent time remained for us the same as at the start. No, our march was important only to us. And when I considered it objectively, it appeared to me now sometimes laughable how we exerted ourselves. What was to come out of East and West Germany was for us a purely theoretical question. That may sound cynical but it was so. For us the wind had significance, likewise our health, the harmony between us. We would find ourselves in this new political situation once the expedition was over.

Such a journey takes you prisoner. Every fibre, every thought, trapped in the ice. It is all so real, demands so much of you physically and psychologically, that the world outside becomes irrelevant. Reality was about saving our skins. All other things lost their significance. What we were doing was a life in itself, completely absorbing us but divorced from the world. What was taking place in

East Germany sounded like a fairy-tale. Nevertheless, it was not our life. Later, some time, the changed reality would impinge on us like an avalanche.

This trip had begun as the most extreme form of journeying freedom. I had perceived it too as a mandate to go where I must, in order to acquire individuality. Now it was just about survival. For that reason my urging, my running ahead. It was imperative. For Arved it bordered on mulishness. I did not want to dwell on the opposite scenario: what Arved would have done if he had been the pace-maker, had been the driver. I had to renounce such speculations. The reality was bad enough.

We had reserved the option to break off the expedition prematurely after a good half of the way from the Pole to McMurdo. Approximately at Gateway, at the foot of the Beardmore Glacier and the beginning of the Ross Shelf Ice. At position 83°30′ south the decision was to be taken.

1.   If by 30 January we have passed 83°30′ south, we continue to McMurdo.

2.   If we reach 83°30′ *after* 30 January and remain at this position for three days (as shown by the Argos), that means: please fetch us from there with the ANI aircraft: landing strip prepared.

I had sent this information from the Pole to Wilhelm Bittorf in Puntas Arenas. Our Argos was a safe but complicated means of communication. And in emergency? If we were immobilized? If one of us broke a leg? A fall into a crevasse? It would be a long time before help could arrive. Perhaps too long. Only when we did not move from one position for four days, was a rescue action to be launched, with the aircraft from Patriot Hills, almost 2,000 kilometres away. To get to us was not only difficult, it would have been dangerous too and impossible in bad weather. That I knew. For that reason too my haste.

I could not imagine anything more beautiful than this movement. This silence, this vastness, this peace! This was heaven.

The desire to march further was one of my motivations. Secondly, curiosity: what did it look like over the horizon? Thirdly, our situation: we were 250 kilometres from the Pole. More than 1,000 kilometres of the route still lay before us.

Arved was a black line behind me. The world around us dissolved into grey mist without the horizon being perceivable.

I had accustomed myself to this black-white land. The differing shades of grey on the snow surface indicated hollows and ridges. The white points were sastrugi, the black, their shadows. Only the sun, often surrounded by two or three haloes, illuminated a section of the sky in rainbow colours. It was as if the spectrum were meant to remind us of water, fire and earth.

The distant view in this snow landscape was not exciting, for all background was lacking and, if it had been there, it would have been swallowed up by this flickering grey that was neither mist nor clouds, but rather indicated a limit to this borderless stillness. The horizon melted away. The only sounds came from ourselves.

Boredom never bothered me, quite the opposite. Often so many ideas ran through my head that I had trouble arranging them. I could only think of one thing at a time. Often I stopped, after a fresh start, to be able to think clearly in one direction. For example, heaven and hell: in his *Divine Comedy*, Dante had placed the damned up to the neck in 'eternal ice'. That was the worst of all imaginable punishments. Worse than roasting in 'eternal fire'. But also too, paradise was here as he had described it – here with us, in the middle of the ice desert:

> . . . In that abyss
> Of radiance, clear and lofty, seem'd methought,
> Three orbs of triple hue, clipt in one bound:
> And, from another, one reflected seem'd,
> As rainbow is from rainbow: and the third
> Seem'd fire, breathed equally from both . . .

Should we run more hours? Sometimes I agreed with Arved that we ought to wait for windy days. However, the wind now often got up

Arved Fuchs sailing. Legs straddled, his gaze fixed on the irregular snow surface, he comes towards my resting place.

to storm force. Then sailing was dangerous. The wind lifted us, threw us to the left, to the right. Travelling at great speed over sastrugi could have resulted in bad falls, broken bones and other injuries.

Seventy-eight years ago today, Scott arrived at the Pole, so we had not too much lead over him; and we had these much too heavy sledges!

In the morning the sun was piercingly hot, although the air was −30°C and we sweated in just our pile suits. The parts of our bodies out of the sun were completely covered with hoar frost and during the stops I froze accordingly. A light southerly wind had got up and the dampness on my skin went right through me.

When the members of Scott's expedition had reached our present position on their return march, they were weakened, ill or injured. The irrevocable tragedy had begun.

> *Sunday, 4 February*. Pulled on foot in the morning over good hard surface and covered 9.7 miles. Just before lunch unexpectedly fell into crevasses, Evans and I together – a second fall for Evans, and I camped . . . We went on skis over hard shiny descending surface. Did very well, especially towards end of march, covering in all 18.1 . . . Every sign points to getting away off this plateau. The temperature is 20° lower than when we were here before; the party is not improving in condition, especially Evans, who is becoming rather dull and incapable.

We noticed too that we were going downhill. The plateau and the highest point of Antarctica lay behind us. I did not notice the terrain falling away but the altimeter showed it hourly. Nevertheless, the sledges remained our main problem. They were so heavy that they hindered us more than everything else. Only with depots, such as Scott and Amundsen had had, would this stage have been bearable without wind. That was no comfort.

Gloomy atmosphere the whole 'day'. Grey, the cloudiness all about us; grey, the snow surface which seemed to oscillate; grey, the whole world around us. The sun was apparent only as a bright spot. We could not see all 'day'. A bad 'night' followed. To take our minds off things, at 'midnight' Arved began to read and I listened to music. This

The British usually pulled their sledges. Falls into crevasses were not entirely avoidable, but they could be guarded against.

non-stop hoping for wind, this staring at the tent walls, this listening with pricked ears drives you crazy. Towards 4 a.m. everything was overcast, a sign of wind to come; wind got up when there were clouds and mist. By 'morning' the sun was shining again.

Again no wind. It was absolutely still. A stillness which was uncanny. On our way to the Pole, on such a day, we would have marched further than usual. Now we rested.

I was constantly having to accustom myself to change. What had been good conditions on the way to the Pole, were now bad; sun, lack of wind, hard snow. For sailing we needed wind and non-skid snow.

We waited for the wind which was to help us pull the heavy sledges. Later on we continued regardless. The snow was soft but frequently patches of bright drift snow lay on the smooth surface, coarse as emery-paper.

The snow surface was now smoother than on the first half of the journey, the way to the Pole. Similar only was the drudgery. The

227

*Much faster than at the Pole, we sailed on towards the Trans-Antarctic Mountains.
More than 100 kilometres in a day was our record.*

fields of hard new snow braked the skis and sledges so that each time
extra thrust was needed to get moving again.

Robert Scott had represented this drudgery in the tawdry light of
morbid self-sacrifice. Sacrifice-seeking adventurers were suspect in
my eyes. I rejected them and smiled at the rites and ideals of the heroic
conqueror; for that reason I had more sympathy with Roald Amundsen than Robert Scott. The notion that drudgery does man good or
even ennobles him is a stupid one. At any rate I am no masochist; on
the contrary; I do what gives me pleasure. As regards my expeditions,
I don't boast about the 'work' done, rather about the correct tactics.

I talked with Arved about it in the tent, but seldom about
motivations, what were we doing here and for what reason. Also, I
did not reflect about God. To myself, however, often I talked for
hours about women. Often it happened that for days nothing else
interested me. One cannot talk about God in infinite space, still less
reflect on Him. In the tent, with Arved, such conversations would
have been embarrassing, but during the day each was alone, and with

oneself one can discuss everything. In this still vastness, to speak with God about God, was still absurd; so I went on by myself and talked with myself about women. 'Ladyless South' the British had called the Antarctic. Such lack of imagination – or a deceit? Had the early polar travellers really no recollections, no longings, no desires?

Time and again, I encountered figures of women; living, obstinate, wanton women. I pictured them in my day-dreams, naked and sometimes as my partner. To have experienced some good relations helped during these hard weeks on the polar plateau. But not as regards death. Against that only one thing helped, pulling the sledge further and not despairing. Despite our hesitation and Arved's weakness, we had to come through.

It had been my mistake, not to have tested Arved's condition before this trip. I had invited him on my expedition. Now I had to go through with him.

That we would get northerly rather than southerly wind more frequently on the plateau had been foreseeable, had I given more credence to Scott's diary. But we had relied on the statements of the scientists at the Pole; thus this disappointment. We were not prepared for head wind and this fact devoured our energy. When I ran 'donkey' for hours and thereby knew that perhaps it was in vain, I began to despair over everything. The absurdity of this trip became not only obvious to me, but I also became painfully aware of it. With the certainty of reaching the other side in time, it would have been much easier to march across this infinity. So again, doubts of success became the trigger for calling into question the whole undertaking.

Always bad weather, wind from the north! We both suffered, sleeping badly, waking up in the middle of the 'night' to read, to distract ourselves.

Not until a strong southerly wind drove us more than 100 kilometres northwards in a single day, did I take hope again. It was a joy to see how the wind swept the snow plumes across the ground. I shouted with enthusiasm. How the snow surface glittered in the contra light! All my doubts were washed away. All my concentration was riveted on the ground. The snow plumes floated just above the ground. You see them only against the light, on the surface towards the sun; a bright fluff which swims over the grey snow surface.

As well as we could, we guided the sledges through the humps. Even so, suddenly I went straight over a sastrugi mound. It shook me up. The sledge behind me rattled like a cattle truck. I paid close attention to my skis and naturally to the sledge which was supposed to scurry over the sastrugi as easily as possible.

As I was pulling the heavier load, my sledge was rather weakened and the bottom began to detach itself from the body. What would happen if it fell to pieces?

Across gigantic ground waves, we travelled down off the plateau. In part it was like a downhill run – skis juddering and chattering. The ribbed surface was a single living snow-drift. Everything was in motion: we, the sail, the drift snow, the ground under our feet.

I would have loved to travel much further on this day. I would have used the wind to the last second. We could have made up the whole delay which we had built up on the high plateau but Arved was so tired after half a dozen hours' sailing that he could go on no longer. His legs were stiff. In his condition sailing was dangerous. We hoped that the wind would hold to the next day. The positional fix in the 'evening' left no doubt: we had run 56 miles on this day. Thus we had covered 400 kilometres in two weeks and were almost on schedule.

We were standing at the upper end of the Beardmore Glacier system. In front of us must lie the Trans-Antarctic Mountains. Just 1,000 kilometres to go to McMurdo, including, of course, 200 kilometres across glacier and crevasses where the sails would be of little use.

Next day it was so stormy that we had to give up sailing after a few hours. For a while we squatted, shivering with cold, by the sledges and tried unsuccessfully to determine our position. In the lee of the two sledges (one on top of the other) we set up camp. We were right on course. Mount Ward, which we had to leave to our left, lay directly ahead of us.

At night when going to sleep, the day's route continued to unwind before me: wind drifts and sastrugi like cinema pictures in front of my closed, inner eye.

In the morning we could see the ranges of the Trans-Antarctic Mountains clearly in front of us but the storm increased hour by hour to hurricane force and we were compelled to stay in the tent: for forty-eight hours, we waited. In the evening the wind certainly dropped but in the gusts it was still so strong that sailing was out of the question, so we stayed in the tent. In our clammy sleeping-bags, we built up body warmth and frowst.

We were both ready to get up as soon as wind and visibility conditions improved. We dozed, waiting to set out. We didn't want to miss the opportunity between the storm and the next dead calm or the next white-out.

We never lost the desire to go on; but also we did not suspect that with the crossing of the mountains something fragile, something irretrievable would be lost: the exposure on the high plateau.

When I looked out of the tent, I saw elevations. Were they mountains or shreds of mist? On the horizon they melted into a grey rise – the Trans-Antarctic Mountains! Their loftiness touched me. They filled me at the same time with shivers. Joy and fear. That was no contradiction in me, although I would have been able to describe the impression of these mountains on the horizon only with contradictions. But I did not want to draw them, describe them or even once photograph them. I wanted only to get on! The desire to get there, to see the summits close up was just as strong as the fear in the presence of these mountains, the glaciers, the crevasses behind them.

We had covered much ground. Again there was a faint hope of completing the expedition. On 18 January we were able to sail again. For two hours we travelled at quite an angle to the wind, steering towards a notch in the ridge which Charles Swithinbank had recommended as the ideal access to the Mill Glacier. As we could not hold the course and were being driven westwards, we had to climb the last part up to the col. Steeply uphill with the sledges on a tow rope. Once up, we were amazed: what a panorama! One mountain range behind the other, with mighty glaciers in between. Right of us must start the Mill Glacier which was to lead us down to the Beardmore Glacier.

Such scenery! And so much strength in our legs. Now we had to shout out our joy into the world. I sensed that people in civilization, so far as they knew about our journey, deplored us. They pictured ice travel as dreary, cold and exhausting. Three hundred years of polar literature have evoked nothing but prejudice in readers. We were to be envied! At least now. In front of us lay mountains of ice and black rock. Above us this skim milk blue sky. Below, to the right, I sensed an ice-fall. Faintly shimmering and monstrous, the many thousands of ice crevasses: irregular grooves across the still, white surface.

12 Decision at Gateway

For three days now we had seen mountain peaks. In our direction of march, a mountain chain was recognizable between low cumulus clouds. They were indefinably far away, but seemed to me sublime and unusually beautiful. After so many days on the flat ice I had become susceptible to shapes, to heights. These mountains seemed to me more imposing than any Himalayan landscape.

How gladly I would have shown this mighty landscape, the blue ice, in which the sun mirrored itself, the black rocks on our left, to my children: Layla, who lived in Canada, nine years old, and Magdalena at home, who was now two. I reflected what we could do, in order that the children of today would be able at least to visualize this undisturbed vastness. If they should never have a chance to visit this 'last world', they must be able to imagine it.

Yet it was only a short step from this overpowering impression to the absurdity of our crawling along. My anger, when Arved did not follow, showed me distinctly how human I was still. I knew that not even I could have gone twelve or fifteen hours non-stop. The absurdity of our delusion, to traverse the last corner of the earth, now contrasted with those high spirits when planning: and still we did it! I went on. I wanted to prove nothing. My 'call' had become a despondent request: 'Arved, follow'. We just went on, nothing more, even though others held it to be impossible: but no longer for that reason.

Here the ice age was alive. The Alps must have looked like this once upon a time. How often within the last million years did the temperature fall to the point where the snow in the mountains also lay during the summer months?

When had the Antarctic last been without ice? Was it astronomical factors, cyclical changes in the eccentricity of the earth's orbit or the altered inclination of the earth's axis which influenced the intensity of the seasons? Certainly, the glaciation had originated through far-reaching changes of climate. All changes, such as air pollution, alter the ocean currents, the heat exchange, the properties of the atmosphere and finally the climate, that is to say, whether glaciation increases or decreases.

Nowhere on earth is there a landscape which is as grandiose as the route from the interior of Antarctica to the coast of the Ross Sea. First the polar plateau, a gigantic domed ice-cap. Then the Trans-Antarctic Mountains which stretch for 3,500 kilometres across the ice continent, not as high but longer than the Himalaya. At last the Ross Shelf Ice, a swimming, frozen sea the size of France. Like policemen, the rock massifs of the cordillera stand in the flood of ice which flows down from the polar plateau. The kilometre-deep ice in the centre of Antarctica moves at a speed of 10 metres per year, faster in many places. This inland ice presses against the mountains and high up their flanks. It forces itself between them. Thus have the greatest glaciers on earth developed. One of these is the Beardmore, 200 kilometres long and up to 50 kilometres wide. The ice stream winds through the mountains, which stand to left and right of it like fortifications. Shackleton, who in 1908 was the first to see this glacier, expressed it reverently:

> It is as if we were really at the world's end and have arrived at the birthplace of the clouds and eyrie of the four winds. And it seems to me that these children of nature observe us mortals with jealous eyes.

Shackleton and his Pole hunters, who penetrated much too deep into the Antarctic with far too few provisions, had to starve on the way back to the coast. Ill and on frost-bitten feet, they ran for their lives. 'Shack' had turned back at the right moment but Scott had forced himself and his men as far as the Pole, without bearing in mind that the return would be much more difficult than the outward journey. On the upper Beardmore Glacier their strength gave out – they stood, as we now, at the threshold of the Trans-Antarctic Mountains.

Shackleton – picture from his attempt to reach the South Pole: rock islands in an ice sea. Since then the scenery has not altered.

Tuesday, 6 February. We've had a horrid day and not covered good mileage. On turning out we found sky overcast; a beastly position amidst crevasses. Luckily, it cleared just before we started. We went straight for Mt Darwin, but in half an hour found ourselves amongst huge open chasms, unbridged but not very deep, I think. We turned to the north between two, but to our chagrin they converged into chaotic disturbance. We had to retrace our steps for a mile or so, then struck to the west and got on to a confused sea of sastrugi, pulling very hard; we put up the sail. Evans' nose suffered, Wilson was very cold, everything was horrid . . . Towards the end of the march we realized the certainty of maintaining a more or less straight course to the depot, and estimated the distance to be 10 to 15 miles.

Food is low and the weather uncertain, so that many hours of the day were anxious; . . . Evans is the chief anxiety now; his cuts and wounds suppurate, his nose looks very bad, and altogether he shows considerable signs of being played out.

235

Arved and I had decided to follow the advice of the British glaciologist, Charles Swithinbank, to descend the Mill Glacier to the central Beardmore. Would that really be easier than the Shackleton-Scott route? From now on there was scarcely any chance of rescue, despite our Argos set with which we were to transmit our daily position. The little transmitter, which I had on my sledge, would have availed us nought however. The signal would have told our sponsors via satellite that we were between the Mill and Beardmore glaciers. On this crevasse-covered glacier, an aircraft could scarcely have landed.

In the following stage I expected the greatest difficulties. From now on katabatic winds must set in and blow down from the mountains across the glacier like an avalanche of air. Plus bare ice.

We were lucky. At last we found the ground which together with favourable wind provided ideal sailing conditions. The descent to the Mill Glacier worked out smoothly. After the problems on the plateau I had been sceptical. I had deceived myself. We went down shallow slopes, slid over steeper flanks. With and without sail. In the late afternoon we crossed a side stream of the Mill Glacier at the 'gallop'. In the evening we came to our first rock campsite and, at the edge of the Mill Glacier, between some rocks, we erected the tent in the lee of a massive block. Blue ice lay round about but for the first time for two and a half months we were camping on stone again. It was like being in the mountains and I felt myself saved. The storm shook the tent. The wind howled. In the morning the storm seemed to want to tear the tent from its anchorages. It hurled the drift snow with such force that it crashed against the walls.

We went on further, wearing crampons. Now the ground descended and the going was less strenuous than in the previous weeks on the high plateau. As I stumbled down the Mill Glacier, I was sure that we were on a better route than Scott. Sure, my feet twisted frequently on the bumpy ice, and sometimes my left knee joint slipped out but the sledge slid well. As I have had a loose knee joint for many years, I had to take care. I could not afford to fall into a crevasse. For that reason I scanned the glittering ice surface far ahead for ice-falls; for bright and dark streaks.

At this point of the descent, Scott's fate was already sealed. Only a rescue column could have still saved him.

236

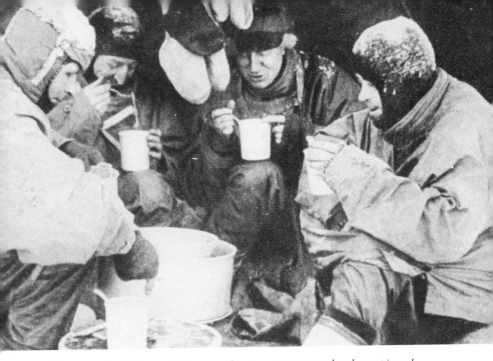

The Scott team in their tent. Their pyramid tents were so narrow that they got in each other's way constantly: when eating, when sleeping, when dressing.

Sunday, 11 February. The worst day we have had during the trip and greatly owing to our own fault. We started on a wretched surface with a light south-west wind. With sail set, and pulling on the skis the horrible light made everything look fantastic. As we went on the light got worse, and suddenly we found ourselves in pressure. Then came the fatal decision to steer east. We went on for six hours, hoping to do a good distance, which in fact I suppose we did, but for the last hour or two we pressed on into a regular trap. Getting on to a good surface we did not cut out our lunch meal, and thought all was going well, but half an hour after lunch we got into the worst ice mess I have ever been in . . .

Monday, 12 February. Here we are, after a very short supper and one meal only remaining in the food bag; the depot doubtful in locality . . . Meanwhile, we are cheerful with an effort.

'Safety Spur', a steep rock buttress on the Mill Glacier. It was a good feeling, running towards a known point.

Arved and I had developed a sort of gallows humour which made us accomplices. We stumbled across the glacier which was bare ice, full of holes. My diversions whilst marching were concerned now with the landscape and less with my dreams. Although I wanted to give up extreme mountaineering, I gazed at all the faces, edges and buttresses at the side of the glacier with all the curiosity of the maker of first ascents, as if they were in the Dolomites. There were fewer crevasses and so I let my eyes rove. We crossed about a dozen.

Frequently now Hercules aeroplanes flew over our route, leaving a white vapour trail behind them. They gave us a rough idea of the direction we had to go in. Apart from that, they were far, far away; for us a sign of another world.

In the contra light the ice shimmered like a lake. Waves, some small, some bigger lay behind one another, as if the wind were travelling over them. Snow plumes hung from the ridges of the mountains. The clouds swept past.

We passed under 'Safety Spur', a good name for the steep, brittle rock edge and a good feeling for us as, for the first time since the Pole, we could identify a real location with a point on the map.

A moraine at the side of the glacier looked flat. There we ought to be able to find a suitable campsite. I climbed down to it over steep ice, on which lay fine sand and light porous rock with, in between, some pieces of lignite! I scuffled in the rubble with my feet. It was a great joy to be able to run over dry land. After living on the ice for nearly three months, rock was a tonic to the eye, to the feet. The sky was milky white and had been for days. The sun now stood deeper than at New Year when we had been at the Pole but it did not set. Not for one moment did it disappear behind the high mountains.

Arved and I recovered well. Although there was a lot of sand in the melt water, we washed hands and face. Our beards were bleached, faces swollen, hands and feet hurt.

Next day we went on. Always fewer crevasses – and these were narrow. We were able to cross them without much problem. That was good. One breaks through especially easily without skis. Again an aircraft floated away over us. Twice a day the same sequence. The machines emerged at the northern edge of our field of vision, drew their white trail in the sky and disappeared half an hour later over the southern edge of the horizon. They took a long time to pass. Four or five hours later they returned.

Far beneath us I could recognize the glittering ice stream of the Beardmore Glacier. I thought of Scott, then forgot him again.

As I travelled across the ice I could not let my imagination roam unbridled because I had to concentrate on the ground. Going across bare ice was in the long run less strenuous than crossing snow on skis but it meant more stress on our joints. When I was tired I had to move carefully if I did not want to fall when my left knee clicked.

Now as before I examined the rock ridges to left and right with a view to their ascent possibilities. Time and again I asked myself whether this summit was attainable or that face climbable. Would the ice gully there go? Unfortunately we had no time to climb in these mountains, although I would have liked to.

How much energy I won back on these successful march days! Since we had reached the Mill Glacier, things had progressed splendidly, as if we had to believe in getting through in order to get

An empty fuel drum and a bamboo marker indicate human activity. This was to be an ice landing strip.

through. Suddenly I thought of the motto of my castle: *Vinciturus vincero*. It stood over the main entrance to the 'Hall of a Thousand Delights', and was a Latin tag meaning 'Because I am determined to win, I shall win'.

Yes, I knew now that this motto was right. Correct also because one success carries energy over into the next success.

At the lower edge of the Mill Glacier, where it flows into the Beardmore Glacier, we were to come to an 'ice runway' which Charles Swithinbank had laid out the previous year. We looked for and found it: measuring sticks, empty fuel drums, bamboo poles with little green flags. Some sticks were snapped off, others stood askew. I checked how far they still rose above the ice. One of the broken sticks I took with me, as a souvenir. It was the only sign of life which we had found on the mainland, apart from our two dumps at the Thiel Mountains and South Pole. Nothing else. No animal, no grass, not even a glacier flea.

When we had reached the foot of the Mill Glacier and turned into the Beardmore Glacier, we ran for a long time along a moraine which had been thrown up by the two glaciers pushing up against one another. There was a short stretch of hard snow on which we tried to sail. On a narrow strip of hard snow between bare ice we went fast with strong wind. It was dangerous and strenuous: our most exciting hour of sailing so far. The bare ice to left and right of the 'sail piste' was rough like desert ground. On each rise, transverse crevasses. Whilst braking, I twisted my knee twice. The wind was at the upper limit of acceptable strength, making it difficult to hold the sail. I had a lot of trouble getting through without injuries.

On this day I was often far ahead, often waiting. Arved was slow. He came on, yet did not arrive! I waited half an hour. After an hour he still hadn't arrived. I could not believe that Arved was so far behind. As if I had an evil presentiment, I said to myself: 'Please, not a fall into a crevasse or a broken foot'. A little mistake and we would have been lost. The absurdity of this journey became clear to me again. I stood there, went back a bit, stopped and gazed intently southwards, fearing the worst. Then I saw Arved emerge as a tiny dot on the horizon. He was on foot, not sailing. I ran back to my waiting point. He had been lifted up by the sail and catapulted into the air. On falling he had jammed a ski in a crevasse. He had almost broken his leg. I didn't know that and plodded towards him without my sledge, worried, despondent.

He had really almost broken his leg. These gusts were dangerous. They seize the canopy which stands vertically above one's head in strong wind and catapult you into the air. Ought we to continue to sail on the glacier? Better not. We camped between scraps of snow on an ice-fall.

Next morning we had hellish trouble crossing a precipitous ice-fall. It was the first of the two ice-falls which we had to overcome on the route described by Charles Swithinbank, in order to get to the other side of the Beardmore Glacier. After starting, I thought we would soon be out of the crevasse zone but the terrain became worse by the hour. Arved and I resigned ourselves to the situation. Doggedly, we searched for a route! A dangerous balancing act with the sledge on the narrow ridge between the crevasses which were hundreds of metres

By my reckoning, Arved and I crossed more than 6,000 crevasses. The bridges were not always so stable, the chasm often bottomless.

long and often 20 metres wide. My sledge was scrap, no longer reparable.

The central Beardmore Glacier to the left of us was dark, the ice cleft like the skeleton of a many-miles-long giant dinosaurus. You look around and see only crevasses. On a surface of several square kilometres nothing but upthrust glacier ice. And you are in the middle of it, with no obvious way out. Of course, we had reckoned on crevasses and associated problems on the Beardmore Glacier but reality surprised us nonetheless. The Mill Glacier had been straightforward and we had gained confidence there. So much greater now was the disillusionment. Again we would be repelled. We had hoped to be able to sail on the Beardmore. Unthinkable! Not only because there was little or no wind, above all on account of the realities of the terrain with its chaotic ice-falls!

With the increasing problems, however, our personal relationship improved again. After the polar plateau it had generally got better.

The constant waiting during the day no longer got on my nerves so much. Naturally, I still expected a reaction from Arved on awakening. I seemed simply a slave driver when it was always I who had to say 'Let's get going!' Meanwhile Arved realized that we had to march. Run on and on and on. During the day I no longer had to press him. The driving was restricted now to an encouragement in the morning on starting. Arved went as well as he could.

We passed between 'camel humps' high as houses. The views were tremendous, likewise the impressions. Individual snow crystals lay on the snow crests in such a way that they reflected the sun. They seemed by this means much bigger, like a thousand small suns.

How many mountains were unclimbed here still? Almost all. But even if someone had been up there, it took away nothing of their stillness and sublimity. As I marched, I kept scanning the faces for climbable routes.

This evening we drank two tots of whisky 'on the rocks' to celebrate the day. The worst lay behind us; as we thought.

On the opposite side of the Beardmore Glacier stood the 'Cloudmaker', that peak to which Shackleton had given the only correct name. Always the first mists clung to it and the clouds built up there. The 'Cloudmaker' made not only clouds, it made bad weather too; and mists would have been disastrous on a crevassed glacier. On a broken glacier and in white-out, unimaginable!

The going was bad too in the twilight. It was strenuous and nerve-racking. Often I went without sun-glasses, so as to be able to distinguish snow from ice. Whilst leading, I could only go around the hidden crevasses and avoid them at the right moment. Crevasses, always crevasses. Would this dance on the snow bridges never stop? Some thousands – between 20 centimetres and 20 metres wide – we had already crossed.

When I got inside the tent of an 'evening', I got the cooker going straightaway, as I was now carrying it on my sledge. I had already put up the tent by myself. Then I took off cap, boots and socks. Next I treated my feet with powder and stuck them in my down boots. I cared for them like an essential tool. By the time Arved arrived, I was already 'at home'.

Just as I had got myself worked up for weeks over Arved's

slowness, now I was amazed at his adroitness, as well as his speed, for even in the ice-falls he was not far behind me. Only his reactions did not alter. In the 'morning', when I woke him, he got up but there never came an encouraging word: 'Today we'll do a bit more! we'll do an extra hour.' How pleasant such an encouragement would have been for me! I too would have loved to lie abed of a morning. The waiting during the rest stops now did not last so long. After ten to fifteen minutes, when I was cooled down, we went on. The only thing which still annoyed me was just that I had to press in the morning. Reluctantly, as I did it, I was obliged to say: 'We must do more. Today we must add a bit.' If only Arved had once taken over this role of driver. Only once. Once a week. Once a month. Once on the whole journey.

Life was reduced to essentials. During the day I was often hungry and enjoyed eating. In the tent I lay down because I was bone tired. In the tent it was always warm and dry. But signs of wear and tear were showing: my left knee, the dodgy one, often jumped out when I turned round with crampons on. The tendons in my feet were swollen. Also my finger joints hurt. It would have been nice, never more to have to go out into the wind, the cold, the ice. No such luck!

We followed a set routine and yet hoped for surprises every day. Perhaps a southerly wind would get up; perhaps we had passed all the crevasses; perhaps all the difficulties were already behind us. We hoped all the time.

The descent over the Beardmore Glacier became ever more difficult. Still bare ice. We had travelled 150 kilometres over bare ice and our crampons were wearing out. Our knees suffered, for this ice was full of irregularities. We were now in the middle of the glacier. Sometimes we went along a gigantic highway of snow, then again across crevasses. Innumerable crevasses. And again we climbed through a precipitous ice-fall.

I was a bit ahead and suddenly found myself between innumerable crevasses. Despair. Broad open crevasses everywhere, left, right and centre. No longer did I have the courage to go on, at least not with the sledge. So I unharnessed myself and continued without it. After ten minutes I gave up. There were too many crevasses around me, some

On the Beardmore Glacier. Bare ice, crevasses in between, filled with drifted snow. One recognizes the crevasses by the colour shading and depression.

as big as a church. I saw no chance of making progress, so back I went, grabbed the sledge and struggled along the barely recognizable track back to Arved, who had stopped. What were we to do? We dumped both sledges. A false route description by Charles Swithinbank made us angry. One went to the left, one to the right. After 500 metres I believed I had found a fairly safe route. So we struggled leftwards. Always further to the left. Ultimately, we had to reach the true left side of the Beardmore Glacier, which once Shackleton and Scott had traversed. We found no way out. All this had cost us a great deal of effort and yet brought us scarcely nearer. At the foot of the mighty ice-fall, we camped. The tent stood in the middle of the blue ice on a small patch of snow. Coming from below we would have been able to go around this ice-fall without great difficulty. From above, however, we had had insufficient preview. Like blind men we had run into the middle of the abysses and holes, into a labyrinth of ice towers and crevasses which were more than 200 metres deep.

245

Had Scott passed over similar ice-falls on his death march from the Pole to McMurdo? With a sledge laden with stones, with geological discoveries. Hard to imagine. What use to Scott were his supply dumps, in which too little fuel and provisions had been deposited, dumps which always he had to search for. And so they dragged themselves down, no longer able to recover. Evans had hurt himself in a fall into a crevasse and there was always this frightful certainty that they were too late. They were marching into the Antarctic winter, into death. Edgar Evans, the strongest to begin with, was the first to die, so weakened through scurvy, hunger and injuries that he could no longer help pull the sledge.

Friday, 16 February. A rather trying position. Evans has nearly broken down in brain, we think. He is absolutely changed from his normal self-reliant self. This morning and this afternoon he stopped the march on some trivial excuse. We are on short rations, but not very short, food spins out till tomorrow night . . .

Saturday, 17 February. A very terrible day . . . Evans started in his place on the traces, but half an hour later worked his ski shoes adrift, and had to leave the sledge. The surface was awful, the soft, recently fallen snow clogging the ski and runners at every step, the sky overcast, and the land hazy. We stopped after about one hour, and Evans came up again, but very slowly. Half an hour later he dropped out again on the same plea. He asked Bowers to lend him a piece of string. I cautioned him to come on as quickly as he could, and he answered cheerfully as I thought . . . Abreast the Monument Rock we stopped and seeing Evans a long way astern, I camped for lunch. There was no alarm at first, and we prepared tea and our own meal, consuming the latter. After lunch, and Evans still not appearing, we looked out, to see him still afar off. By this time we were alarmed, and all four started back on ski. I was first to reach the poor man and shocked at his appearance; he was on his knees with clothing disarranged, hands uncovered and frostbitten, and a wild look in his eyes. Asked what was the matter, he replied with a slow speech that he didn't know, but thought he must have fainted.

*Edgar Evans. Petty Officer Evans
was the strongest man in Scott's party
on the way to the South Pole. He was
the first to collapse and die on the
return march.*

We got him on his feet, but after two or three steps he sank down again. He showed every sign of complete collapse. Wilson, Bowers and I went back for the sledge, whilst Oates remained with him. When we returned he was practically unconscious, and when we got him into the tent quite comatose. He died quietly at 12.30 a.m. . . . . It is a terrible thing to lose a companion in this way, but calm reflection shows that there could not have been a better ending to the terrible anxieties of the past week. Discussion shows us what a desperate pass we were in with a sick man on our hands at such a distance from home.

We continued on our self-appointed route. For us, death by hunger was not so nakedly obvious, and winter was still a month away. Nevertheless, things were not going well. Death still did not enter our thoughts. Not once did it occur in my day-dreams, neither as ideal nor as figure of terror. Failure was still a possibility, however.

In the 'morning' there were often singular lighting effects. The humps and hollows were then yellowish, bluish, greenish – all in pastel colours. A land like Tibet.

Gateway campsite. The sails had to be rolled up, the tent erected. Beyond the saddle, between the rocks, the Ross Shelf Ice begins.

Our equipment suffered terribly with the dragging and tearing between the crevasses. On one occasion we lifted our sledges one at a time over narrow ice bridges, helping each other, all the time in danger of being pulled backwards by the heavy sledge into a crevasse. Another time we pulled the sledges for hours around ice-falls. Just before Gateway, a strong wind got up once more and, despite the icy piste, we sailed northwards, between steep rock slopes and the glacier. I steered towards that small saddle which is ensconced between Mount Hope and a row of smaller granite rocks: Gateway. Arved followed well. We were two tired men who stumbled around the tent in front of Gateway. Together we put it up and unpacked our sledges, each his own; in a leeward hollow on the south side of Gateway.

When we marched away next day, it was grey again. The landscape was grey because the sky was grey. No mist. One could not see far though. Arved ran ahead for a bit. At last! For that he needed no compass. Gateway, a high pass, lay before us. After I had packed my sledge I followed him, trying not to overtake him, enjoying the role of follower. How pleasant it was to run behind a black strip. To see a trail ahead of you! Not constantly having to seek out the route. Arved chose the best possible route between crevasses and sastrugi; and I followed him. Following him on this climb up to Gateway, I had more time for reflection again, hence my wish that we should alternate the trail breaking on the last 700 kilometres to McMurdo. We were still behind schedule, nevertheless I felt that we would make it. I had arranged with Wilhelm Bittorf that we would run to McMurdo if we crossed Gateway before 30 January. It was 26 January when we crossed the pass. The die was cast.

During this expedition there had been constant doubt. At first, would we get to the Pole? Then, would we get to Gateway? Now, is the route across the whole of the Ross Shelf Ice still possible? Granted, at the start of the journey, if I had known that we would reach the Pole, I would have been content. Nevertheless, I had always proceeded in the hope that perhaps we would complete the whole route. Now I was driven by the compulsion to carry on to McMurdo. And I was curious. Curious about our endurance, curious about Scott's burial place, curious about this flat snow land that all our predecessors had described as dreadful. I knew that there was no other choice than to see it through. Not much more than two weeks' time remained to us to cross the gigantic Ross Shelf Ice.

I gazed southwards. I could not see far, yet I sensed the extent of the land mass. It is not true that all myths on earth have evaporated. They were here yet. No civilization, no tourism and no mass media. The undisturbed, the overwhelming, the sublime were one here. But would it remain for me what it had been as I passed through the heart of it? Would only fragments of the myths remain when I reached the other side? Was not all lost thereby?

13   Vanishing Point McMurdo

When I too reached the top of Gateway, I gazed into a grey north. Arved had arrived there ahead of me and was just as disappointed with the view as I was. To the right, far below, I suspected a broken ice-fall where the Beardmore Glacier plunged down to the shelf ice. To the left below us, a single sea of mist, beneath which must lie the Ross Shelf Ice. I was thinking now only of McMurdo. That vanishing point lay 700 kilometres further north, where drudgery and lust for ice travel were to come to an end.

A little later we reached the Ross Shelf Ice which stretched as far as our journey's end. The Trans-Antarctic Mountains had been overcome, the Antarctic winter was approaching. We had three weeks at the most to cover the stretch to the sea. Before the pack ice paralysed traffic, we had to reach the ship which was to take us to New Zealand. Besides, our provisions would last only until 15 February.

The weather was bad. All the same we tried to sail the first few kilometres of the Ross Shelf Ice but the wind was so weak that the sails wouldn't stay up. We went on a bit. At the foot of Gateway, where the glacier ran out flat, we erected the tent and camped on the edge of the mainland, with shelf ice beneath us. Next 'morning' we got up at 2 a.m. We must get on! There was a sailing wind. By 4 a.m., when we wanted to leave the tent, the wind had grown to storm force. Whiteout. Sailing or marching was unthinkable. All we could do was wait. This last stage, which remained to us, had to be mastered quickly with sailing on a good snow piste. We were to be mistaken.

The distance corresponds to the crossing of Greenland by Nansen's route. Still we were confident, although the bad storm, all the powers of nature, were against us. The storm increased to hurricane force. For twenty-four hours. Tens of thousands of ice grains crackled simultaneously on the tent walls. The wind tore ceaselessly at the tent as if it wanted to carry it off in shreds. At first you are afraid. You try to brace the tent from inside to compensate for the gusts. Then you resign yourself to your fate. Now you only hope. Worst were the gusts which could have snapped the tent poles. What if the guy-ropes tore? If the outer skin burst? We could not have been rescued.

After hours the storm became routine. It was as if there had always been storminess. Would it ever stop again? Fear gave way to hope. This feeling, that it had always been stormy, calmed us, although it was now somewhat stronger. The question was whether we could find our way in this storm. It overlayed the fear that the tent could rip.

The storm covered up our tent more and more into an igloo-like cosiness. Drift snow built up around the sledges and on the lee side of the tent entrance.

The armour of snow outside was a comfort. A further consolation was my partner near me. And my own strength. But we were losing valuable hours and were still behind schedule. Although we had made good progress on the Mill and Beardmore glaciers, we were limping along. We had to cover more than 35 kilometres per day if we were to be at McMurdo in time, an average which could not be maintained without sailing wind. And if the weather remained bad? If grainy powder snow slowed our progress, as had happened to Scott and his men in February 1912? What if a series of blizzards and white-outs heralded the 'autumn' weather prior to the Antarctic winter? Rescue was out of the question.

We did not know that the New Zealander, Max Wenden, was supposed to 'visit' us in the one-engined Cessna stationed at Patriot Hills. Wilhelm Bittorf had given the instruction. Wenden and Mike Sharp attempted to fly the 1,700 kilometres to Gateway, to wait for us there. They were to collect our films and ascertain our arrival time at McMurdo. First of all they constructed a fuel dump and flew back to Patriot Hills. For the attempt to reach us they needed two intermediate stops on account of the bad weather in order to get to the dump again. On landing, one of the runners of the Cessna was damaged. The repair lasted nine hours. There were still just 500 kilometres to Gateway. But meanwhile the weather worsened. Moreover, because of the enforced intermediate landings, the fuel would not have sufficed to Gateway and back. And if they had had to fly a search pattern? Max

Marching in 'white-out'. Although it is bright, one stumbles as if in darkness. All contours are wiped out. Only one's partner is still just visible.

and Mike decided to turn back. We were unreachable. A flight to Gateway would have been completely impossible!

The tent was still standing, a yellow point bending to the storm. We made no progress and remained there all day. Arved went outside twice. Once to fix the tent, once to fetch food. The two sledges on the south side of the tent stood firm, one on top of the other.

When the storm diminished somewhat we set out at once. Still mist and white-out. It was like walking in the dark. If there were a hole in the ground, we'd fall in. If the ground rose, we'd notice it only by the weight of the sledge. If we crossed a slope, our skis slipped. But we didn't see it. We saw nothing. We didn't know where we were. We didn't know if we were going straight ahead, in a circle or upside down. Were it not for the force of gravity and the compass, we would have gone out of our minds. It was no consolation to be on the shelf ice. The landscape was as flat as the sea; and just as wavy.

I marched without any reference point. Only when I turned round, did I see behind me the black dot that was Arved.

In this lack of orientation, I was concentrating again only on two things: on Arved, whom I must not lose, and on reaching McMurdo in time! Sailing was impossible. Flat calm. We remained wholly dependent on our strength. Each on his own. Again our hopes dropped. I went stubbornly on into the mist. Often crevasses, then mighty snow waves. I waited, stared. Arved shouted that I should stop where I was. I went on. Then, between great walls of snow, no more way forward. I stopped. Arved followed. He tried to navigate. The GPS set gave us a position. We studied the detailed map and decided that we were too far to the right. So we turned off leftwards and went around the snow waves. More crevasses. Often I was on the edge of a crevasse without noticing it and once I had one ski over the abyss before I saw the tell-tale light and shadow. The tints in the firm snow were brighter than those over the dark holes. I pulled my ski back.

It was now warmer and damper, yet for us colder, because it had been difficult to dry our things in the tent. Often we went out of a morning into the cold in damp clothes – they stiffened at once into an ice crust.

Suddenly it became brighter. No more mist. Behind the grey, tightly packed fleecy clouds I sensed the sun. The snow surface, a cold whiteness. In the north at the edge of the steely blue horizon licked steely blue flames of light. But still no wind. Everything was now limited: visibility, our rations and our strength. Especially our time. The food shortage was painful. We had allowed only forty-five days for the 1,430 kilometres from the Pole to McMurdo Sound. Food and fuel would last at the most for two weeks. No provision depot awaited us. By 16 February our rations would be exhausted, if we did not begin to starve before. It was going to be difficult to escape from 'White Mama'.

McMurdo was also controlled by Americans who, just like their colleagues at the Pole, afforded no sort of support to private adventurers like us. 'We have to rescue these madmen with our aircraft if they get into trouble', was the official explanation of their policy. 'Why should we entice them with dumps and other logistical aids?' Therefore we had to be faster. The possibility of being picked up by the Greenpeace ship *Gondwana* was nil, for by the time of our arrival at

McMurdo, the *Gondwana* would have long since put to sea. The Italians were more generous but unsympathetic if we should arrive too late. From their station at Terra Nova Bay, only 300 kilometres away from McMurdo, they would take us home. 'We'll gladly take Reinhold Messner and his German companion with us', said Roberto Cervellati, head of station, to Wilhelm Bittorf. 'But we can't wait for him. If he's late, we take no responsibility.'

We had to be at McMurdo by 15 February, with enough breathing space, weather notwithstanding, for the helicopter flight from McMurdo to Terra Nova and the charter ship *Barken*. Most of the passengers on the *Barken* wanted to fly on to Italy as soon as possible, to wives and children whom they had not seen for months.

I rationed the food, at first without Arved knowing, then with his consent. Soon we were constantly hungry. In the tent of an 'evening', Arved and I talked of our favourite dishes. Hunger! Whilst marching now – our vitamin and hazelnut bars no longer sufficed to quell our hunger during the day – I thought of all the invitations which I had declined in the months before departure: at home with my mother, with Witzigmann in Munich, with South Tyroler Winkler, et. al., et. al., et. al. . . .

'For breakfast, bacon and eggs!' That was Arved's start to the day in this fool's paradise. So far away and yet we could talk about it without getting depressed.

'Smoked salmon and a glass of champagne. And cheese – Gorgonzola and a little bit of fresh Parmesan', I said.

'And butter', interjected Arved. What wouldn't we have given now for a bit of butter!

Soon our dreams went further, beyond eating. 'Imagine', said Arved, 'you're sitting in the bath – for hours in hot water, listening to music, with a drink nearby and reading.'

It was not the recollection of past enjoyments that conjured up these desires in the tent, it was hunger. Food smells projected into the future. I didn't mind. Hunger was part of the job; I looked forward to future meals.

Frequently now, we heard the movements of the shelf ice. The cracking and groaning in the ice came suddenly. Often I fancied I

254

could feel a shaking under the floor of the tent. A shiver went through me, like a rent in a paper-bag in which I had packed my fear. When I was marching or lying down, and all was quiet, there were no fears. As if they had never been. But suddenly in the night – a split in the ice, a cracking of the tent poles in the storm – fear broke out.

How little it needed to push the most hidden fears to the surface. They were always there. I had only concealed them from myself. My heart beat faster, I could feel it in my throat. This disquiet drove me on. Out of the tent. Onwards! Like a hunted animal.

Then I drove Arved on. Worried at not going fast enough, I ran far ahead. Sometimes full of compassion, then angry again, obsessed. We must get on! I could not grasp why Arved could not run with the same energy as I. But the wind slowed me too. Against the storms and the heavy snow, neither my obsession nor my fury could accomplish anything.

How despairing Scott must have been, at that time, seventy-eight years before, on 24 February 1912:

Friday, 24 February. A little despondent again. We had a really terrible surface this afternoon and only covered 4 miles . . . It really will be a bad business if we are to have this pulling all through. I don't know what to think, but the rapid closing of the season is ominous . . . It is a race between the season and hard conditions and our fitness and good food.

Scott's diary occupied me more and more; and, in between, the early years of my childhood.

'I no longer know what I am to think', complained Arved during a rest stop. 'I am stuck in the past. I lacked new ideas after the North Pole. Once everything is thought out, one does not simply start again from scratch. It would be as monotonous as the wall of mist in front of us.'

'Yes', I confirmed: 'One's whole life rolls through one's head. Backwards and forwards.'

I thought about my life in many variations. First the past, the irreversible, then the future.

As a child, I had already pulled loads. A rack-wagon laden with

A sketch, drawn by Wilson, which shows tent life on the Scott expedition. Arved and I had a dome tent and much more space.

roost ladders from St Peter in Villnöss to St Magdalena; wood from the forest; stones from a rubble pit for the path in front of our hen-houses. My father had kept us children busy all the time. As a six-year old I 'worked' eight hours per day. I did not deplore this life. Not the present. Not the future. Whether there was a 'fate', whether I went against my 'destiny', did not interest me. To have the fantasy of free rein, to see what came out of it, only this made me oblivious to the agony of sledge pulling.

No, I expected no assistance. No help from outside. Scott, with his three survivors, had dragged himself on because he hoped continually for a rescue:

Monday 27 February . . . Pray God we have no further set-backs. We are naturally always discussing the possibility of meeting dogs, where and when, etc.

The dogs would never come! Scott had given no definite instruction that a relief column was to come to meet him on the way back.

How good it was still, to be entirely dependent on oneself!

256

Counting on extraneous help is always dangerous. We too did not have enough food and had to ration ourselves, for I would not risk breaking into the reserves which I had packed at the Pole.

Now again we argued frequently. Disputes over the length of the day's march. Disputes over the speed. Although Arved was running better than I had expected, we were always too slow. With relentless stubbornness, I went ahead. I knew that I could compel Arved to follow because the tent was on my sledge. I knew too that I was pushing him to the limit of his ability but I had to do it, even though I regretted it. Mostly I was so far ahead after the first four and a half hours' march that he could no longer catch up with me; not even in the rest stops. So I could not weaken my resolve if he wanted to shorten the time by an hour.

I knew now why Scott had come to grief on this march. Eroded by the long route, exhausted and sick, the team collapsed, weakened by scurvy and vitamin and mineral deficiencies. Condemned to death by the approaching winter. Discipline alone could no longer have saved them.

Friday, 2 March. Misfortunes rarely come singly. We marched to the depot [Middle Barrier] fairly easily yesterday afternoon, and since then have suffered three distinct blows which have placed us in a bad position. First we found a shortage of oil; with a most rigid economy it can scarce carry us to the next depot on this surface [131 kilometres away]. Second, Titus Oates disclosed his feet, the toes showing very bad indeed, evidently bitten by the late temperatures. The third blow came in the night . . . It fell below −40° in the night, and this morning it took one and a half hours to get our foot gear on . . . Worse was to come – the surface is simply awful. In spite of strong wind and full sail we have done only 5½ miles. We are in a very queer street since there is no doubt we cannot do the extra marches and feel the cold horribly.

Saturday, 3 March. The wind at strongest, powerless to move the sledge . . . God help us, we can't keep up this pulling, that is certain. Amongst ourselves we are infinitely cheerful, but what each man feels in his heart I can only guess.

257

Arved and I were not broken men. And we had, like Scott, a last trump card: wind assistance. Luckily our sails were better than his. At least once a week, every time we were about to run out of time, a favourable wind got up, as if there were still a compassionate God. That gave us new self-confidence and strengthened us in our belief in getting through. A day's sailing doubled the distance covered. Scott had not been able to employ his sail as skilfully as Shackleton or us. His sail was mounted on the sledge and it is very difficult to manoeuvre a sledge with fluttering sails.

Always, as I lay in the tent of an evening, I saw the snow surface rush by under me, like in a film before my closed eyes. The endless little bumps! The colour of the snow when it was not glittering in the sun was grey to shining white. Meanwhile, the colour of the snow told me whether it was heavy or non-skid, whether it was fast or slow. Small nuances in the shades of grey constituted the distinction. Often light played across the snow surface: greenish streaks, yellowish, an ochre-coloured spot, all in pastel colours. The overcast sky above. As if we were again somewhere on the high plateau of Tibet.

The mountains now lay far to the left of us, like the steel-blue frontier wall of a forbidden kingdom.

The temperatures were just below freezing point. Everything was wet: sleeping-bag, clothes, tent. The water ran down the tent walls. No more drying out. We could burn the cooker as long as we liked but everything remained damp. When we packed the sledges in the morning, we had the impression that it was much colder, 15°–20° below zero. The dampness got into everything, even in our bones. Our fingers swelled up. Our gloves were icy lumps. On top of this, the drudgery of sledge pulling. Generally, there was no wind.

In his book, *The Worst Journey in the World*, Apsley Cherry-Garrard describes similar sufferings. The winter march to the breeding grounds of the Emperor penguin had been for him and his companions a trip into hell. That was eighty years ago. The world here and the suffering was still the same.

The trouble is sweat and breath. I never knew before how much of the body's waste comes out through the pores of the skin. On the most bitter days, when we had to camp before we had done a

Bowers, Wilson and Cherry-Garrard before their winter march to Cape Crozier: it was to be 'the worst journey in the world'.

four-hour march in order to nurse back our frozen feet, it seemed that we must be sweating. And all this sweat, instead of passing away through the porous wool of our clothing and gradually drying off us, froze and accumulated. It passed just away from our flesh and then became ice; we shook plenty of snow and ice down from inside our trousers every time we changed our foot-gear, and we could have shaken it from our vests, and from between our vest and shirts, but of course we could not strip to this extent.

We did the only thing which could be done in the circumstances: we marched. Daily more than 30 kilometres, even 40 kilometres, for seventeen days without a single rest day. The snow stuck to our skis and balled up on the bottoms. The sledge ploughed deep into the new snow. It was a brutish job breaking trail. We lost weight. Each morning a first anxious look outside: wind rising? Mostly it came from the north. Thus head wind, as with Captain Scott:

Saturday, 10 March. With great care we might have a dog's chance, but no more . . . Our gear gets steadily more icy and difficult to manage. At the same time of course poor Titus . . . keeps us waiting in the morning until we have partly lost the warming effect of our good breakfast, when the only wise policy is to be up and away at once. Poor chap! It is too pathetic to watch him; one cannot but try to cheer him up.

Once, when Arved announced, in an argument over our speed, that he no longer wanted to run as many hours as previously, I threatened to leave him behind alone.

'You can have the tent and the Argos set. They will come and fetch you. I am going on. I am going to McMurdo.'

Arved said nothing and went. His pride was greater than his exhaustion. We went seven hours per day, eight hours, nine hours. Arved went to the point of collapse. I felt bad, when often I was several kilometres ahead and noticed how he became slower by the hour. But I did not wait for him. Pity helped neither him nor our progress. Now only an exact marching timetable could help and the will to hold to it. Like Scott we were completely dependent on ourselves:

Sunday, 11 March. I practically ordered Wilson to hand over the means of ending our troubles, so that any one of us may know how to do so . . . We have thirty opium tabloids apiece and he is left with a tube of morphine. So far the tragical side of our story.

. . . Know that 6 miles is about the limit of our endurance now . . . we have seven days' food and should be about 55 miles from One Ton Camp tonight, $6 \times 7 = 42$, leaving us 13 miles short of our distance . . .

Monday, 12 March. The surface remains awful, the cold intense, and our physical condition running down. God help us!

This tragedy now lay seventy-eight years in the past, but I was

'Bill' Wilson. *Wilson was a doctor and great friend of Scott. His drawings are works of art and evidence of his deep understanding of nature.*

pre-occupied with it all the time. Although Captain Scott and his men had been dead a long time, their heroic epic had survived. All other adventures of this century in the Arctic and Antarctic, including Amundsen's dog-sledge journey to the South Pole, are forgotten. Only Scott's report has stood the test of time, and is still alive.

> *Friday, 16 March or Saturday, 17 March.* Tragedy all along the line . . . It was blowing a blizzard. He [Oates] said, 'I am just going outside and may be some time'. He went out into the blizzard and we have not seen him since.

Arved and I were standing now before the scene of this tragedy. The same ice sea, the same shimmering blue mountains in the background, the same violet-coloured sky above. A mighty stage. A reality which moved me emotionally. That Scott had elevated himself to the status of hero, I could forgive. That he had obviously compelled his companions to play their roles to the end, in order to quash any doubt as to their British heroism, I did not comprehend.

> *Sunday, 17 March.* We are . . . only two pony marches from One Ton Depot.

Was not my criticism of Scott true also of me? I was forcing Arved to an act that he no longer wanted. Nevertheless, we spoke also of our homeward journey, as of a flight from Rome to Paris, not as though we had still to get through the ice sea and might thereby starve, freeze or die of thirst. Scott and his men had:

> . . . the last *half* fill of oil in our primus and a very small quantity of spirit – this alone between us and thirst . . . Our strength is almost exhausted.

On 19 March 1912, ten days before his death, Scott was still noting only factual information in his diary. Nothing more about the condition of his comrades, nothing about his sensations.

> *Thursday, 22 and 23 March.* Blizzard bad as ever – Wilson and

262

'Titus' Oates. Oates cared for the ponies in winter quarters and on the first part of the march to the South Pole. He had recognized the deficiencies in Scott's tactics.

Bowers unable to start – tomorrow last chance – no fuel and only one or two bits of food left – must be near the end. Have decided it shall be natural – we shall march for the depot with or without our effects and die in our tracks.

Death for Scott had become a theatre piece. Scene: the loneliest place in the world. The public: mankind. Once and for all, we were to learn of what sacrifice the British were capable. This death, beyond the frontiers of sense and pain but reconstructable in the sparse sentences of the final diary pages, was thought of as a symbol: tragedy was not an edifying game; death was much more the living proof of the self-sacrifice of a handful of men.

Thursday, 29 March. Outside the door of the tent it remains a scene of whirling drift . . . We shall stick it out to the end, but we are getting weaker, of course, and the end cannot be far.

It seems a pity, but I do not think I can write more.

R. Scott

For God's sake look after our people.

263

'Birdie' Bowers. Perhaps Bowers still had the strength to get to the next depot. Who knows. The details of this tragedy remain shrouded.

This was Scott's last diary entry. The exact background to his end is unknown. When I thought now of the dismay of these men, the horror that must have seized them when they grasped that they would never make it to the depot, I ran faster. Arved too increased his speed on this day, although he still tried to talk me out of the maxi-stages which I felt to be necessary.

To the end, he succeeded in somehow concealing his inadequate condition quite convincingly. That was good. What Arved would not admit to himself, because he did not want to, could therefore not be true. Avowed weakness would have weakened him still more.

We were ready to get up at any time of 'day' or 'night' to make use of the wind. But mostly it remained calm. So we marched 16, 17, 18 miles per day. Those were long, hard days. I led the way all the time. Arved could follow only with difficulty. We were no longer travelling over crevassed areas and we could not get lost. It was, therefore, not dangerous if each went along by himself. It was only hard work for both of us. We might not spare ourselves an hour of going, not a minute.

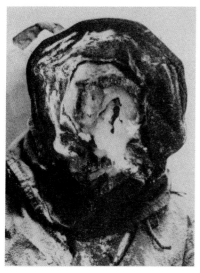

Iced-up face. Damp breath, snot and driven snow often freeze into a mask of ice in the Antarctic.

Arved and I had now spent three months together. Running one behind the other in the 'daytime', in the confined tent at 'night'. That was not so difficult if you sweep before your own door. You each smell only the stinking socks of the other person, not your own. If you don't learn to accept your partner as he is, you lose fast. A marriage can be parted, a team like us not! It was that which made things both difficult and easy: to be dependent on one another in often hopeless situations, for better or worse, makes for tolerance. Egoism swiftly turns against you. This knowledge was as strong as a law of nature. We both respected it.

The art of bringing such a difficult journey to a successful conclusion, lies above all in getting on with your partner. Argument, pent-up aggression or even hatred consume energy reserves, like sugar and vitamins, which we both needed to progress. He who remains tranquil in spirit, has also more strength. This recognition, collected in half a hundred trips to the mountains of the world, helped me to keep calm when our progress was hopelessly slow.

In these hostile suroundings, we were no more and no less people than at home. Each knew the pressures which would arise out of the

265

remaining stretch, the approaching winter and the reserves in the sledge. But when I reflected with whom I could have made this journey, there remained only Arved.

Arved Fuchs was the ideal partner for the crossing of the Antarctic continent. To be sure, we had a different rhythm of march and are by temperament even opposite types, but we wanted the same thing with all the energy and enthusiasm we possessed. Arved is rather introverted. He confided his anger at me to his diary. As I did likewise. When, nevertheless, pent-up aggression broke out in a stressful situation, that was a relief and we quickly forgot it. My respect for Arved never flagged for one day of the long journey and it was to be greater at the end than at the start. Such self-understanding, such calm in critical situations. When it was necessary, he could demand of himself to the point of exhaustion.

I am in this respect otherwise. Not only on account of tactics do I prefer to run a further 10 kilometres today than tomorrow. Running is for me a physical pleasure, when tendons and joints are not overstressed. That has nothing to do with masochism or ability to suffer – I am a pedestrian and will remain one all my life. Also, I like to provide for the future. To do more than absolutely necessary in a day means for me security, satisfaction, calmness. As a mountain farmer provides for the winter, so I like to store up reserves of time when weather and energy allow. I like to have a cushion against stormy days, an accident or other imponderables.

Perhaps that was the essential difference between Arved, the seaman, and me, the mountaineer. The sailing ship is dependent on wind, the kayak on the current. You trust yourself to nature and try, with all your experience and intelligence, to make it work for you. The mountain farmer on the other hand can only survive the winter if he provides in summer, if he stores in autumn what he needs in winter.

Arved is a seaman and I am a mountain farmer. These partly opposing means of living have stamped us and for that reason we will remain opposites in many situations in our lives.

The doubtless necessary conflicts which there were during this journey had their origins deep in this completely different view of things. But it was this difference which also had brought us so far. If

266

this journey were to succeed, then it were because Arved's seaman's mentality and my mountain farmer's instincts mutually stimulated each other to a higher performance. We did not hold each other back, we complemented each other in many respects. In this connection, I shall accept criticism only from those who are capable of following in our footsteps.

What lent me wings during this expedition was the daily living together on the ice. What was to come afterwards – the provoked disputes between us, the imputed inability to get on with one another, sensations hawked around – had nothing to do with the Antarctic traverse. Also superficial assertions, such as 'Messner the slave-driver, the wrangler, the egoist', could not tempt me out of my reserve. In Antarctica I had learned to keep calm, to be amazed, to be silent.

In all my expedition books I have tried to stick to reality as far as recollection permits. And just because I write quite openly about fears, egoism and aggression, I have been frequently styled as the 'all-consuming (kilometres, summits, successes, people) Super-Neandertaler'. My claim, to be sincere *vis-à-vis* myself and my readers, was construed continually as me showing off. I know that only the word that you have torn out of your soul has power. I prefer to write about my weaknesses rather than about records and I am suspicious of heroic tales, as also of those which others make up about me.

During my difficult expeditions there has never been any quarrel between me and the 'summiters', perhaps because life and survival at the limit would have been impossible. Also now on this journey across the Antarctic continent, there was an understanding beyond all the divisive words.

What was to come afterwards, when the monovision of outsiders dissected an experience like ours, for morning reading or as 'bed-time sweets', was certainly interesting but not true. It had to do with our ninety-two days on the ice as little as the Mediterranean with Antarctica.

For two weeks we marched at the limit of our abilities. Provisions were rationed. We divided our food very precisely. Nevertheless, we

Minna Bluff. Beneath the vast sky it is difficult to estimate distances. How far were we from the mountains?

showed no signs of deficiency. We just lost weight. My fingers hurt as the tendons needed rest. We were hungry. Although the wind seldom helped us on, every day we caught up some of what we had lost on the plateau.

There were no more crevasses. Suddenly, another good sailing day. The mountains stood before us: Minna Bluff, the smoking volcano Erebus, close by to the right the smaller Terror. We were in high spirits, were now certain to reach McMurdo. From this point on there was no more doubt. We would arrive in time. After a second favourable sailing day we felt completely safe and tucked into the food reserves which we had kept for an emergency.

The piste became increasingly worse. At first it was icy. Then glacier sump, sastrugi. Visibility poor. We sailed hard in the wind. My knees hurt. Our Achilles tendons were swollen. Arved's feet were no longer as raw as in the 'Thiels', although he still had pressure points and blisters, right up to the last day. But he went on, without slowing.

Again exciting lighting effects, rays of sun broke through the clouds; the horizon blue-violet, the valley below yellow. Or was the hollow only an optical illusion? Steely blue, the snow spread out in front of us. The changes were an effacement and a lighting up, a game between green and orange. Such views I knew from the mountains – thundery, and the land pastel-coloured.

Steadily, I had travelled across this snow surface – for almost a hundred days. Now suddenly, the feeling that each snow grain here symbolized a living organism. Were all people, animals and flowers, which had ever lived on the earth, preserved here? Crystalized in tiny, deep frozen drops of water? That which the wind drove across the Antarctic – there were at every instant a thousand millions – were still not come to rest. I tried to expel this thought play from my head but it pursued me. Was the Antarctic perhaps still a sort of heaven? Not only a place of peace and quiet, a paradise, as Dante describes it:

> But the flight was not for my wing;
> Had not a flash darted athwart my mind,
> And, in the spleen, unfolded what it sought.
> Here vigour fail'd the towering fantasy:
> But yet the will roll'd onward, like a wheel
> In even motion, by the Love impell'd,
> That moves the sun in Heaven and all the stars.

Past Minna Bluff, we came to a labyrinth of crevasses. Partly sailing, partly skiing, we crossed the many kilometres' wide obstacle. A dried-out glacier sump with many holes and gullies held us up again. We camped just under the saddle between Black and White Island. It was at the most a day's run to McMurdo. In the stillness I apologized to Arved for having driven him on for ninety long days. But had I not done it, we would not have got here. Now it was unimportant who had been ahead, who behind; who had driven, who had held back. The sum of our energies had brought success.

On 12 February we crossed the pass between Black and White Island. On the other side we travelled over a humpback piste down to the

First meeting with people after leaving the South Pole. Scientists from the New Zealand Scott Station greet us.

shelf ice. It was poor snow with dry 'sump' in between. We made for Willies Field, the American airport at the big McMurdo base. We could recognize it with our binoculars.

Suddenly a vehicle came towards us. Some men and women got out and waved. We went towards them and were greeted by New Zealanders. They were on their way to Black Island to make geological investigations. After they had radioed their Scott Base, they told us that mail was waiting for us there and that we were the New Zealanders' official guests. The Italians would fetch us soon in their helicopter, to travel back to New Zealand with the Italian expedition on the Dutch ship *Barken*. In a few weeks we would be back in civilization again.

The New Zealanders went off southwards in their snow vehicle. We went north, along a real 'road' which had been constructed for vehicles. As I went along this piste, hour after hour, I was simultaneously relieved and sad. The so-called road, the marker poles, the knowledge of a bath, a bed, a beer took the strength out of my legs.

270

Arved Fuchs on the edge of Willies Field, the US airstrip on the shore of the Ross Sea at McMurdo. From here Hercules aircraft fly to the Pole.

I knew now that the time between familiarity and strangeness was past. When you drag your whole home behind you for three months, you live another life; a life according only to nature's criteria. The Antarctic is a serious place. For that reason a serious journey now was coming to an end. It would have forgiven us no mistakes. No adventure had given me so much fun as this three-month-long journey: despite the drudgery, despite the exertion, despite the fears.

It was warm. I took off everything as far as my pile suit. What easy going it was on this piste! Scattered on the sledge were two pairs of gloves, a face mask, a scarf, sun-glasses. Like the requisites of a lost existence. I was no longer the same person as a few hours before. We were no longer in the wilderness.

The next people we met were again New Zealanders. They gave us presents of oranges, bananas. They gave us accommodation. We recovered fast.

271

The first American I met asked whether this crossing constituted a record. 'The Antarctic is not a race track' I answered tersely.

The first Canadian asked whether we had brought all our rubbish out again. I was able to confirm it.

The first Japanese photographed my equipment and wanted to know everything about the logistics.

The first Italian embraced me and called me a hero.

The first Russian came with a flask of vodka in his hand and we celebrated the success.

The first Frenchman I met only wanted to know whether Frenchmen had made this journey before us. 'Perhaps', I said.

The first Englishman asked whether we had pulled the sledges all the way ourselves. 'Yes', I said, 'all man-hauling'. 'Just like Captain Scott!' – 'Just like', I said, 'but unfortunately it killed him!'

The first German I met asked 'Why?' – and I had no answer.

III. The Journey on the Ice

Time-Span

Dec. 1986	Ascent of Mount Vinson. Plan for crossing Antarctica worked out.
1987–1989	Investigations, financing, special equipment developed and tested. Contract with 'Adventure Network International' (ANI). Arved Fuchs becomes my partner and concerns himself with sledges, navigation and (in part) provisions. Sailing practice.
Sept./Oct. 1989	Packing. Press conferences. Expedition cargo goes off to Chile.

Penguin chick. On my first Antarctic trip I was able to watch penguins. Later I studied Antarctic literature and Dr Wilson's drawings.

With Arved Fuchs at the South Pole: the fact that we followed a common goal made us a team, all other differences apart.

16 Oct.	Flight Frankfurt–Santiago, Chile.
17 Oct.	Flight Santiago–Punta Arenas (advanced permanent quarters).
18 Oct.–6 Nov.	Delay in Punta Arenas with two false starts in the direction of Antarctica, in each case on account of problems over Drake Passage. First change of route.
7 Nov.	Third start succeeds, flight to Patriot Hills. Meeting with the 'Trans-Antarctica' dog-sledge expedition. New change of plan on account of fuel shortage (?).
7–13 Nov.	Row with ANI. Another change of plan. Packing. Waiting.
13 Nov. 1989– 12 Feb. 1990	Journey on the ice.
12/13 Feb.	Arrival at Scott Base at McMurdo.
13 Feb.	Helicopter flight to Italian station at Terra Nova Bay.
18–27 Feb.	Return journey on the *Barken* from Terra Nova Bay to Christchurch, New Zealand, together with Italian expedition.
27 Feb.–4 Mar.	New Zealand. Holiday with Christine, Sabine and Arved.
5 Mar.	Arrival in Frankfurt. Press conference.
6–10 Mar.	'Aftermath'. Press conference and other public appearances (with Arved and alone) in Germany and Italy. End of the expedition.

My Diary

Here follows the unaltered 'day-by-day' diary which I kept during the march across Antarctica.

13.11.89
Landed: 1313hrs
Sun; hardly any
wind
Pos.: 82°04.99′S
71°58.46′W
Temp. −16°C
Pos.: 82°08.22′S
72°08.76′W
Air pressure 942mb
height: 110m

Hurried departure.
'Trans-Antarctica' needs fresh dogs. (80°40′S). Our set down will be combined with that. Brydon (pilot of Twin-Otter) is to fly from Patriot Hills to the edge of the Weddell Sea, set us down and then push on further to the 'Trans-Antarctica'. We are soon alone in the solitude (infinity). Bolz and Jaeger film and photograph the departure. Everything is hurried. The operation with 'Trans-Antarctica' interests us only peripherally. Three-cornered flight. In tent – after three hours. Marching – is congenial.

14.11.89
−12°C
Pos.: 82°04.79′S
74°26.64′W
950mb
250m

Sky overcast; wind; snow; complete white-out. At first I didn't sleep; could observe from inside the tent how the sun disappeared. After midnight the wind increased constantly. We want to wait until we have three satellites and can determine our exact position. Started about 2 p.m. Sailing wind from south-east. Covered about 20 miles. Unfortunately, it is driving us too far west, so we have only gained 7 miles. Wind from south-east.

15.11.89
−9°C

White-out. Wind out of south-east. We stay in the tent. At midday we get a positional fix. We

Pos.: as before
937mb
370m

have come much too far west. Reading, dozing, cooking. It is difficult to stay sitting down when I think of the enormous stretch which lies ahead of us. Uninterrupted, the storm sweeps over the tent surface. Later – 6 p.m. – the wind comes out of the south. In the 'night' the wind decreases steadily. At about 5 a.m. the sun is shining.

16.11.89
−15°C
Pos.: 82°13.99′S
**   74°42.45′W**
934mb
300–350–450–370m

6–7 a.m. Breakfast. Fine weather. Slippery. Scarcely any wind. (From south-east.) 5.45 a.m. – on the march. Plus 5×15-minute rests. 20 kilometres covered. The first half went well (pleasant terrain). Many sastrugi in the second half. We become slow and tired. How great the distinctiveness of the terrain is irrespective of whether the sun is shining or not. We get inside the tent about 4 p.m. Cooking – eating – drinking. Today is radio day. Bad contact.

17.11.89
−8°C
949mb
270m
Pos.: 82°18.76′S
**   75°27.17′W**
938mb
370m

10 centimetres new snow. Late breakfast. At 8 a.m. still white-out. Start about 11 a.m. Marched two and a half hours to start with. Bad terrain. Sastrugi. The ground rises quite easily in gigantic waves. The waves crests are at more than 4-kilometre intervals. After 2 p.m. we sailed for about two hours. Wind from south-south-east. We are off the right line. Nevertheless, we have gained something. In the evening the wind is somewhat more favourable. It is snowing. After a short while the wind backs from south-south-east to south-east. We are living well. Still getting on too slowly.

18.11.89
−10°C
942mb

Overcast. Wind from south-east. We try to sail but give up after 1 kilometre. Wind is too strong and clearly out of south. We march five

350m
Pos.: 82°25.38′S
        75°49.36′W
929mb
460m

hours with sastrugi, new snow and wind against us. It can't get much worse. We have covered about 15 kilometres. Tomorrow we are going to reduce food rations, mostly to half. The sledges are too heavy. It's as if one were pulling an exhausted man. Also, the snow is still heavy and irregular. A real grind.

19.11.89
−14°C
922mb
Pos.: 82°30.36′S
        75°49.64′W
911mb
600m

Stormy after a stormy night. The wind has moved through 20° to south-south-east. Too little for sailing. Meanwhile, it is too squally and strong. The situation is a bit bloody awful. Started about 11 a.m. and marched for three hours, always against the wind which is developing into a storm. When we put up the tent we had difficulty holding it completely. One of my two mats (sleeping underlay) was torn from my hands by the storm. It vanished northwards at once. Too fast to catch. I replaced it with the spare mat on the sledge.

20.11.89
−15°C
Pos.: 82°39.07′S
        75°53.92′W
900mb
720m

Southerly wind. It is alternately sunny and overcast. Light snowfall in evening. The weather is unsettled. Five hours march; at first many sastrugi and hard, icy snow. In the east a cloud bank comes up and then suddenly, during our third rest, the sun is overcast; a little later everything is grey. On the horizon a narrow streak of light-blue shines through here and there. Like a Fata Morgana. We have travelled through a gigantic, flat valley trough. Like embankments, elevations converge ahead to left and right of us.

21.11.89
−15°C
900mb

Long day. Cloudy weather that held us up (white-out) at first and later overcast. A dark edge to the encircling horizon. After an attempt

Pos.: no reading
899mb
−8°C

to sail (wind from south-east) we used the broad skis. Wind is too weak, coming later from north. A fresh attempt to sail failed – wind not strong enough. Marched six hours – often without visibility and that with steamed-up glasses. It is enough to drive one to despair. But no one is without hope, especially not us.

22.11.89
−15°C
Pos.: 82°56.52′S
**   77°03.17′W**
893mb
800m

That was a really catastrophic day: Arved's sail split; I have lost the distance measuring wheel; Arved's Omega watch seemed kaput but luckily it's going again. We marched southwards three and a half hours in two stages and sailed twice. Wind south-south-east and south. Sailing across sastrugi is like descending a hump-backed piste. If I didn't know that the earliest our depot in the Thiel Mountains can be set up is 3 December, this long march would be too slow for me. Now I feel good and can go for eight to ten hours.

23.11.89
−18°C
Pos.: same as
22.11.89
897mb
770m

Storm the whole day. We stay where we are. Worry in the 'night' from time to time that the tent would tear. We had not prepared for this storm. In the gusts (Strength 7 and more) the blizzard sweeps snow dust over the tent. Including yesterday we have eaten only one food ration (as a saving measure). Radio time in evening. Wind slowly decreasing. In the tent a smell of cooking and damp things. It is more snug than I had pictured it whilst still at home.

24.11.89
−15°C
Pos.: 83°08.51′S
**   77°19.06′W**
889mb

Strong wind in morning. Thus later start. Marched six hours. The wind left off in afternoon. The sastrugi increased. Often small ice sheets in between. However, we are making good progress. Arved's feet (heels and balls of) are sore

840m

and/or bloodshot. Each step hurts him. We must doctor them this evening. Feeling good and could run three to four hours more. Perhaps this were in the long run too much. Also Arved is right to put on the brakes. At the present speed of march we are making 12 miles per day. Decidedly too little.

25.11.89
−18°C
Pos.: 83°15.24′S
77°27.11′W
883mb
910m

Storm again! Towards 3 a.m. it began to blow and it is increasingly stormy. Ran only three and a half hours against the storm: stubbornly, bent over forward, icy wind in the face. We are too slow. If only one could turn this wind into usable energy! We are camped now in the lee of a sastrugi. As a precaution we have placed the sledges cross-wise like a snow plough so that the tent cannot be hit by the full strength of the storm. I would have preferred to run on further in the storm, in the hope that it would finally leave off. Sadly, for Arved that is too risky.

26.11.89
−18°C
Pos.: *c.* 83°27′S
77°40′W
876mb
970m

Didn't set off until after midday. A night of blizzard and a stormy morning lie behind us. Marched six hours; in broad waves the terrain approaches the mountains. In the first half, many sastrugi (up to a metre high), then less. Wind constantly decreasing. Running ahead with the compass is my usual position. The going intrigues me. Always this curiosity as to what is to come, although neither nunataks nor mountains are in sight. Am always thinking of the faces of people close to me; or looking back over the past. I miss neither greenery nor warmth.

27.11.89
−16°C

Again a windy, otherwise good day for marching. After a late start, marched for six hours.

281

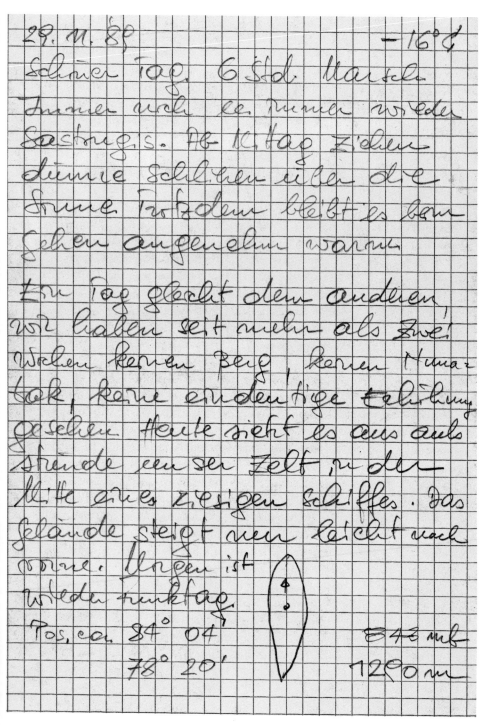

29. 11. 89   −16°C

schöner Tag. 6 Std. Marsch
Immer noch ee. immer wieder
Sastrugis. Ab 10. Tag ziehen
dünne Schleier über die
Sonne. Trotzdem bleibt es beim
Gehen angenehm warm.

Ein Tag gleicht dem anderen,
wir haben seit mehr als zwei
Wochen keinen Berg, keinen Nunatak, keine eindeutige Erhöhung
gesehen. Heute sieht es aus auf
stünde unser Zelt in der
Mitte eines riesigen Schiffes. Das
Gelände steigt nur leicht nach
vorne. Morgen ist
wieder Funktag.
Pos. ca. 84° 04'
$78° 20'$ 842 mb
      1290 m

Page from my diary. My diary consisted of chequered school exercise books. I wrote it up always in the 'evening' in pencil, with facts and impressions. (See diary entry for 29 November 1989.)

Pos.: *c.* 83°40′S
78°00′W
864mb
1,090m

Too stormy in the morning. We are again going upwards in gigantic waves. The crests must be now 10 kilometres apart. On the north slopes there are many large sastrugi; on the southern sides glassy snow ice. The wind blasts us continually, sharply in the face. With difficulty I find a tent site on the hard terrain between the sastrugi. Today is a radio day. All work with radio apparatus and aerial in vain.

28.11.89
−18°C
Pos.: 83°51.82′S
78°11.39′W
856mb
1,170m

At last a fine day. After some wind (very cold) in the morning it was really pleasant in the afternoon. If only there weren't so many sastrugi! Ran for six hours. The terrain climbs on towards the mountains in waves. These waves are now flatter and further apart than hitherto. I try to film over long stretches. We are in camp early and cook, eat, rest. Get on well with Arved. We are now balanced and confident, although still too slow. Pity – yesterday no radio contact – no news from outside.

29.11.89
−16°C
Pos.: *c.* 84°04′S
78°20′W
843mb
1,290m

Fine day. Marched six hours. Still more and more sastrugi. From midday thin streaks drawing across the sun. Nevertheless it stays pleasantly warm whilst on the move. One day like another. For more than two weeks we have seen no mountain, no nunatak, no definite elevation. Today it seems as if our tent were standing in the middle of a gigantic ship. The terrain rises easily ahead. Tomorrow is radio day again.

30.11.89
−18°C
Pos.: 84°17.86′S
79°19.54′W

At last, far ahead to the right, the first mountains – a range like glimmering teeth on the horizon. The summits are scarcely discernible with the naked eye, they are so small. It must

838mb
1,330m

be the Thiels. At right angles to our direction of march is a nunatak. In silhouette, it looks like a flat tree stump. Went for six hours. New direction of march (more west). Still sastrugi. The weather is very good. The sun even has strength in the afternoon. Radio day!

1.12.89
−17°C
Pos.: 84°30.63′S
      80°24.00′W
845mb
1,270m

Again a magnificent day. More streaks in the sky than yesterday but towards evening they all went. Light breeze from south. Now and then the sun goes behind the clouds. It is then cold and damp. Time and again to the right we see ahead of us hints of mountain chains – like Fata Morganas. Mirages of mountain ranges must look like that. We run for six hours on a course of south-south-west (160°). Nevertheless we get no nearer to the mountains.

2.12.89
−18°C
Pos.: *c.* **84°43′S**
      82°00′W
834mb
1,380m

A day like the last. Similarly, we did our six-hours march and advanced about 13 miles. The sastrugi increased again. Sadly, the film which I took of Arved on the move won't come out because the new cassette isn't working properly. A big nunatak stands out clearly to the right of us. At an angle of 60° to our direction of march. In the south-west there hangs a crescent-shaped bank of mist. Perhaps the Thiel Mountains are behind there. The clouds remain unchanged. Evidently there is bad weather.

3.12.89
−17°C
Pos.: 84°50.43′S
      82°22.70′W
836mb
1,360m

It is cloudy and damp cold. A poor day. Wind in gusts from south. We go only four hours because one of Arved's ski bindings is defective. After 10 minutes a strap breaks and, as he cannot call after me, he follows to the rest stop with only one ski. He changes the touring skis for telemark skis and is now wearing kamiks

(Eskimo boots). It is strenuous going on sastrugi terrain with narrow trail skis. Added to that, we have bad visibility. With the Thiel Mountains always ahead of me, I advance relatively easily. Thus I don't have to stare uninterruptedly at the spherical compass on my chest. We hope to be able to radio at the scheduled time today.

4.12.89
−16°C
Pos.: *c.* **85°00′S**
     84°00′W
832mb
1,390m

Overcast. In the morning it is relatively warm. I am using the patched-up binding. We try to sail, but don't get far with the feeble wind and on account of the sastrugi. After I ran into a sastrugi and went head over heels (bruises) we gave up sailing and marched south-south-west. The Thiel Mountains are (almost) always in sight, but they hardly get any nearer. Despite the miserable conditions (bad visibility, sastrugi, snow in between) we march six hours. How far we have come we only guess. The satellites show our position (on our GPS).

5.12.89
−14°C
Pos.: **85°11.00′S**
     85°26.65′W
826mb
1,450m

Grey sky. Relatively warm. We went southwest, always over sastrugi, for six hours. In bad visibility it is a torment for the skis, sledges, feet, ankles, hips and above all the eyes to run further. We progress only slowly. The mountains come imperceptibly nearer. Now with a half-empty sledge it's going well without sastrugi. Also, I would have liked to hand over the compass, at least for a few kilometres. In the evening we put up the aerial again in the hope of being able to contact Patriot Hills or 'Trans-Antarctica'. Arved speaks with Etienne and asks him to pass on our position and situation to Jaeger in Patriot Hills. We must reach our depot tomorrow, if it is there.

6.12.89
−16°C
Pos.: 85°19.00′S
 87°40.00′W
818mb
1,600m

Arrival in depot. From a distance of about 4 miles I can see something dark between ice and snow. The Twin-Otter is distinctly recognizable with binoculars. It must have brought our supplies. We run on almost two hours. Brydon is on his way to the Pole, flying material to Stegar and his people ('Trans-Antarctica'). He has brought us a new tent and food. I speak with Ulrich (Jaeger) in Patriot Hills over Brydon's radio. They don't understand why we are so slow. From now on we want to use an Argos set instead of radio. Because of the few radio opportunities until now, I send the *Der Spiegel* reporter my diary entries. Arved refuses to send his. March to the depot: five hours. Sailing at first, then running. Bad sastrugi. Time presses. The pilot must be off to the Pole. Resting.

7.12.89
−18°C
Pos.: as yesterday
828mb
Altitude: as
yesterday

Rest day. Storm. We dry our clothes. Above all, our boots must be treated inside and out. Meanwhile we drink Pisko-Sauer. The used equipment as well as all rubbish remains here in containers and is to be fetched away later. Storm all day. Our cooker burns almost uninterruptedly. We have enough fuel. We read mail, newspapers, *Der Spiegel* and re-calculate the rations for the second leg at 5,000 calories per day. Strange − after the mail from home is put aside, the tent is home. And no home-sickness.

8.12.89
−19°C
Pos.: as yesterday
825mb
1,600m

Good weather. Little wind. Rest day. Arved doesn't want to move. Pity. We repack the sledges. Early next morning the Twin-Otter arrives. We shuffle the containers around: 1× empty; 1× rubbish; 2× private, destination

Punta Arenas and Europe; 1× food for Patriot Hills; 1× Pole depot. Brydon is in a hurry. He talks about the Pole, drinks coffee and is obviously in a good mood because 'Trans-Antartica' (at Pole with the Yanks) is receiving so much support (USSR, USA). In a day or two he will fly to the Pole and back again, to fly in journalists and further equipment for Steger.

9.12.89
−10°C
Pos.: *c.* 85°27′S
89°20′W
806mb
1,800m

The deviation is now 54° east. Mist, light snowfall in morning. We cannot orientate ourselves by the mountains. 'White-out'. If only we had run yesterday. We make 200 metres height. It is a relentless grind (partly zigzagging) to reach the height of the Thiels. We are going south-westwards in the hope of avoiding too much up and down. In the evening the weather opens up on the horizon and we can see the Thiel Mountains hazily behind us. Long day, as Arved often stayed far behind. There are crevasses and sastrugi again.

10.12.89
−22°C
Pos.: 85°39.66′S
88°36.31′W
88mb
1,850m

Horribly cold and strenuous day. Storm from south-west. Sastrugi. It is a misery, having to run this stretch in bad visibility: once we walked round a hole, once braked the sledges down into a valley without skis and pulled them high up again. Once we crossed a gigantic ice sheet with crevasses. We set off today an hour earlier, so as to get a firm position in the 'evening'. The satellites are now ahead of us in the daytime. Still stormy, the weather is good, went for six hours. From tomorrow it must get better!

11.12.89
***c.* −22°C**
Pos.: 85°51.05′S

Mist in morning. Nevertheless it is a relatively clear day. Streaks over the main Thiel range. We got up an hour earlier, lost the time through

88°28.01'W
786mb
1,990m

Arved's late arrival at the rest stops. I have taken his petrol can from him although my sledge was already heavy. We must have the same rhythm and run more daily! Many ups and downs and many sastrugi (they run south-west to north-east) which we must cut across at an angle of about 30°. Now a vast, white land lies before us! I insist on seven hours' march from tomorrow.

12.12.89
−15°C
Pos.: 86°05.57'S
88°27.45'W
793mb
1,930m

At last a fine day once again. Good weather, little wind. At midday we came across the tracks of 'Trans-Antarctica' which we followed here and there. It is more curiosity than help which they offer us. We run seven hours (2+ 1¼+1¼+1¼+1¼). In between 15 minutes' rest each time. This speed and the hours marched are a good basis for the coming weeks. The time is well filled out: eight hours' (with rests) march: six hours' (2½ in morning; 3½ in evening) cooking and drying in the tent; one hour (½+½) tent putting up and taking down; nine hours' sleep.

13.12.89
−23°C
Pos.: c. 86°18'S
88°00'W
784mb
2,040m

Wind! We sail. After an hour Arved determines our position: 86°05.80'S, 87°38.27'W, i.e. we are travelling east and gaining nothing towards the Pole. Therefore we keep going. Much wind against, relatively deep snow, scarcely any sastrugi. Today we do only six and a quarter hours. How far we have come we do not know as in the tent it is too late for the GPS fix. From 6.30 p.m. there are only two satellites. We move easily to the south-west in the hope of meeting Steger's tracks in two to three days' time.

14.12.89	Gorgeous day. Little wind. At first we go
c. −23°C	south-west. In the hope of finding Steger's
Pos.: 86°33.95′S	tracks, we deviate from the correct course.

14.12.89
c. −23°C
Pos.: 86°33.95′S
87°59.88′W
774mb
2,110m

Gorgeous day. Little wind. At first we go south-west. In the hope of finding Steger's tracks, we deviate from the correct course. Then we give it up and proceed exactly southwards. The snow is not so heavy. Now and then crystalline new snow in hollows, as no wind there. Finally, harmonized with Arved: both running at almost the same rhythm. Seven hours' march with one and a quarter hours' rest in between. No mountain, nothing to see. In the west, on the horizon, an elevation shows sometimes as a silver streak. Or is it a mirage? In the evening, cloud streaks come up in the south, west and north – is the weather changing?

15.12.89
−24°C
Pos.: 86°48.28′S
87°58.48′W
765mb
2,200m

Beautiful day. Light south-east wind. We march with telemark skis. (During the last hour I switched to touring skis because my right heel was hurting. The pressure on my foot, when pulling, causes a sharp pain, particularly when the pressure is not equally distributed.) Seven hours' running time. Many sastrugi which run in all directions. In the evening again streaks in the south and west. Weather seems to be holding, however.

16.12.89
c. −24°C
Pos.: 87°02.73′S
88°01.45′W
749mb
2,370m

Cold, windy day. I am still using the patched binding. Have bad pain in my heel (bone bruised?) After going for 10 minutes Arved breaks both bindings of his touring skis. He changes to telemark skis which he uses with his heavy boots. Many sastrugi, steep slopes. Bad terrain. After two hours I go ahead without waiting longer for Arved than the 15-minute rest stops. At the camp site I erect the tent. Arved's proposal that I should go ahead, in good visibility naturally and because of the track, so as not to cool down in the rest stops, is a blessing for me. Seven hours of going. No vexation and no worries. Arved arrives one and a half hours later. He struggled through with an iron will. For that he has (despite lack of fitness) my admiration.

17.12.89
c. **−25°C**
Pos.: as before
748mb
2,370m

Rest day. Storm. The wind has risen continually since the hours of yesterday afternoon. We rest in order to go easy on feet and joints. It is good for once not to have to put up and take down the tent. We sleep, read, eat and drink a lot. For some days I have been hungrier when sledge pulling and also tired somewhat faster. We are definitely feeling the altitude. It is not only the donkey work which wears one down in the long run, it is this constant repetition that fatigues (whilst resting it becomes clear); moving tent, cooking, camping.

18.12.89
−25°C
Pos.: *c.* 87°17′S
   89°30′W
734mb
2,470m

Very cold day. In the morning we sailed for one and half hours and crossed the Steger route which is scarcely recognizable. Then we ran for five and three-quarter hours. The Steger track runs too far west.
Whilst sailing my fingers almost froze. Also when marching it is cold. Wind from southeast. Fewer sastrugi. Constant climbing. Sadly we missed the three satellites in the evening. Therefore tomorrow we must depart earlier so as to know exactly where we are. Uneven tent site, all corners and edges.

19.12.89
−25°C
Pos.: *c.* 87°30′S

Lovely day. Relatively windless. Very many sastrugi. Occasionally they are giant sized. There are hump backs which are 10 metres long

89°50′W
723mb
2,640m

and up to 2–3 metres high. Seven full hours of going. Nine hours on our legs. We followed the Steger track which is not always recognizable. We want to stay on it until we catch three satellites again. We are travelling (87°28′S, 89°50′W) through a gigantic amphitheatre. There is a hole in the white infinity like a crater and on all sides the slope climbs steeply. Tremendous!

20.12.89
−26°C
Pos.: 87°46.21′S
91°19.59′W
710mb
2,770m

Lovely day but very cold. Sastrugi almost the whole stretch. After two hours the improvised binding broke on the ski I took over from Arved when it first broke. I patch it in the open without gloves. Twice my fingers go white. Nevertheless I can carry on before Arved arrives. Thus we lose no time. Seven full hours' march. For me the rest stops are the worst part because then I cool down completely. Wait each time 10–15 minutes, until Arved is there and then another 10 minutes. We must find a better solution. It is not about going fast or slow, it is about making 15 to 16 miles southwards in the seven hours, and that will only happen at my speed. We could run more hours slower. Arved refuses more than seven hours' running time.

21.12.89
−28°C
Pos.: 88°00′S
91°00′W
705mb
2,849m

Storm. We move nevertheless. It is late, 10 a.m., before we depart. The storm increases. After two hours I wait 20 minutes for Arved and nearly freeze. He has a white nose when he arrives, frostbite? At once I continue. Thus we go six and a half hours. It is a problem putting up the tent alone in a strong wind. I fix it with skis and ice-axe. It takes an eternity. Then I take the spare cooker and crawl into the tent. Arved arrives one and a half hours later. He is brave, does not complain. His frostbitten nose turns blue-red in the tent. Basically it is hellish to move in such conditions, but if we want to get to McMurdo we may not spare ourselves any more and I do want to get there.

22.12.89
−29°C
Pos.: 88°15′S
91°00′W
704mb
3,840m

Lovely day. On account of wind (south-east) we start late. We make good progress although sastrugi predominate over wide stretches. Arved running well! Now we have an ideal speed. It is fun to be underway with this man, above all when we are equally fast. From the north a bright belt of clouds rises in the afternoon, and rolls over us in the evening. It turns grey, snows lightly. Wind from north-east. Tomorrow there will be a good sailing wind! Seven full hours marched.

23.12.89
−15°C
Pos.: 88°26.33′S
92°24.44′W
708mb
2,800m

Sadly no more wind. Cloudy, but warm. For the first time on this trip I go without anorak and overtrousers. Later when the wind (east) gets up, it becomes acutely cold. We run seven hours with exactly an hour's rest (4×15 minutes) At this speed running on ahead doesn't bother me. On the contrary, I am glad to do it. Heavy snow. Twice the sky clouded over and both times it cleared again in between. The terrain is flatter but always many sastrugi. We wished for a Christmas present of a smooth running surface. In vain.

24.12.89
−25°C
Pos.: same
700mb
2,880m

Christmas Eve. Rest day. It cleared in the night. Weather good, wind from south. We read, write letters, dry boots and windproofs. We photograph life in the tent. Arved knows how to produce cosiness. For that I am forever thankful. In the tent it is acutely cold, but still cosy in our sleeping-bags. As there is no Christmas goose we must see what there is good to eat with a shot of whisky. I try a muesli cake. Still six days to the Pole.

25.12.89
−23°C
Pos.: 88°40/41.91′S
92°32.09′W
691mb
2,990m?!

Storm the whole night through. It chased the fine grained snow across the heavy surfaces. Until nearly midday no hope of continuing. We doubt whether we should set out. Started after midday. At first still strong wind which luckily decreased. Fewer sastrugi, relatively flat surfaces. The snow is as heavy as flour. The sledge seems to weigh several hundredweight and the skis – the skins are now almost worn through – seem to stick to the ground. Seven hours' real marching time. When shall we finally get normal conditions?

26.12.89
−10°C in 'morning'
−25°C in 'evening'
Pos.: 89°12.40′S
(89°12.50′)
92°02.11′W
(92°12.65′)
688mb
3,040m

Warm in morning. We started late. Heavy snow. After three and a quarter hours, north wind got up. Little at first, then more. We sailed continuously at first and made ever quicker progress. Sadly Arved remains far behind. I waited for him after two and a quarter hours and got quite cold, as I am dressed for marching. Although I don't feel good about it, we must use this first good wind. Therefore I sailed on three hours more and waited – after putting up the tent alone in the storm – one hour for Arved who rails over my sailing ahead. He is right. Hope we have gained ground. Arved's anger is quickly exhausted. YES!! We have advanced more than 30 miles.

27.12.89
−25°C

Stormy night. The wind turned through about 100°. Nevertheless, we try to sail in view of

Pos.: 89°31.96′S
104°33.15′W
696mb
2,940m

yesterday's sailing success. We ran just three hours on the Steger route and then at an angle of about 30° west to it. All in all we run five and a half hours. Wind from east-north-east. No sun. Bad visibility. Now and then small sastrugi. Heavy snow, then again soft snow. We endeavour to stick together on account of the miserable visibility. It seems to me as if we are travelling in a circle. Tomorrow we shall see how far we have come when we take the fix. We have cold hands whilst sailing, also cold feet in the evening.

28.12.89
−28°C
Pos.: 89°44.94/97′S
113°09.39/
28.30′W
681mb
3,120m

Windy day. Storm, now and then in gusts, from south-east. It blasts in our faces. Therefore we march seven full hours. The snow is so heavy, that I constantly have the feeling of climbing a mountain. The sledge feels as if it had a double load. Perhaps we are also feeling the altitude. On account of the negligible atmospheric pressure, the effect of altitude on the body at the South Pole is much more noticeable than at 3,000 metres in the Alps or Himalaya. Arved 'laments' over the altitude and his injured right knee. Yet he struggles through. He runs the seven-hour stretch without grumbling. Tomorrow at the Pole?

29.12.89
−20°C
Pos.: c. 89°54′S
113°53′W
687mb
3,040m

Storm. We stay in the tent until afternoon. In mist we would not find the Pole today. At 3 p.m. we go on despite everything. Although the wind has abated somewhat, we have trouble taking down the tent and packing the sledge. We run four and a half hours through mist banks and heavy snow. Time and again sunbeams break through the white-out. The scene is excitingly uncanny. When the tent is up, the wind abates, it gets brighter. I fetch the binoculars and gaze southwards. 'The Pole!' 8.20 p.m. local time. We dance around the tent and shout: 'The Pole!' Arved goes wild. I am grateful to him because I have learned so much from him.

30.12 same day as 31.12.89 on International Date Line THE POLE – 25°C Pos.: 90°S 693mb 2,990m

We run three hours in bad visibility. This slow poking around towards the Pole – wind, mist, clouds – is thrilling. Now and then worries that we are running false. Suddenly again the Pole directly in front of us: 90° south. We see the Pole (the station) for the first time in the last hour. In the ANI camp Bolz and Jaeger are asleep. Everybody is asleep – here it is not 2 p.m., Chile time. Here it is about 5 a.m. – New Year! All on account of the International Date Line and the change to New Zealand time.

Reinhold Messner. At the South Pole we celebrated Arved's achievement as the first to reach both Poles on foot inside twelve months. The Americans produced wine to drink to his health.

1.1.1990
c. −20°C
Pos.: same
693mb

We are staying in J-5, a barracks with curtained cubicles. After a long day answering questions, a mad New Year party in the dome – a gigantic aluminium cupola with several compartments – and a lot of wine, I am turned on. There were a few scientists and lots of technicians at the New Year party. (Joiners, drivers, hydrraulic engineers, electricians, radio operators.) Everyone is being very nice to us. The fancy dress costumes are 'End of the World' theme: chains around the shoulders, fetters, nakedness and armour. Post-punk-era. After beer, wine and champagne, we got to bed at 1 a.m. Two days have passed without sleep and yet I cannot sleep because it is too hot for me in the tent barracks and people are constantly coming and going. I would like to rest.

2.1.90
−20°C
Pos.: Pole = 90°S
686mb
3,060m
Weight: 68kg
(150lb)

Ulrich (Jaeger) flies home. Arved has again not yielded his diary. Pity. Spent the night in the tent in front of the barracks in order to be able to sleep. If tent life becomes a necessity for me in Munich and Juval, Sabine will desert me too. After a sauna (fainted briefly on account of low blood pressure) finally a good night. I am sleeping in the tent in front of J-5. Nevertheless, I wake up frequently, because the South Pole is like a shunting yard. Twice I hear a C130 (Hercules) come in. Frequently worried that a bulldozer could roll over me and the tent. We clean up the sledges, re-pack everything afresh. The sledges now weigh a good 120kilos. With that we have to do the 1,400 kilometres to McMurdo. (Maximum fifty days' survival rations.) Wilhelm (Bittorf) tells me in a one-sided conversation (I cannot answer) that we must be at McMurdo on 15 February *at the latest*, otherwise the Italians will leave without us. Option with ANI to fly out remains open. Sadly, I receive no permission to radio 'Terra Nova'. I press for departure.

3.1.90
−22°C
Pos.: 89°35.14′S
         175°33.72′W
689mb
New altitude:
2,830m

Breakfast in the dome. We are provided with all manner of dainties. Now suddenly we are officially welcome. Our secret attendants – the simple artisans, girls, drivers of J-5 – are pleased. Arved and I are more than grateful to these people. Start 11 a.m. on the landing strip. The sledges are so heavy that it takes two men to pull each one from the camp. Little wind. All our friends are here to see us off. Each wants to give us something: chocolate, cake, two tots of Grand Marnier. We travel laboriously northwards with sails for six hours.

4.1.90
−25°C
Pos.: *c.* 89°S160°E?
672mb
3,010m

White-out in morning after snowy night. After breakfast we stayed in the tent and got into our sleeping-bags again. Towards 3 p.m. we start in thick mist: miserable visibility. The wind is good though. Therefore we risk it. We sail – being extremely careful not to lose ourselves – softly and fast. Each time Arved did not follow. I had to stop and wait. After half an hour the visibility became somewhat better, then the sun came through and the wind dropped. With the sails swinging before us, we ran on further, five full hours. We call this technique 'penguin' sailing. Out of a lost day came a successful one. Unfortunately no exact position.

5.1.90
−18°C
Pos.: ?88°33.93′S
         165°46.14′E

In the morning it's windy and overcast. Ideal for sailing. We sail fast, i.e. 'swallow'. Later, with clear sky and sun, the wind decreases. Sailing and running with sail five and half

665mb
3,090m

hours. My knees hurt. In the stops we move around like old men. My hips are rubbed raw from the sledge harness – also the seat harness of the sail rubs. When the wind is weak, it requires effort and skill to move it. We swing the sail in front of us, up and down or to and fro. Sitting in the tent, we hear a Hercules which is flying somewhat to the right of us, on its way to the Pole.

6.1.90
−28°C
Pos.: as yesterday
666mb
3,100m

Already this morning a Hercules is flying over our tent. That is a good feeling after no GPS fix for three days. We are apparently on course but how far have we got? I wanted to go on, Arved didn't. Lovely weather but no wind. We stay in the tent. I am reading Friedell's *Modern Cultural History* until my arm goes to sleep, holding it outside the sleeping-bag. Arved finds the problem with the GPS (Magellan) set. We are now east not west. We get a fix and are satisfied. In the afternoon clouds come up, the wind unfortunately only in puffs.

7.1.90
−28°C
Pos.: approx. as yesterday
667mb
3,080m

Yesterday 'evening' we tried to move: too little wind. After 2 miles we gave up. This morning the same game. Arved believes, correctly, that we should save strength. We want – tactically speaking – to wait for wind and then run and not be lying in the tent dog-tired from sledge pulling when stronger wind arrives. Calm the whole day. Now, when we would most prefer storm, we experience the serene, warm days which we lacked on the march to the Pole. We read and film 'life in the tent'. When reading I forget completely where we are.

8.1.90

Again no wind! We run with and without sail

Arved Fuchs and I at the main entrance to the dome, heart of the Polar station, where we were officially welcomed shortly before departure.

−35° C.
Pos.: 88°24.42′S
      165°33.92′E
659mb
3,180m

but not far. Three hours' actual going. Once the sun has burned off all the clouds and mist, the last of the breeze drops. From today we want to run at 'night'. During the past three days, it was cloudy and windier at 'night' (from 2 a.m.) than 'daytime'. We are not hoping for sailing wind but assistance with pulling the heavy sledges through the soft, heavy snow. We are already behind schedule. Every hour we waste now means 4 kilometres too little at the other end. These timid attempts to sail and being left hanging in windless space is like swooning. Better seven to eight hours' marching than hoping, waiting, marching, stopping.

9.1.90

We start late afternoon (8 January 1990) and run

−40°C
Pos.: 88°10.02'/
   87°52.66'S
   162°17.67'/
   159°02.75'E
660/663mb
3,190/3,140m

until 5 a.m., a good six hours' 'penguin'. It is so cold that I get white flecks in my fingers while putting up the tent. Still windy. Arved is motivated, despite his weariness. Start once more at 1.30 p.m. four hours' march: 'penguin' and 'donkey' (i.e. pulling without sail aid). It remains overcast and the wind comes in gusts, drops, comes again. The first sastrugi. The ground is now harder but time and again this soft, heavy snow. As the wind is from the west, it drives us leftwards away from our route.

10.1.90
−20°C
Pos.: as yesterday
666mb
3,110m

Magnificent day, light northerly wind. It is so warm – even outside – that one could lie naked in a snow hollow and not freeze. The most peaceful, warmest day of the trip so far. We must get on. Arved wants to wait for wind. So we stay where we are and eat, read, enjoy life, as if 1,200 kilometres of ice did not lie ahead of us. I agree with Arved, there is a limit to masochism. We have no desire to slave hard, so we wait for the wind to change direction. After a few hours' hoping in the morning (wind must come) I forget where we are.

11.1.90
−31°C
Pos.: as yesterday
666mb
3,100m

Again a magnificent, windless day. Although it is 'warm' – or so it feels – we measure the shade temperature at −31°C. We are induced – in the hope of wind getting up from the south – to wait. We are still not much behind schedule. Patience one more day. It is not laziness which keeps us in the tent, but the knowledge that we are squandering strength and time if, after eight hours' tugging sledges, the wind should get up. If the wind doesn't come we shall be gambling with the expedition's success. At least clouds are coming up across the sun.

12.1.90
−30°C
Pos.: 87°45.83′S
        159°08.62′E
665mb
3,120m

North-east wind! It is unbelievable how the conditions hold us back. Always wind against us! We go four hours ('donkey') in bad, heavy snow. Again, I had to take something from Arved's sledge load. Although heavy mist comes up in the north, the wind direction remains the same. It ought to be almost always southerly wind here. So far we have had south-east or north/north-east winds. Then two days almost completely windless. With these heavy sledges, at 3,100m above sea-level, with grainy snow under our skis and the wind in our faces we are marking time.

13.1.90
−21°C
Pos.: 87°38.32′S
        159°23.86′E
672mb
3,040m

North-east wind again. For the first time I doubt whether we shall make the whole stretch to McMurdo. Not like this! Arved thinks we ought to drop the original plan and only run to Gateway. This would also be an Antarctic crossing. I understand why he refuses to do more than five hours per day. If the wind continues to blast in our faces we have no chance one way or the other, but if it changes and gets stronger, we are rested so as to sail maxi-stages. Then we would have a chance still. A relative one at least. I only want to march to McMurdo! We must get on. It is terrible leg work pulling the sledges through the soft snow. Although I have run only four hours ('donkey'), ahead all the time, my thighs and hips are hurting! The clouds come and go.

14.1.90
−35°C
Pos.: 87°22.03′S
        161°09.11′E
673mb

After an unpleasant dispute in the morning (Arved: 'I'm not going more than four hours') we run for seven hours. At first 'penguin' with light south wind. After three hours we put up the tent and wait two hours for better wind. It

3,020m

is clear and the ground underfoot changes constantly (e.g. soft snow, sastrugi fields, half-hard wind-blown ground and expanses of ice). All the time too little wind. It has got extremely cold. The sun burns when there is no wind. If one is damp and touching metal there is a constant danger of frostbite.

15.1.90
−32°C
Pos.: 86°26.16′S
      164°32.57′E
695mb
2,780m

At last, a dream day. In the morning it is extremely cold, the tent totally iced-up (for the first time we slept with the inner door closed), but the wind is strong enough the whole time to pull us with our help (swinging the sail). Not until 'evening', in the last of the seven hours' run did it drop away. After the first four hours Arved is too tired to sail safely. I wait gladly. The ground underfoot varies: from smooth to sastrugi which run across our line of travel. We cross gigantic wave troughs. In the hollows, unfortunately, it is always dead calm. We both fall down and getting up is particularly difficult. Generally, it is only possible to get on one's feet after releasing sledge and skis.

16.1.90
−35°C
Pos.: 85°54.52′S
      166°10.51′E
710mb
2,610m

Stormy day. The whole night the wind whipped the walls of the tent with its snow plumes. I scarcely slept. Late start. We sail 'swallow'. Course 215°. The wind is so strong that we have to be very careful. We sail at an angle of 60° to the wind and are easily dragged along or overthrown. Once I trip badly over a sastrugi. After two hours we see the first mountains. They lie, shimmering blue, exactly in front of us. We sail towards them. Over waves, now with the mountains in sight, now again not, we advance quickly. After a further hour new mountains emerge and yet more. Where is the entrance to the Mill Glacier? Where are we! we need an exact fix before we go any further. We must not overshoot.

17.1.90
−28°C
Pos.: as yesterday
712mb
2,580m

Storm! The whole night the tent walls flapped. It crashes, sprays, howls. In the morning it is nearly impossible to open the tent flap, the snow-drift has it 'walled up'. Outside white-out. Not mist, but snow plumes so thick that we can see only a few metres and the storm prevents us continuing. We wait. In the 'even-ing' the wind comes in gusts. In front of the mountains is a wall of mist, only the summits are free. Our tent is completely iced-up and snow lies in the inner entrance. It is impossible to keep it dry. Perhaps we can set off 'at night'. No. Another day lost.

18.1.90
−25°C
Pos.: 85°25.02′S
168°19.47′E
771mb
2,000m

Hard but beautiful day. The most exciting so far. For about two hours we sail at an angle against the wind, climb high to a pass (naviga-tion: OK) and travel down to the Mill Glacier. All three types of locomotion ('donkey', 'pen-guin', 'swallow') come into use. It is a joy to see that, despite problems with his sail, Arved copes. The landscape is gigantic, dimensions (mountain ranges, desert, glaciers) which no one can imagine. And the knowledge that there is nobody anywhere gives to the whole an elevated mood. The wind is changeable so that we have to unfurl and take in sail at least ten times.

19.1.90
−25°C
Pos.: 85°10.15′S
167°29.74′E

Ice travelling. Beautiful, hard day. We march seven hours with instep crampons. Two short sailing attempts (sadly without success) over rough, bare ice. Many crevasses on the hump

801mb
1,800m

backs. The sledge is relatively easy to pull on the bare ice but our feet 'swim' and the ground is uphill, downhill. We camp between stone blocks at the edge of the glacier ice. Familiar surroundings for me. Less wind in 'evening'. We have tired bones and I (again) a dodgy left knee joint, evidence of youthful wear and tear.

20.1.90
−24°C
Pos.: 84°51.57′S
    168°06.09′E
820mb
1,580m

Hard and good day. The streaks in the sky come and go. Not much wind. We run five hours with crampons (Arved loses three spikes) and then sail a bit. A narrow, hard snow track (often crevasses, often bare ice) meanders between ice-falls. Our speed becomes alarmingly fast. No room here for mistakes. Tremendous views. Unfortunately, Arved hurts his left knee (the sail lifts him and he falls into a crevasse) and he follows on foot. Worried he may be hurt, after a long wait, I go back a fair way. Luckily he is OK. Thus we lose a lot of time. Camp between Mill and Beardmore glaciers. All around noisy crevasses. This running on bare ice is gruelling. Added to which my sledge (on account of the extra weight) is bust. (Cracks between base plate and belly.)

21.1.90
−15°C
Pos.: 84°44.08′S
    169°27.97′E
857mb
1,270m

Hardest and most dangerous day so far. For the most part we move between and over gigantic crevasses. We have to overcome an ice-fall which looks like the upper part of the Khumbu Glacier on Mt. Everest. Wind from north; mostly sunny. Arved running very well and shows instinct in dealing with the crevasses and no fear. I am enthusiastic. Swithinbank has described a 'pure' route for us. We run eight hours and clearly don't get far, going to and fro, up and down. Often snow lies between bare ice, often the crevasses are 10 and 20 metres wide; luckily, they all run in one direction. We find the way out between two giant-sized crevasses.

22.1.90
−16°C
Pos.: 84°30.01′S
    170°01.52′E
881mb
1,030m

North wind again. In the morning a thick cloud hangs on 'Cloudmaker' (a mountain) and soon the sun is overcast. Scarcely any cloud to the south. The cold and wind now come from the overcast shelf ice. Seven hours' march ('donkey'). The up and down is terrible. Also we go 2 miles to get 1 mile north. From above we have no view of the route. We try to reach the middle of the Beardmore Glacier by crossing side streams. Arved running well, although he has taken the bacon from me, so that my busted sledge will be lighter. We understand each other (without many words) very well.

23.1.90
−10°C
Pos.: 84°16.59′S
    170°19.34′E
904mb
830m

Strenuous and dangerous day. In the morning snowfall and mist. Wind again from north. We go two hours on skis, then three hours with crampons on bare ice and, finally, we torment ourselves for two hours across a wildly shattered ice-fall, which is marked on no map. We get stuck, go slowly back and at last get around it on the left. In part the crevasses are so big that one could put a church inside. Coming from above, these ice-falls are invisible, suddenly you're there and there's no way out. We are united in our vexation about the unexpected dangers.

24.1.90
−15°C
Pos.: 84°00.69′S

North wind! Bad day. We march on skis and with crampons. To begin with we have really good visibility; in the afternoon it shrinks to

170°29.39'E
922mb
650m

less than 50 metres. Navigation becomes hard work for me. The constantly changing ground (snow, ice, sastrugi, crevasses) is a grey mass. Time and again I step in holes. Running by compass means constantly overcoming gigantic ridges; without a compass we would now run round in circles in the mist. Will this ice never end? Where does the hard snow foundation begin? Ran seven hours. With detours, that is surely more than 30 kilometres. But how far have we actually come north in the direction of McMurdo?

25.1.90
−19°C
Pos.: 83°33.15'S
171°02.57'E
967mb
200m

Good weather. The sun is burning hot. In the morning we try to sail – unfortunately, all in vain. Then we march and sail ('penguin') three hours more in the evening. All in all, we are on our legs more than ten hours. We make it to just before Gateway. Twice one of my legs goes in a crevasse despite the skis. There are evil holes under a thin layer of snow. Now I have swellings on knees, backside and elbows and am always hungry. Already we are eating bacon rinds. No more rest stops. We must economize because, at our present speed, our rations will not be sufficient to reach the first station on the Ross Sea.

26.1.90
−9°C
Pos.: 83°29.73'S
170°56.15'E
977mb
230m

Rest day. Nevertheless we cross Gateway Pass. Arved runs ahead for the first time since 14 November. Bad visibility (sun and mist), wind from all directions. We climb at first and then run down towards the Ross Shelf Ice. We have tested, repaired, sorted all pieces of equipment. In twenty days we must be at McMurdo. At the moment everything has closed in and it is snowing on the surrounding mountains. The winds apparently have local characteristics. I expect little help from them for the time being. That the south wind should predominate here, I take to be a fairy-tale. Who measured it? It is warm. I sweat all the time: in my sleeping-bag, whilst running. Nevertheless, we are not icing up as we did on the plateau.

27.1.90
−15°C
Pos.: as yesterday
988mb
70m

Blizzard. We begin to cook at 2.30 a.m., because good wind rising. We want to get on. Bad visibility with overcast sky. At 4 a.m., when we want to leave the tent, snowstorm raging, which increases for twenty-four hours. In the gusts the tent almost rips and is pressed down. Arved goes outside twice to position the sledges as a wind shield and to fetch provisions. The storm almost overwhelms him. Hour after hour we support the tent walls from within. Later we place a sail on the inner south side of the tent so that it cushions the gusts of wind on the walls from inside. We hope and wait, read, doubt.

28.1.90
−5°C
Pos.: 83°20.78′S
170°39.55′E
988mb
80m

White-out and changeable, light wind. Snowing. It makes one despair! We march ('donkey') and in new storm (about 20 kilometres) make very slow progress. Breaking trail is strenuous for me. Twice we lose ourselves in massive drifts between the mountains and the Ross Shelf Ice. The ice walls are as big as the Great Wall of China. Arved determines our position and we wander around on the ice ridges. In a white-out you can never see whether a crevasse is coming. Once I found I was standing 20 centimetres in front of a crevasse with one of my skis cantilevered over the abyss. You can distinguish no horizon. Sky and ice surface look alike. How gladly I would swap places with Arved, *vis-à-vis* running ahead. We sweat and everything is wet. This journey is the trip of a lifetime. Too much or too little wind, too much or too little cold . . . warmth . . . visibility.

29.1.90
−6°C
Pos.: 83°06.11′S
    170°09.35′E
975mb
200m

Again no visibility, no wind. It comes variably from all directions (a little) only never from the south. It is too warm. New snow and at each step my skis break through to the underlying hard layer. We go just seven hours (many hollows) and must get on well tomorrow if no south wind comes. Our dawdling on the plateau after the Pole is taking its revenge. We have only two chances of getting through:

1.   Ration food and run four days more than planned.
2.   Go longer stages and put in no rest days.

Everything is wet, sleeping-bag too. Accordingly, tent life becomes uncomfortable.

30.1.90
−15°C
Pos.: 82°54.44′S
    169°55.84′E
967mb
70m

North wind! We run six hours in bad visibility against the wind which towards evening turns a little west. It is damp and cold and as all our clothes are clammy they freeze at once when we rest or stand still. A few times the clouds break briefly on the mountains, then again grey landscape, grey sky, a grey wall in front of you, into which you run. The weather is against us like the wind and time. Grimly, I plod on. Slowly our situation is becoming hopeless. A spark of hope for a southerly wind remains. By all the statistics there should be constant wind from the south here. Have we dragged the sails 1,000 kilometres for nothing?

31.1.90
−16°C
Pos.: 82°30.63′S
    169°18.89′E
974mb
Sea-level

First fine day for a long time. We get up at about 3.30 a.m. and are ready to start by 6.30 a.m. For a bit we can even use the sails ('penguin'). At midday it clears and the big mountain chain to the left of us is visible. Tremendous view. We run on for just eight hours. From today we want to alter our routine. Get up at 'midnight' and run until early 'after-noon'. We are hoping for south wind in the mornings. Now in the 'evening' we have north wind and the sky is again overcast. With our food we drink Eskimo wine (snow water) once more.

1.2.90
−16°C
Pos.: 82°13.04′S
    169°01.40′E
977mb
40m

Again no sailing wind! Often I look out of the tent 'nights'. North or north-east wind. I sleep only lightly, registering each breath of wind. Then – when moving – we have weak south wind. Too little to sail. So we march ('donkey') a good seven hours in the hope of doing 16 miles. The route to McMurdo is simple enough but still almost as far as Nansen's 1888 crossing of Greenland, and the snow is heavy. The sledges slow us down and in eighty days we have already covered almost 2,000 kilometres.

2.2.90
−12°C
Pos.: 81°55.67′S
    168°47.18′E
974mb
60m

It is a misery. Everything is damp, visibility bad and the wind variable from all directions. Our sailing hopes dwindle. It takes a lot to go stubbornly northwards all day – in front of you a grey wall of mist, behind you a sledge which gets heavier by the hour. It is as if one were going uphill. The surface here is flat as a board with gigantic slates, the sastrugi. At each step the snow crust gives way, gigantic snow slabs collapse. Despite all, we allow ourselves not a moment's rest. Always I march the full spell (one and a quarter hours) and wait for Arved.

3.2.90
−18°C
Pos.: 81°26.08′S
168°31.00′E
980mb
10m

Really good day. It is indeed mostly overcast and cold but wind (breeze) from south. We can't sail but the sail helps pull the sledges and thus we run at Langlauf pace ('penguin') northwards. We start early and run the whole day. Arved puts in a lot of effort. Far to the left of us the mountains appear as a silhouette. The clouds are like little holes. Now and then it snows lightly. The snow on the ground is like heaped-up hoar-frost. A deep track lies behind my sledge for Arved to follow. Three such days and we are saved! More and more I begin to think aloud, especially when moving. Arved hopes that in emergency (no wind) we can call out the Italian helicopter from McMurdo. For days I try to talk him out of it.

4.2.90
−21°C
Pos.: 81°08.61′S
168°13.46′E
982mb
Sea-level

Lovely, very cold day. Perhaps it is the damp air which makes the cold so cutting; more likely it is our lack of fat. We are now only skin and bone. The cold sets my teeth on edge. In both the first two hours' march I freeze terribly, run quicker to warm myself up. Then I dress myself more warmly. We run the whole day. North wind! Two aircraft fly almost exactly over us to and from the Pole. It takes more effort each day to do the spells exactly to the minute between rests – but if we once begin to deviate, it is all up, then we are trapped.

5.2.90
−12°C
Pos.: 80°52.27′S
168°08.11′E
980mb
20m

Again a strenuous day's running, again north wind, again grinding drudgery. I feel awful because I drive Arved relentlessly. We would not have to march such long stretches now had we done seven or eight hours per day earlier on. Signs of deterioration (body and equipment) appearing. We both have inflammation of tendon

310

sheaths and hunger, hunger, hunger. The almost 5,000 calories per day are now too little in our emaciated condition with 30–40 kilometres' each day; heavy snow as well. We eat all of the day's ration including bacon rinds. We must be at McMurdo by 15 March. Streaks from north and the mountains on the right are still visible. Vapour trails from the DC 130 direct us to McMurdo.

6.2.90
−15°C
Pos.: 80°35.87′S
⠀⠀⠀**168°08.74′E**
973mb
70m

North wind and hunger! The striae in the north remain unaltered the whole day. The mountains to the left are always recognizable as blue silhouettes, as if we were marking time. We run two hours (plus 4 × 1¼hours). When I think that we put in eighty paces a minute and each step causes pain in foot, knee, hip joints, shoulders, elbows, at 6,000 paces per spell (one and a quarter hours), that is too much pain to endure. If someone had forced me to go through this miserable drudgery to the end, I would have given up already. But we are doing it voluntarily and day by day determined to keep going.

7.2.90
−22°C
Pos.: 80°14.19′S
⠀⠀⠀**168°25.36′E**
971mb
90m

Again a long run more appropriate to dog sledging. In leading I make a deep track, like a grave in the soft snow. I am used to the compass, but it is still a burden. South-west wind. Too little wind for sailing. When running ('penguin'), it pulls me again and again to the right (wind direction). We mix the methods of locomotion and so get off course. Lightly overcast, the mountains are clear. The wind is very cold and as all our clothes are damp, we freeze more. Towards evening the wind increases. We hope it will increase further in the night and camp so as to be rested for the ideal wind. So I won't think about it: good sailing wind?

8.2.90
−23°C
Pos.: 79°57.88′S
168°26.23′E
967mb
120m

Miserable day. Only Scott had it worse at this stage. No visibility, it is as if you were stumbling over clouds. The wind is out of the southwest but so weak that the sail collapses time and again. We run with and without – the whole cold day. The sky is overcast, the air damp cold and our clothes iced up. Running ahead is tiring, although I am not vexed if Arved follows well. We develop a dry gallows humour and starve with composure. Arved is harder and tougher than I thought at the Pole and can drive himself to the point of exhaustion. We talk almost only now of McMurdo and the homeward journey. We never thought that this easy section would turn out to be the hardest.

9.2.90
−15°C
Pos.: 79°10.89′S
168°31.81′E
967mb
110m

South wind at last! After morning dead calm and bad visibility a strong wind picked up in the 'afternoon', which rose to storm by 'evening'. We run and sail 'penguin' and 'swallow' until our fingers and feet threaten to freeze. The ground is whipped up by the wind and time and again we travel over breakable crust. Dark clouds all around us. Feels thundery (like in Europe). Arved follows on my heels. We fix up the tent and listen to the storm which whistles and howls and sings. Now it is getting colder like on the plateau. Perhaps winter is coming already. In four days we could be at McMurdo. That would be more than lucky at the last minute.

10.2.90
−18°C

After a stormy night – I slept badly and lost my Xi-Stone (Tibetan barometer of the soul) – a

312

Pos.: 78°35.31′S
168°37.86′E
976mb
60m

clear day. In front of us the mountains: Minna Bluff, Mt Erebus with its smoke plume. Unfortunately, the wind comes from the south-west. We sail hard at an angle to the wind. Over ice slabs and patches of heavy snow we make good progress, but cannot hold the right course. Nevertheless, we are saved! All vexation is forgotten. We are a good team when there is no pressure. We put up our camp early and tear into our reserve rations which we have kept for 16 February and later. In three days we shall be safely at McMurdo. Therefore the days of hunger are past and already forgotten. It's amusing.

11.2.90
−15°C
Pos.: 78°15.19′S
167°02.12′E
980mb
30m

Exciting day. After two hours' weak sailing wind we travel (with reduced power) in miserable visibility through an ice-fall. Then we run once more for two hours through a dried-up glacier sump and after a further two and a half hours reach the deep saddle between Black and White Island. Unfortunately, not quite. We have let ourselves be diverted by the morning wind into this longer route and are running rather in zigzags. Now we are here and resign ourselves to the cold, to the wind (now from the north) and to our fate. At least we can eat, eat, eat. We both know that we have made it. Arved is full of the joy of living and I am grateful to him for everything I have learned from him: fixing our position, putting together provisions, relaxing in the tent. Later on he will forgive me for driving him on so often.

12.2.90
−9°C
Pos.: 77°51.00′S

North wind. We start late, cross the pass between Black and White Island and march two hours across the ice slabs in the direction of

166°45.00′E
984mb
20m

McMurdo. Everything is OK (timetable, route). At the latest we shall be at McMurdo by evening. We struggle on towards Willies Field. Now a tracked vehicle is coming in our direction – New Zealanders going to Black Island. They tell us that we are guests in Scott Base and that letters are waiting there. They notify their New Zealand station (Scott Base) over the radio. We run on three hours and meet another New Zealand vehicle that catches up with us an hour from the base. We film, photograph and finally travel over a metalled road to Scott Base, where we are enthusiastically received and taken in. We have arrived!

IV   The Antarctic Treaty of 1 December 1959

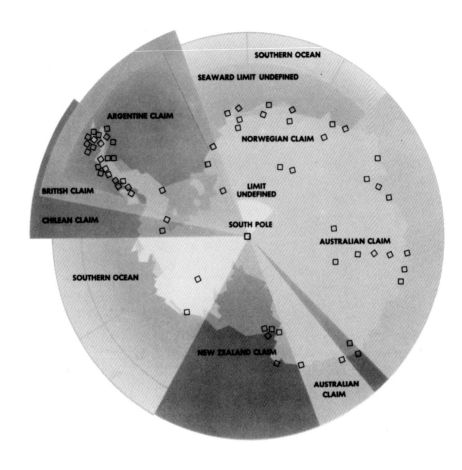

SOUTHERN OCEAN

SEAWARD LIMIT UNDEFINED

ARGENTINE CLAIM

NORWEGIAN CLAIM

BRITISH CLAIM

LIMIT
UNDEFINED

CHILEAN CLAIM

SOUTH POLE

SOUTHERN OCEAN

AUSTRALIAN CLAIM

NEW ZEALAND CLAIM

AUSTRALIAN
CLAIM

Seven nations (Argentina, Chile, France, Great Britain, Norway, Australia and New Zealand) claim territory in Antarctica. A danger for the 'World Park'.

316

The Governments of Argentina, Australia, Belgium, Chile, the French Republic, Japan, New Zealand, Norway, the Republic of South Africa, the Union of Soviet Socialist Republics, the United Kingdom of Great Britain and Northern Ireland, and the United States of America,

Recognizing that it is in the interest of all mankind that Antarctica shall continue forever to be used exclusively for peaceful purposes and shall not become the scene or object of international discord;

Acknowledging the substantial contributions to scientific knowledge resulting from international co-operation in scientific investigation in Antarctica;

Convinced that the establishment of a firm foundation for the continuation and development of such co-operation on the basis of freedom of scientific investigation in Antarctica as applied during the International Geophysical Year accords with the interests of science and the progress of all mankind;

Convinced also that a treaty ensuring the use of Antarctica for peaceful purposes only and the continuance of international harmony in Antarctica will further the purposes and principles embodied in the Charter of the United Nations; have agreed as follows:

Article I

1. Antarctica shall be used for peaceful purposes only. There shall be prohibited, *inter alia*, any measure of a military nature, such as the establishment of military bases and fortifications, the carrying out of military manoeuvres, as well as the testing of any type of weapon.
2. The present Treaty shall not prevent the use of military personnel or equipment for scientific research or for any other peaceful purpose.

Article II

Freedom of scientific investigation in Antarctica and co-operation toward that end, as applied during the International Geophysical Year, shall continue, subject to the provisions of the present Treaty.

Penguin colony on the ice; a drawing by Dr Wilson. Wilson, who had already accompanied Scott on his first Antarctic expedition, was also a vertebrate zoologist.

Article III

1. In order to promote international co-operation in scientific investigation in Antarctica, as provided for in Article II of the present Treaty, the Contracting Parties agree that, to the greatest extent feasible and practicable:

(a)   information regarding plans for scientific programmes in Antarctica shall be exchanged to permit maximum economy of and efficiency of operations;

(b)   scientific personnel shall be exchanged in Antarctica between expeditions and stations;

(c)   scientific observations and results from Antarctica shall be exchanged and made freely available.

2. In implementing this Article, every encouragement shall be given to the establishment of co-operative working relations with those Specialized Agencies of the United Nations and other international organizations having a scientific or technical interest in Antarctica.

Article IV

1.   Nothing contained in the present Treaty shall be interpreted as:

(a)   a renunciation by any Contracting Party of previously asserted rights of or claims to territorial sovereignty in Antarctica;

(b)   a renunciation or diminution by any Contracting Party of any basis of claim to territorial sovereignty in Antarctica which it may have whether as a result of its activities or those of its nationals in Antarctica, or otherwise;

(c)   prejudicing the position of the Contracting Party as regards its recognition or non-recognition of any other State's rights of or claim or basis of claim to territorial sovereignty in Antarctica.

2.   No acts or activities taking place while the present Treaty is in force shall constitute a basis for asserting, supporting or denying a claim to territorial sovereignty in Antarctica or create any rights of sovereignty in Antarctica. No new claim, or enlargement of an existing claim, to territorial sovereignty in Antarctica shall be asserted while the present Treaty is in force.

319

Article V

1. Any nuclear explosions in Antarctica and the disposal there of radioactive waste material shall be prohibited.

2. In the event of the conclusion of international agreements concerning the use of nuclear energy, including nuclear explosions and the disposal of radioactive waste material, to which all of the Contracting Parties whose representatives are entitled to participate in the meetings provided for under Article IX are parties, the rules established under such agreements shall apply in Antarctica.

Article VI

The provisions of the present Treaty shall apply to the area south of 60° South Latitude, including all ice shelves, but nothing in the present Treaty shall prejudice or in any way affect the rights, or the exercise of the rights, of any State under international law with regard to the high seas within that area.

Article VII

1. In order to promote the objectives and ensure the observance of the provisions of the present Treaty, each Contracting Party whose representatives are entitled to participate in the meetings referred to in Article IX of the Treaty shall have the right to designate observers to carry out any inspection provided for by the present Article. Observers shall be nationals of the Contracting Parties which designate them. The names of observers shall be communicated to every other Contracting Party having the right to designate observers, and like notice shall be given of the termination of their appointment.

2. Each observer designated in accordance with the provisions of paragraph 1 of this Article shall have complete freedom of access at any time to any or all areas of Antarctica.

3. All areas of Antarctica, including all stations, installations and equipment within those areas, and all ships and aircraft at points of

discharging or embarking cargoes or personnel in Antarctica, shall be open at all times to inspection by any observers designated in accordance with paragraph 1 of this Article.

4. Aerial observation may be carried out at any time over any or all areas of Antarctica by any of the Contracting Parties having the right to designate observers.

5. Each Contracting Party shall, at the time when the present Treaty enters into force for it, inform the other Contracting Parties, and thereafter shall give them notice in advance, of

(a) all expeditions to and within Antarctica, on the part of its ships or nationals, and all expeditions to Antarctica organized in or proceeding from its territory;

(b) all stations in Antarctica occupied by its nationals; and

(c) any military personnel or equipment intended to be introduced by it into Antarctica subject to the conditions prescribed in paragraph 2 of Article 1 of the present Treaty.

Article VIII

1. In order to facilitate the exercise of their functions under the present Treaty, and without prejudice to the respective positions of the Contracting Parties relating to jurisdiction over all other persons in Antarctica, observers designated under paragraph 1 of Article VII and scientific personnel exchanged under sub-paragraph 1(b) of Article III of the Treaty, and members of the staffs accompanying any such persons, shall be subject only to the jurisdiction of the Contracting Party of which they are nationals in respect of all acts or omissions occurring while they are in Antarctica for the purpose of exercising their functions.

2. Without prejudice to the provisions of paragraph 1 of this Article, and pending the adoption of measures in pursuance of sub-paragraph 1(e) of Article IX, the Contracting Parties concerned in any case of dispute with regard to the exercise of jurisdiction in Antarctica shall immediately consult together with a view to reaching a mutually acceptable solution.

Article IX

1.   Representatives of the Contracting Parties named in the preamble to the present Treaty shall meet at the City of Canberra within two months after the date of entry into force of the Treaty, and thereafter at suitable intervals and places, for the purpose of exchanging information, consulting together on matters of common interest pertaining to Antarctica, and formulating and considering, and recommending to their Governments, measures in furtherance of the principles and objectives of the Treaty, including measures regarding:
(a)   use of Antarctica for peaceful purposes only;
(b)   facilitation of scientific research in Antarctica;
(c)   facilitation of international scientific co-operation in Antarctica;
(d)   facilitation of the exercise of the rights of inspection provided for in Article VII of the Treaty;
(e)   questions relating to the exercise of jurisdiction in Antarctica;
(f)   preservation and conservation of living resources in Antarctica.
2.   Each Contracting Party which has become a party to the present Treaty by accession under Article XIII shall be entitled to appoint representatives to participate in the meetings referred to in paragraph 1 of the present Article, during such times as that Contracting Party demonstrates its interest in Antarctica by conducting substantial scientific research activity there, such as the establishment of a scientific station or the despatch of a scientific expedition.
3.   Reports from the observers referred to in Article VII of the present Treaty shall be transmitted to the representatives of the Contracting Parties participating in the meetings referred to in paragraph 1 of the present Article.
4.   The measures referred to in paragraph 1 of this Article shall become effective when approved by all the Contracting Parties whose representatives were entitled to participate in the meetings held to consider those measures.
5.   Any or all of the rights established in the present Treaty may be exercised as from the date of entry into force of the Treaty whether or not any measures facilitating the exercise of such rights have been proposed, considered or approved as provided in this Article.

Article X

Each of the Contracting Parties undertakes to exert appropriate efforts, consistent with the Charter of the United Nations, to the end that no one engages in any activity in Antarctica contrary to the principles or purposes of the present Treaty.

Article XI

1. If any dispute arises between two or more of the Contracting Parties concerning the interpretation or application of the present Treaty, those Contracting Parties shall consult among themselves with a view to having the dispute resolved by negotiation, inquiry, mediation, conciliation, arbitration, judicial settlement or other peaceful means of their own choice.

2. Any dispute of this character not so resolved shall, with the consent, in each case, of all parties to the dispute, be referred to the International Court of Justice for settlement; but failure to reach agreement on reference to the International Court shall not absolve parties to the dispute from the responsibility of continuing to seek to resolve it by any of the various peaceful means referred to in paragraph 1 of this Article.

Article XII

1(a)   The present Treaty may be modified or amended at any time by unanimous agreement of the Contracting Parties whose representatives are entitled to participate in the meetings provided for under Article IX. Any such modification or amendment shall enter into force when the depositary Government has received notice from all such Contracting Parties that they have ratified it.

(b)   Such modification or amendment shall thereafter enter into force as to any other Contracting Party when notice of ratification by it has been received by the depositary Government. Any such Contracting Party from which no notice of ratification is received within a period of two years from the date of entry into force of the modification or amendment in accordance with the provision of sub-paragraph 1(a) of the Article shall be deemed to have withdrawn from the present Treaty on the date of expiration of such period.

2(a) If after the expiration of 30 years from the date of entry into force of the present Treaty, any of the Contracting Parties whose representatives are entitled to participate in the meetings provided for under Article IX so requests by a communication addressed to the depositary Government, a Conference of all the Contracting Parties shall be held as soon as practicable to review the operation of the Treaty.

(b) Any modification or amendment to the present Treaty which is approved at such a Conference by a majority of the Contracting Parties there represented, including a majority of those whose representatives are entitled to participate in the meetings provided for under Article IX, shall be communicated by the depositary Government to all Contracting Parties immediately after the termination of the Conference and shall enter into force in accordance with the provisions of paragraph 1 of the present Article.

(c) If any such modification or amendment has not entered into force in accordance with the provisions of sub-paragraph 1(a) of this Article within a period of two years after the date of its communication to all the Contracting Parties, any Contracting Party may at any time after the expiration of that period give notice to the depositary Government of its withdrawal from the present Treaty; and such withdrawal shall take effect two years after the receipt of the notice by the depositary Government.

Article XIII

1. The present Treaty shall be subject to ratification by the signatory States. It shall be open for accession by any State which is a Member of the United Nations, or by any other State which may be invited to accede to the Treaty with the consent of all the Contracting Parties whose representatives are entitled to participate in the meetings provided for under Article IX of the Treaty.

2. Ratification of or accession to the present Treaty shall be effected by each State in accordance with its constitutional processes.

3. Instruments of ratification and instruments of accession shall be deposited with the Government of the United States of America, hereby designated as the depositary Government.

4. The depositary Government shall inform all signatory and acceding States of the date of each deposit of an instrument of ratification or accession, and the date of entry into force of the Treaty and of any modification or amendment thereto.

5. Upon the deposit of instruments of ratification by all the signatory States, the present Treaty shall enter into force for those States and for States which deposited instruments of accession. Thereafter the Treaty shall enter into force for any acceding State upon the deposit of its instruments of accession.

6. The present Treaty, done in the English, French, Russian and Spanish languages, each version being equally authentic, shall be deposited in the archives of the Government of the United States of America, which shall transmit duly certified copies thereof to the Governments of the signatory and acceding States.

Member States of the Antarctic Treaty

+ United Kingdom	31.5.60		
+ Republic of South Africa	21.6.60		
+ Belgium	26.7.60		
+ Japan	4.8.60		
+ United States of America	18.8.60		
+ Norway	24.8.60		
+ France	16.9.60		
+ New Zealand	1.11.60		
+ USSR	2.11.60		
+ Poland	8.8.61	(29.7.77)	
+ Argentina	23.6.61		
+ Australia	23.6.61		
+ Chile	23.6.61		
Czechoslovakia	14.6.62		
Denmark	20.5.65		
Netherlands	30.3.67		
Rumania	15.9.71		
+ East Germany	19.11.74	(5.10.87)	⌐
+ Brazil	16.5.75		
Bulgaria	11.9.78		(now united as one nation)
+ West Germany	5.2.79	(3.3.81)	⌐
+ Uruguay	11.1.80	(7.10.85)	
Papua-New Guinea	16.3.81		
+ Italy	18.3.81	(5.10.87)	
Peru	10.4.81		
Spain	31.3.82		
+ People's Republic of China	8.6.83	(7.10.85)	
+ India	19.8.83	(12.9.83)	
Hungary	27.1.84		
Sweden	24.4.84		
Finland	15.5.84		
Cuba	16.8.84		
South Korea	28.11.86		
Greece	8.1.87		
North Korea	21.1.87		

| Austria | 25.8.87 |
| Ecuador | 15.9.87 |

The first twelve named States are the original signatories to the Treaty; the dates signify date of ratification.

+ Consultative States. To the original signatories eight more have been added. The dates in parentheses indicate when these States received consultative status.

Papua-New Guinea acceded to the Treaty as the first Asiatic Developing Country when it became independent of Australia.

V World Park Antarctica

Pack ice. In the Antarctic winter, icebergs, floes and snow freeze into a single girdle of pack ice. Tremendous pressure develops through ice compression.

Antarctica – the 'last' continent – is in danger. After 200 years' research the parcelling out and exploitation of mineral wealth on the ice continent is to begin.

When in 1773 the seafarer James Cook crossed the southern polar circle with his ship – on course for the legendary southern land 'Terra Australis Incognita' – he was disappointed. There was nothing to be gained 'down under'. In his famous words, 'I have never seen so much ice', are summarized the results of his explorations.

The glacier continent comprises 12.4 million square kilometres, and millions upon millions of floes and icebergs surround it winter and summer. In the Antarctic winter the girdle of pack ice solidifies in a surface of around 20 million square kilometres. The concept of mainland becomes relative in the Antarctic.

(Previous page)   The penguin is the symbol of Antarctica. It resembles a gentleman in evening dress. It should be treated with corresponding respect.

On the true land called Antarctica lies the greatest ice mass in the world. The armour is up to 4,500 metres thick. Its weight: 27 thousand billion tons. Over millions of years, this weight has caused the continent to sink by 800 metres. Under the pressure of the ice the earth's crust has been depressed.

The ice cap is a single, mighty glacier, with over 100,000 years' accumulation of compressed snow. It is in constant motion, flowing at a speed of up to 2.5 kilometres per year towards the coast. There it crashes in skyscraper-sized pieces into the sea. Blizzards, with top speeds of 200 kilometres per hour, rage across the interior. Lowest temperature recorded: minus 89.2°C. Winter in the Antarctic is as cold as in the corresponding regions of the north, the summer considerably colder. The average annual temperature at the South Pole is less than −50°C.; south of 60° latitude it is below freezing point. Only 2 per cent of Antarctica is free of ice.

After the first man had set foot in Antarctica in 1895, there began the 'heroic phase' of South Pole exploration. With ponies, huskies, later with motorized sledges, armoured vehicles and aircraft, the 'conquerors' penetrated into the until then greatest undisturbed biotope on earth.

Roald Amundsen reached the South Pole on 14 December 1911, a month before Robert F. Scott. Full of satisfaction, he hoisted the Norwegian flag there. Man had wiped out the last 'white spot on the world map'. Amundsen found neither animals nor plants in the interior of the land.

On the mainland there is not one mammal. A region that is bigger than Australia and which has at least the same surface area as Europe and the USA put together, accommodates today not a single higher species of animal. Antarctica's few mammals all live in the water. In the sea it is 'warm', yet 'warm' in the Antarctic is a relative term. A hardened man would survive only a very brief bathe. But when a seal glides from the ice into the water, it must experience approximately the same as we do when we go into the sauna.

Arved Fuchs and I did not see a single animal on our 2,800-kilometre journey across the interior of the ice continent; not even a glacier flea.

The combination of cold and strong wind on the ice is extremely

Seals sunbathing. At the edge of the mainland, where the ice is thin, seals, sea lions and sea leopards have their bathing spots.

unfavourable to the development of organic life, added to which is the negligible humidity and, in winter, the lack of sunlight.

Only an umbellate plant, a variety of pink and a sort of grass withstand the extreme climate of the Antarctic. Here and there moss and lichen grow exuberantly on rocks.

The water, on the other hand, is rich in life, with big fish stocks and swarms of mini-crayfish called krill which flow around the coastal waters in massive shoals. Krill makes up the basic diet of the Blue and Fin whales which filter the little rose-coloured crayfish out of the waters by the ton.

The most famous inhabitant of Antarctica, its animal symbol, is the penguin. Millions of them nest on the coasts. These flightless birds live in colonies of tens of thousands, and for thousands of years have nested at the same spot on the edge of the water. Protozoons, mites, springtails (*Colembolan*) belong to the Antarctic fauna; and of course seals which sun themselves in groups on the ice.

For the last thirty years man has lived there constantly. Altogether

332

McMurdo is the biggest base in Antarctica: a small, dreary town on Ross Island at the edge of the ice continent.

he has constructed seventy research stations on the white continent. The biggest research base (USA) is located at McMurdo on the edge of the Ross Shelf Ice. In the summer some 1,500 people live there.

The interest of Antarctic researchers, apart from their scientific work, is in the rich oil and mineral wealth which they find under the gigantic covering of ice. How much fossil fuel lies in the ground, no one knows but since it has been established that Antarctica broke away from the super-continent Gondwana 200 million years ago, researchers conclude that raw materials similar to those known in South Africa will be forthcoming.

Mining of raw materials by the industrialized nations is impossible for the time being because of the 1959 Antarctic Treaty. Some of the nineteen Consultative States now want to obtain free access to the raw material deposits. The Treaty is due for renegotiation in 1991.

To guard against the danger of large-scale environmental damage through mining and oil shipment, Greenpeace and other organizations have created and propagated the 'World Park' concept.

During the Second World Conference on National Parks, held in 1972 in Yellowstone National Park in the USA, the first serious proposal for World Park status for Antarctica was developed. In a resolution, 'the great scientific and aesthetic value of the unspoiled natural ecosystem of Antarctica' was emphasized and all signatories to the Antarctic Treaty were requested 'to enter into negotiations with the aim of proclaiming the Antarctic continent and the surrounding oceans as the first World Park under the auspices of the United Nations Organization'.

Already, within the frame of the 1959 Antarctic Treaty, people were at one in their desire to protect 'for all time' the world's natural biotope. In 1972, in the context of the Convention for the Protection of the World's Cultural and Natural Heritage, it was pointed out that the Antarctic as a region is, on the whole, of priceless value to humanity:

> To be protected, a place must represent an important step in world history; it must represent a fundamental currently wasting geological process or a biologically evolutionary process, or the interaction of man with the natural environment; it must embrace exceptional natural phenomena or geological formations or regions of unusual natural beauty; it must concern a region with important natural biotopes, in which threatened animals and plants of exceptional universal worth survive.

As the excellent Greenpeace book about the Antarctic demonstrates, Antarctica fulfils all these conditions. Many scientists, nature lovers and adventurers who know Antarctica subscribe today to the 'World Park' idea. So also do 'Trans-Antarctica' and the two of us who traversed the continent in the 1989–90 Antarctic summer, at the same time and by different routes. We are now as before in contact with one another so as to give our requests more weight.

The reconnaissance and exploitation of mineral wealth must be prohibited because otherwise the original wilderness of the Antarctic landscape will be lost. The transport of raw materials through the pack ice girdle of the Antarctic is so risky that it cannot be justified. Water, climate and all life would be thereby extremely endangered, as the *Exxon-Valdez* disaster in Alaska has demonstrated recently.

'Trans-Antarctica' and we have experienced a wild, white continent. Through our pictures and reports, many people have gained an insight into a landscape which is worth preserving. We did not want to recruit for tourism in the Antarctic and are united in our view that such should be allowed only under careful control.

This is expressed in our mutual congratulations:

To Trans-Antartica, congratulations! All our respect for completing one of the Great Polar Journeys of all time. Let's now fight together for World Park Antarctica. Safe journey home. Polarcross.
Arved Fuchs.   Reinhold Messner

Reinhold & Arved.
Congratulations on your successful completion of your expedition! Sounds like you had a very interesting time. I am looking forward to hearing about it in more detail. I would like to talk with you about a few items that concern us both.
Trans-Antarctica.

A World Park Antarctica concept must take into consideration that:

1.   Antarctica must not be divided up politically. It belongs to the whole of mankind. Enshrined territorial claims are not acceptable.
2.   Antarctica must remain free of weapons and military installations. There must be no sort of nuclear activities.
3.   All mining of raw materials must be prohibited.
4.   Scientific research work is to be carried out only in a restricted co-operative and co-ordinated way amongst all the scientific stations in the Antarctic.
5.   Any form of tourism which relies on machines is to be prohibited.

335

The US station at the South Pole. A Hercules aircraft in the air. The Antarctic is an ideal place for scientific work. Certain observations are possible only there.

6. No sort of rubbish may be buried in the Antarctic or remain there.

There must now be developed mechanisms for carrying through such provisions. Also in future there must be an international court of control which ensures that the provisions of the Antarctic Treaty are complied with. Hitherto only Greenpeace was on the spot for the protection of the Antarctic environment. In future, not only must independent courts examine the ecological damage caused by scientific and logistical actions, but also the supervision of fishing must be regulated.

New Zealand, Australia, France and Italy (especially President Andreotti) support the World Park concept. Personalities like Jean-Jacques Cousteau, Jean-Louis Etienne and Will Steger have, by their actions, acquainted sections of the population with the problems of division and exploitation of Antarctica. The process of enlightenment has just begun. When documentary film-makers like the Grimme

Dr Edward Wilson's drawings have enthralled many people with the beauty of Antarctica, and contribute to its protection.

prizewinner Axel Engstfeld intercede for a World Park Antarctica, they can do a great deal to alter people's consciousness:

> For me, Antarctica has a powerful symbolic character concerning the conflict of mineral wealth *vis-à-vis* a stable ecosystem. It is really the last place on this planet that is not colonized, the last place that does not belong to any nation and that is not divided up. And for me the question is this: is man in a position to accept that and perhaps so to leave a piece of land on this planet, or must man walk off with that too? Fundamentally, what has happened in other lands is repeating itself exactly: discovery, conquest, plundering. It is an icy mirror of our understanding of the world.

Protection of the Antarctic is, nevertheless, only possible if we restrict our wanderlust. The same applies to the Arctic. A recent offer of a polar trip, announced in all the newspapers, is like a blow in the face

337

for every nature lover. It costs not only a lot of money, it costs so much in polar wilderness that nobody can justify it to us.

Luxury Cruise to North Pole
Departing Hamburg. For the first time, in August, western tourists can participate in a trip to the North Pole with the biggest ice-breaker in the world, the Soviet *Rossja*. As a spokesman of the Polar Shipping-Consulting GmbH in Hamburg-Wedel intimated on Monday, the 75,000hp atomic ship offers, along with Soviet scientists, around sixty passenger places for a fortnight's luxury cruise. Included in the fare of DM35,000 per person, is a barbecue party with salmon, caviar and vodka actually at the Pole.'

Despite all the criticism of our Antarctic crossing, I venture to hope that potential followers will be ready to take upon themselves the same restrictions that Arved Fuchs and I took upon ourselves. So as not to disturb the white wilderness of Antarctica, we went on foot. Our journey on the ice was not planned as a protest march – it developed along the way into a 'propaganda spot' for the World Park idea. Our pictures prove that the Antarctic is unendingly beautiful and on that account worthy of protection.

VI Ralf-Peter Märtin/ Reinhold Messner Chronicle of Antarctic Expeditions

'Who can bear everything can risk everything.'
Vauvenargues

350 BC   It was the Greeks who 'invented' Antarctica, thereby enabling it to be discovered almost 2,000 years later. Everything in the world, so taught the Greek philosopher Aristotle (384–322 B.C.), has somewhere its equivalent, as if ordained by a law of symmetry. As there was in the north of their imaginary sphere-shaped world, under the starry picture of the Bear (Gr. *arktos*), a cold zone, the Arctic, there must likewise be a correspondingly cold zone on the southern half of the sphere. The ancient geographers took up the model and developed five climatic zones. Cold ones in the north and south, adjacent to that temperate zones, which again were separated from one another by a hot one. But only the temperate latitudes were habitable. In the northern hemisphere this meant the area between the Baltic Sea in the north and the Sahara Desert in the south.

AD 100   Claudius Ptolemaeus (*c.* 100–161), the most famous exponent of ancient geography, added two substantial amendments to this model. In his writings he maintained that the southern latitudes would be fruitful and richly populated, but nevertheless separated from the northern hemisphere by a hot girdle of fire. Both additions increased the ambition to search for the unknown southland: the key to the riches was courage.

   In the Christian Middle Ages this blueprint was not developed further. Mostly, people believed that the world was a flat disc. Theologically, the existence of people in the inaccessible southern

Scott Statue in Christchurch, New Zealand. I didn't want to shake the Scott image with my expedition; I wanted to learn to comprehend and judge his historical Antarctic adventures.

341

hemisphere was also not justified, for how could these have descended from Adam and Eve and thus be God's creation.

Not until the fifteenth century, when the age of discovery dawned, did men reconsider Ptolemaeus. The Portugese voyagers did not only want to find India, as they slowly groped their way southwards down along the African coast, but also the 'Terra Australis Incognita', the unknown southland.

1497　To begin with everything seemed to agree with Ptolemaeus. The tropical heat equated well with his girdle of fire. But Africa was not a new continent separated from the northern hemisphere. Vasco da Gama proved that as he sailed round the Cape of Good Hope in 1497 and actually found the sea route to India.

1519　Interest now turned to South America, whose eastern coast the Spanish explored. In 1519 Magellan discovered the strait later named after him, the through way to the Pacific, and reported that he had sighted mountains with many fires in an unknown land in the south, which he named Tierra del Fuego. Was this the northern tip of the undiscovered Terra Australis? At about the same time the French seafarer Paulmyer de Gonneville returned to the little northern French harbour Honfleur. He reported miraculous things. True stories? On the voyage to America he had been driven ever further southwards by a mighty storm. At last he had reached the coast of an unknown land. For him this was without doubt the sought-after Terra Australis. For six months he had dwelt in this country. Loudly he proclaimed he had found Eden, a paradise, in which people lived in contentment and did not need to work. As proof he produced furs of unknown type, pigments and plumes. The effect of his report was enormous. It lasted for over two centuries. The hope of material gain, of gold, drove on ever more new expeditions. Amundsen expresses this frankly, almost cynically, when he says: 'Power hungry rulers hoped to enlarge their possessions. Men, who struggled for fortune, dreamed of fantastic quantities of the alluring metal.' Time and again French expeditions attempted to verify Gonneville's report. In vain.

1578　Finally, the English queen Elizabeth I was induced to send her admiral Sir Francis Drake on the search. Drake reached Tierra del Fuego, set course southwards and ascertained that, south of Cape Horn, Atlantic and Pacific flowed into one another. Here too Terra Australis was not to be found.

1769/70 Almost two centuries passed until the British Captain James Cook appeared to be successful at last. On his first voyage to the Pacific he had discovered New Zealand in 1769 and Australia in 1770. Was thereby the question revealed, the legendary southern continent located? The British Admiralty wanted an answer. Once and for all. Again they commissioned Cook. He was to search systematically the stretches of the South Atlantic and South Pacific. The captain knew what awaited him in this region, the 'Roaring Forties'. Powerful westerly winds blow there. Carefully Cook fitted out his ships *Resolution* and *Adventure*. This voyage was to last more than three years.

1773/75 In the three Antarctic summers 1773, 1774 and 1775 Cook circumnavigated the last unknown continent of the world. He was the first to cross the southern polar circle and sail along the border of the pack ice. Despite intensive search he found no through channel. His ships (the *Resolution* about 30 metres long, the *Adventure* even less) time and again found themselves amongst icebergs. In gigantic fields of drifting ice, captain and crew experienced the most dangerous situations. Cook was an excellent navigator. Also, he had spent a long time preparing the expedition. He led it excellently and lost only four men.

The practical outcome of these two journeys was meagre, however. Cook announced to the Admiralty that there was no further continent in the southern oceans. He did not exclude, however, the possibility that an ice continent stretched around the South Pole. If this were true, the land were inaccessible and worthless on account of the ice. This view held for 120 years.

1819 The 1,200-kilometre peninsula develops like a finger. This part of the continent reaches furthest in the direction of South America to the north. From its tip to Cape Horn the distance is only

1,200 kilometres. In 1819 the British merchant ship *Williams* was driven so far south when rounding Cape Horn, that her captain, William Smith, believed he had sighted land.

1820 This claim had to be investigated and in 1820 the British brig *Andromache*, with Smith on board was sent to the South. He sighted land as before. Nevertheless today he has to share the fame with Captain N.B. Palmer (USA) and with Baron von Bellingshausen (USSR), who saw the Antarctic peninsula through their telescopes at the same time. Although it remains debatable who was the first man to see the continent, all three are today immortalized in Antarctica – in the form of geographical designations.

It was clear, at any rate, that the Antarctic was totally an ice continent. The dream of a fruitful southland was ultimately destroyed. The land down there, whether a single continent or an ice covered group of islands, was inaccessible, extremely cold, hostile to life and uninhabited. From then on, only one group of people was to interest itself in Antarctica – whalers and seal hunters. They had wreaked so much havoc amongst the animal population of the northern hemisphere that they urgently needed fresh fields. From now on the explorers took a back seat.

1824 One of these whalers, James Weddell, an excellent captain, who kept his crew in good humour with three glasses of rum a day, broke through the girdle of pack ice in 1824 and found open water behind it. By great good fortune he had sailed south during one of the warmest Antarctic summers. He discovered the sea today named after him and reached the most southerly point on earth to date.

1838/42 The years 1838–42 saw the first American Antarctic expedition under Charles Wilkes on its way south. It was not to be particularly successful, Wilkes losing four of his six ships. He sighted the eponymous Wilkes Land.

1839/43 The British advanced more professionally, fitting out two ice ships, *Erebus* and *Terror*. Specialists provided them with double decks and stern walls. The external planks were shod with copper and the interior was divided up by watertight bulkheads. The commodore was James Ross, an experienced Arctic captain. He knew his way about in ice and in 1831 had discovered the magnetic North Pole. Now he was to find the magnetic South Pole, the approximate position of which the German mathematician Gauss had already calculated.

Ross navigated his way along the limit of the pack ice. Then he found a through passage and sailed into an enormous bay which is called Ross Sea after him. The British reached the Antarctic mainland at Cape Adare. On trying to push further south, a gigantic wall of ice over 50 metres high barred the way. Ross had come up against the biggest shelf ice-field in the world, known today as Ross Shelf Ice. It is a drift ice-pack as big as France and Belgium combined and it lies further south than the Weddell Sea. Further penetration was, on account of the drift ice, impossible. However, the thirst for knowledge was for the time being quenched: the whalers picked up rich harvests.

1895   At the end of the nineteenth century, interest in Antarctica took up again. A young generation of explorers set about the last white patches on the map of the world. Everything unknown was to be conquered. The spirit of the industrial age could brook no *terra incognita*.

On 24 January 1895, modern man set foot on the soil of Antarctica for the first time, i.e. the Norwegian Carsten Borchgrevink (1864–1934). Whether South American Indians had been there already remains controversial: arrow heads found later on the peninsula would suggest this.

1898   In 1898 a ship overwintered in the Antarctic for the first time. Her captain, Adrien de Gerlache, was Belgian and his ship was called *Belgica*. The expedition set out much too late and was badly equipped. Probably the *Belgica* became involuntarily trapped in the pack ice of the Bellingshausen Sea. From 2 March 1898 to 14 March 1899 the ship drifted with the pack ice. Anxiety, panic and illnesses spread. That ship and crew survived the Antarctic winter, the expedition had to thank two of the members: Frederick Cook and Roald Amundsen.

Both were yet to cause a stir. The American ship's doctor, Dr Cook, later was to claim, against Robert Peary, to be the first to have reached the North Pole (1908). The Norwegian, Roald Amundsen, chief petty officer on the *Belgica* and a pupil of Fridtjof Nansen, was at twenty-six already an experienced adventurer and was to become the most successful ice traveller of all time.

1899   What the *Belgica* had been obliged to suffer, Borchgrevink voluntarily took on a year later, his expedition deliberately overwintering in the Antarctic. This was an experiment that brought important findings. Subsequently, Borchgrevink travelled with dog sledges over the Ross Shelf Ice to the Murray Glacier. Two Finns cared for the dogs which had been introduced into Antarctica as draught animals for the first time. They reached latitude 78°50' south, the most southerly point man had yet achieved.

1902/04   Three scientific expeditions followed in the next few years. From 1902 to 1904 a German expedition, under the leadership of Erich von Drygalski, explored the Atlantic coastline of Antarctica (Kaiser Wilhelm II Land): a Swedish one, under Otto Nordenskjöld, devoted itself to the Antarctic peninsula: and a Scottish one under William Bruce was active in the Weddell Sea and in Coats Land. At the same time, there began the Antarctic career of the man who, more than all others, was to become the 'hero' of the ice continent.

British-born, Robert Falcon Scott (1868–1912) came from a lower middle-class background. His father was a brewer, his mother adored her sons. In 1881 Robert, just thirteen years old, entered Royal Navy academy as a cadet. He got through his studies and took up the customary career as an officer, and served in the Pacific and Caribbean. He was thirty-one years old and held the rank of lieutenant when he met Clements R. Markham, the doyen of Antarctic research and then President of the Royal Geographical Society. Markham was looking for a leader for his Antarctic expedition, while Scott was seeking an opportunity to shine and make his career.

Robert Falcon Scott in the 'togs' of an ice traveller. Scott, a persevering and strong-willed man, was to become the 'hero' of the South Pole.

1901/04   The coastline of Antarctica was known, by and large, as a result of the foregoing expeditions. Now it was all about exploring the interior. At the same time about taking possession of the last ownerless continent. Concrete gain Markham did not promise, rather more the fame which would arise with each new expedition under Britain's flag. Scott was the right man for the job. He was not only ambitious, strong and capable of radiating enthusiasm, he was a British officer and proud of it. Scott received for his mission a brand-new ship, specially constructed for this expedition, the *Discovery*. When he set sail on 31 July 1901, the King and Queen saw him off. To underline the importance of this large-scale voyage of discovery, Markham had got half of Britain enthusiastic about it.

On 8 January 1902 the *Discovery* reached Cape Adare. On McMurdo Sound the crew erected their winter quarters, a sturdy pre-fabricated wooden hut. Scott carried with him a balloon which he used for atmospheric research. On 4 February he climbed up with it to inspect the Ross Shelf Ice. Sadly, the ice surface was not as flat as a board, as he had hoped. Mountains and a range of wavy hills spread out before him. Scott thought of overcoming these 'plains' with ponies and dogs. After the first wintering, Scott commenced a serious attempt to reach the vicinity of the Pole. His companions were Ernest Henry Shackleton and Dr Edward Wilson. The two sledges with provisions, fuel and equipment were drawn by nineteen huskies. The expedition started on 2 November 1902. On 3 February 1903 the men returned to the *Discovery*. In the ninety-three days they had covered 1,500 kilometres, which meant an average daily performance of 16 kilometres. In the closing stages, the men dragged the sledges themselves; the dogs were not up to the strain and all had to be shot.

> The British had either poor dogs – or they couldn't get on with them . . . The British have loudly and unmistakably declared to the world that skis and dogs are useless in these regions and that hide clothing is nonsensical. We shall see – we shall see.

Thus later did Amundsen judge Scott's and Shackleton's first expeditions. History was to prove him right.

Scott, Wilson and Shackleton had indeed covered less than half the

Shackleton, Scott and Wilson (from left to right) setting out on their land journey, which established the friendship between Wilson and Scott and the rivalry between Shackleton and Scott.

distance to the Pole, but had thereby set up a new southern record. Scott described this 'heroic act' in an impressive diary; also the worries. The physical condition of the participants was miserable by the end of the march. All were suffering from snow blindness, Shackleton and Wilson had scurvy. Only the fact that they had good weather during the last 100 kilometres back to the ship saved the party. They were totally exhausted. A snowstorm would easily have finished them off. Despite his protests, the sick Shackleton was taken on board the supply ship *Morning*. Furious, he sailed back to England. That was the beginning of the rivalry between 'Shack' and Scott.

After the second Antarctic winter, from October 1903 Scott reconnoitred the Trans-Antarctic Mountains and pushed on into the hinterland, Victoria Land. The six men of this expedition put 1,160 kilometres behind them in fifty-nine days and reached a height of 2,700 metres (average speed 20 kilometres per day). The temperatures were murderous, 40°C. below zero. From the first they had renounced the use of dogs. 'Man-hauling' – dragging the sledges themselves – was Scott's tactic. It was to become his creed. On 24 December 1903 the group was back on the *Discovery* safe and sound. Scott was the undisputed 'hero' of the Antarctic. As Scott's ship entered the New Zealand port of Christchurch on 1 April 1904, an enthusiastic crowd awaited him. The practical results of the expedition were plain to see. The Ross Shelf Ice, the Trans-Antarctic Mountains and Victoria Land had been reconnoitred. Now more was known about the ice continent, much more. The South Pole, however, was still far away, unexplored. It became a fixed idea with 'Shack', his goal. Ernest Henry Shackleton (1874–1922), nicknamed 'Shack' by his friends, was born in Ireland. He was six years younger than Scott, but a real old soldier. At seventeen he enlisted in the British merchant marine. Quickly he rose to be Third Officer. When he met Scott and accompanied him to the Antarctic, he was curious, fond of life and ready to learn. As one of the best men on the expedition, it galled him unspeakably that he had not been able to cope with the physical stresses. He knew that he was superior to Scott, but first had to prove it. Henceforth he made his way as a journalist, gave lectures, and canvassed unsuccessfully for a seat in Parliament. Also as a businessman he was not successful. Finally, he decided to go to the Antarctic a second time on his own account. This time he wanted to conquer the Pole, cost what it might. The funds that Scott had been amply provided with officially by the Royal Navy, naturally were harder to come by for 'Shack'. Still, they sufficed to buy the expedition's equipment (sledges, sleeping-bags, skis, etc.), which he organized mainly in Norway. There they had experience on ice. His ship, the *Nimrod*, was forty years old.

1908/09 On New Year's Day 1908 the expedition set out from New Zealand. At Cape Royds, 20 kilometres away from Scott's wintering point, he set up his camp. Shackleton took a motor car to Antarctica. It was the first motorized ice vehicle. This absurd 15hp vehicle did not stand the test, however. Instead of dogs, 'Shack' decided to use Manchurian ponies and had them transported half-way round the world, in order to try them out as draught animals. The route to the Pole he proposed, over the Ross Shelf Ice to the

350

Shackleton's motor car didn't function in the Antarctic as he had expected. After some test runs it was dispensed with.

Beardmore Glacier, was the one which he had got to know with Scott. From the glacier he hoped to reach the polar plateau and press on towards the South Pole. On 20 October 1908 he departed with half a dozen ponies and three companions. Fuel and provisions were calculated for ninety-one days. Also on the sledges was fodder for the ponies. On the Ross Shelf Ice, 'Shack', Marshall and Adams already had to shoot the first animals. Unlike dogs, ponies sweat and are thus unsuited to extremely low temperatures. On 26 November they reached the southernmost point of Scott's expedition. Shackleton was triumphant. Onwards! It became colder, the snow softer. As they fought their way up the Beardmore Glacier, the situation became really depressing. One pony after another collapsed. The meat was stored in depots against the return. The last of the hard-pressed beasts fell into one of the many crevasses which became ever more enormous.

The rations became increasingly scantier. The marching performance·of an average 20 kilometres per day was far too little to reach the

351

Pole and get back to the *Nimrod* before the Antarctic winter. 'Shack' realized that they were not quick enough. On 9 January 1909, only 175 kilometres away from the Pole, they gave up. The return march became a race against death. The weather worsened all the time. Pony maize now served almost exclusively as food. Shackleton did not order, he ran ahead, thus drawing his men on. Although they hoisted sails on the sledges and thereby achieved a daily performance of from 31 to 47 kilometres, they were too slow. The return march lasted until the fourth day of March. In 128 days they had covered 2,736 kilometres (average 21 kilometres per day). Half-starved, they climbed aboard the *Nimrod*. During Shackleton's push for the south, a second group from his expedition, led by Douglas Mawson, had reached the magnetic South Pole. At the time this was some 500 kilometres away from the spot where the ship was anchored.

Back in England, 'Shack' too was hailed as a hero. He enjoyed the glow of publicity, wrote a successful book about the expedition and became a professional adventurer. Edward VII knighted him and gave him £20,000. He had debts nonetheless. The expenses of the expedition had become so great that he had to give lectures for years.

1911/12   Three and a half years later came the final race for the South Pole which was to result in two successes and one tragedy. The two principals were Scott and Amundsen. The Norwegian Roald Amundsen (1872–1928) had been born near Oslo. Originally he was going in for medicine but gave up his studies and went to sea. He became an explorer and adventurer, *the* specialist on Arctic ice. In 1898 he had overwintered in Antarctica on board the *Belgica*. During the years 1903–06 he became the first to master the North-west Passage which, above all, brought him recognition in Britain. He was just as much at home in the Arctic as Antarctic, possessed outstanding leadership qualities and was a precise planner. His tactics were based on small, fast expeditions. In every respect he was a professional. Amundsen was on the point of setting off for the North Pole, and Fridtjof Nansen had lent him the famous ship *Fram* for it. When,

The Norwegian Roald Amundsen was a brilliant skier, planner and seaman. His tactics: fast expeditions with Eskimo equipment.

352

suddenly, the news spread around the world in 1909 that the American Robert Peary had already reached the North Pole, Amundsen changed his plan without saying anything. He wanted the South Pole. It was in the same year, almost at the same time, that Robert Scott set out for Antarctica a second time. This time Scott had to get to the South Pole. He wanted to 'beat' Shackleton and, as he said himself, 'secure for the British Empire the honour of having achieved this exploit'. He himself wanted to raise the Union Jack above the South Pole. On 15 June 1910 Scott sailed from Cardiff in his ship *Terra Nova*. When he put in at Melbourne, the following telegram was waiting for him: 'Permit me to inform you that the *Fram* leaves for Antarctica. Amundsen'. Scott knew what that meant; the Norwegian was also after the Pole!

Amundsen had kept his plan a secret until the last minute. His crew thought at first that he wanted to sail around South America to get to the Bering Sea. Once on the high seas he disclosed to his people his real intention and the goal of the voyage. He left to them the choice of joining him or returning home at his expense: no one was to go to the Antarctic unwillingly. Not a single man refused to follow him. On 14 January 1911 Amundsen's ship entered Bay of Whales. From here, from the eastern edge of the Ross Shelf Ice, the shortest route led to the South Pole. On the ice the crew erected the winter camp 'Framheim'.

Scott, who had reached Antarctica ten days earlier, chose as his camping ground Cape Evans, 30 kilometres north of his first landing place. The rivals were 800 kilometres away from each other, but Amundsen's base lay 100 kilometres nearer the Pole. Scott comforted himself with the thought that he would be able to make faster headway on the already known Shackleton route.

Amundsen knew nothing about his route, only that he was 1,300 kilometres from the Pole. Both groups used the remainder of the Antarctic summer to place supply depots along the planned routes. The Norwegians got much further than the British. Amundsen had brought more than a hundred of the best sledge dogs with him. He wanted to operate exclusively with dog-hauled sledges. Scott was equipped with motorized sledges, ponies and dogs.

A hard winter set in. While this was familiar to the Norwegians,

Amundsen's dog-sledge expedition near the Trans-Antarctic Mountains. The route was furnished with depots and marked with snow pyramids.

Scott shut himself off from his crew. Amundsen had installed a daily programme which had to be strictly adhered to, whereby each man had his task. All the equipment was tested and overhauled. Everything was discussed, including a precise arrangement as to how much alcohol should be allowed. In the quarters of the Scott outfit the hierarchical structure of the Royal Navy prevailed. Boxes of provisions divided the space into officers' and crew's messes. In the evening, the officers and scientists gave erudite lectures.

Amundsen's first attempt miscarried, a false start. On 20 October 1911 weather conditions were favourable for the first time for the march to the Pole. Amundsen had selected four men to accompany him: Wisting, Bjaaland, Hassel, Hansen. Four sledges, loaded with food and fuel for months, were to be pulled by a total of fifty-two dogs. The animals came from the Arctic, mainly from north Greenland. As Eskimo dogs they were used to ice; pulling sledges was their speciality.

Scott started almost two weeks later. On 2 November 1911 he set

355

off with all he had: motor sledges for the first stage across the shelf ice, plus ten ponies and twenty-three dogs. All in all, thirteen sledges and sixteen men. Dogs and ponies came from Siberia. The men of both expeditions used skis.

Amundsen advanced extraordinarily quickly across the shelf ice. At each degree of latitude he constructed and marked depots. At the foot of the Trans-Antarctic Mountains, 500 kilometres from the Pole, he still had forty-two dogs. With these he systematically overcame the steep ascent to the South Pole plateau. Once arrived on top he had the twenty-four weakest dogs, whose pulling power he no longer needed, shot. They had no longer to be fed, rather served in their turn as fodder. Cold and sastrugi made hard work for Amundsen. 'The Devil's Dancing Floor' his men called the most dangerous stretch of the polar plateau, a region of crevasses with soft snow. On 14 December 1911 Amundsen and his companions reached the South Pole. They shot six more dogs as food for the remaining twelve which were to get them back to the *Fram*. Without great difficulties they were back in base camp in Bay of Whales on 25 January 1912 with eleven dogs and two sledges. The Norwegians had needed ninety-nine days for the 3,000 kilometres. This gives an extraordinary average performance of 30 kilometres per day and it remains to this day the fastest dog-sledge journey of this kind. Amundsen's 'victory' was no accident. It was based on the correct assessment of the South Pole problem and on precautionary planning. Amundsen's tactics, calculated with mathematical exactitude, had proved right. As he selected all components to his best advantage – men, dogs, sledges, food – he had from the first a better chance than Scott, even though he had started with the drawback of an unknown route.

Scott followed Shackleton's tactics, using ponies as draught animals and Shackleton's route. He thought less about his competitor Amundsen, much more about his British rival 'Shack' who had once been his 'pupil'. When Scott reached the Beardmore Glacier, he had already lost five of his ten ponies. The rest he now shot and with the meat set up another depot for the return march. After the ascent to the 3,000-metre plateau he sent home the dog team. The British couldn't get on especially well with the dogs and didn't want to kill them. They held them to be unreliable. Pulling one's own sledge did credit to a man.

A transient tomb for Scott, Bowers, Oates and Evans. When the three remaining bodies were found, a headstone of snow was erected. The wind has long since carried it away.

With only two sledges and seven men he continued on foot. Unfortunately, many difficulties accumulated: storms, sastrugi, heavy snow. Scott's expedition, completely different from that of the 'technician' Amundsen, was ideologically overburdened. Amundsen wanted to reach the Pole, or nothing. He wanted the fame too, to be the first. That presupposed, however, that he survived his undertaking. But Scott and his companions wanted to prove something more than geographical facts. They wanted by their mission to show the world that the British were in no way decadent, rather still a 'race of heroes', ready to die for 'their thing'. Bowers, one of Scott's companions, stylized the sledge pulling in his diary as high proof of that. And Scott wrote: 'The journey has once again shown that Englishmen bear hardship, help one another and can look death bravely in the eye as in the past'.

This form of self-sacrifice was now necessary. On the South Pole plateau with its sastrugi, deep heavy snow and cutting south wind, Scott's team was a worn-out bunch. The group's exhaustion became ever more obvious. Daily stages of only 10 kilometres were commonplace. On 4 January 1912 Scott finally had to split up his small troop once more. With only one sledge now and four men, among them his friend of many years Dr Wilson, he pressed on for the Pole. In spite of everything he reached his goal on 17 January 1912. He had indeed 'beaten' Shackleton, but lost the race for the South Pole. Near the Norwegian flag which fluttered there, Scott planted the Union Jack. The return march of the demoralized group became a catastrophe. Two, Evans and Oates, died on the way. Thirteen kilometres away from the life-saving One-Ton-Depot the theatrical story of heroism ended on 29 March 1912. Deadly weakened and pinned down by snowstorms, Scott, Wilson and Bowers could go no further. No rescue column could reach them. When their frozen corpses were found eight months later, 16 kilos of rock samples were discovered on their sledge and, in the tent, Scott's diary which was to 'immortalize' him. In Britain the headlines read: 'Fateful Defeat!'. Scott's death, and his ability to relate his suffering graphically, satisfied the need for a tragic hero. For decades the description of the unending drudgery mercifully covered up all the painful questions. Discussions about the inefficient means of transport, the insufficient planning and the men who, lacking training, could not manage their Norwegian skis properly, were stifled. But to compare Amundsen with Scott is false too, because their methods are not comparable. What remained after the 'conquest' of the South Pole?

1912/13   Wilhelm Filchner (1877–1957), a Bavarian First Lieutenant, formulated the next Antarctic challenge. The goal of the two German Antarctic expeditions led by him was to cross the ice waste from the Weddell Sea to the Ross Sea. A crazy idea, whereby they wanted to establish whether the continent was a single land mass or split by a channel of ice. Filchner had little experience on ice. He had ridden alone through the Pamirs and had led an expedition across the Tibetan plateau. For training he took himself and his men off to Spitzbergen. Everything was ardently practised: skiing, management of the huskies, tent life. Nansen and Nordenskjöld helped with the choice of ship, and Shackleton advised Filchner about the strengthening of the stern. So much prominent support gave self-confidence. A Norwegian ship, built for polar travel, was renamed the *Deutschland* and was equipped for the ice sea.

The Weddell Sea is notorious for its miserable weather conditions. The drift ice along the coastline is treacherous. But bravely, from 10 December 1912 to 27 January 1913, the *Deutschland* fought her way through a labyrinth of icebergs and floes.

When at last Filchner sighted the coastline, which is fronted by the shelf ice later to be named after him and until then unknown, he believed he had success on his side. But scarcely had the men erected a wooden hut from prefabricated parts as base camp at the beginning of February, than the ice under them broke into gigantic floes. Dogs, hut and men drifted northwards towards catastrophe; yet they were successfully rescued. However, they were no longer in time to reach the open sea. Filchner had originally wanted to sail the *Deutschland* to South Georgia, so as to be able to overwinter at the whaling station there. Too late – already by the beginning of March the sea froze over surprisingly quickly. The ship became shut in by ice and did not free herself again.

Involuntarily, the *Deutschland* drifted a whole Antarctic winter in the ice. Not until the end of September 1913 did she free herself again. Back in civilization, Filchner categorically declined all invitations to start for the Antarctic once more. There was nothing there worth having and Tibet interested him more. Besides, he was of the opinion that the really spectacular successes in the Antarctic ice could only be achieved by teams with polar exploration traditions: Scandinavians, Russians, Canadians; and the British naturally. Shackleton listened with pleasure; he had been fired up by Filchner's plan and noted his failure with satisfaction.

1914/17   Sir Ernest Henry Shackleton, now forty years old, took up Filchner's idea. His polar expedition was to put all previous ones in the shade. He planned the adventure of his life. In a propaganda campaign without equal, he raised so much money inside two years that he was able to outfit two ships. Five thousand adventurers applied to take part in his new Antarctic expedition. 'Shack' selected. In the spring of 1914 preparations were complete. The *Endurance*, under the command of Shackleton, was to run into the Weddell Sea and overwinter there on the edge of the Filchner Shelf Ice. At the start of the Antarctic summer, Shackleton would then cross the continent, accompanied by six men and dog sledges. A novel snow vehicle, a forerunner of the modern Ski-doo, was to support them. The planned route led over the Filchner Shelf Ice, to the South Pole, the Beardmore Glacier and across the Ross Shelf Ice to McMurdo Sound.

A second expedition was come to meet him. Its task was to set up a station at McMurdo Sound, using a second ship, the *Aurora*, and from there to construct provisions depots on the Ross Shelf Ice. The Beardmore Glacier was assigned as the meeting point for both parties. Such a bold traverse was only to be contemplated after Scott had reached the South Pole and Filchner had established the starting point. Did 'Shack' want to prove that he was better than Scott? Did he want to restore British honour after the disaster of 1912, or did he want to experience an adventure – 'the last trip on earth'? Everything was ready. What he certainly had not taken into account was the outbreak of the First World War. Patriot that he was, Shackleton placed ships and crews at the disposal of the Admiralty. This body, however, decided on the continuation of the bold scheme. The war would soon be over, thought 'Shack'. He was to be deceived. On 8 August 1914 the *Endurance* left Plymouth harbour. Without any intermediate port of call the ship reached South Georgia on 26 October. 'Shack' at once set course for the Weddell Sea.

Hemmed in by pack ice and icebergs, the *Endurance* was man-oeuvred south with bravura for three long months, but they were unable to penetrate as far as the coast. On 19 January 1915 they were conclusively frozen in. Although the mood of the 28-man company remained excellent – with dog training, organized pony races, football on the ice, and reading the purposely taken *Encyclopaedia Britannica* – the elements played havoc with the *Endurance* and drove the ship and the ice masses 2,410 kilometres off course. On 24 October 1915 they found themselves 917 kilometres north of where they had got trapped.

Things got worse. The ship was no longer able to free herself. Not at the beginning of the Antarctic summer, not in the autumn. She had got amongst the ice compressions which slowly crushed her. As if made of pasteboard, she splintered into a thousand pieces. Luckily, this unfortunate process lasted a month. The equipment, lifeboats, all provisions could be safely taken out of the ship. Shackleton's expedition had foundered, delivered up to the ice, perhaps condemned to

For his expedition across the ice continent, Shackleton developed a snow vehicle, a forerunner of today's Ski-doo.

death. The entire crew had at its disposal now only three ship's boats, five tents and a little food. By way of comfort, 'Shack' handed out an extra half sausage per man. On 21 November 1915 the *Endurance* sank.

Was it the irony of fate that exactly at this time – with the advancing summer – the ice became soft and brittle?

'Shack' ordered a march across the drift ice. Despite great dangers the men dragged the ship's boats across the ice. Further and further northwards. The greatest care determined the choice of camp sites and the route. Once more Shackleton's deputy, Frank Wild (1874–1930), proved himself. He was at this time by far one of the most experienced Antarctic explorers. He had taken part in Scott's first expedition during 1901–04. In 1907–09 he had been with Shackleton and from 1911 to 1914 he had participated in a further Antarctic expedition. Wild had spent almost a decade on the ice continent. 'Shack' and his people knew the value of that. Shackleton attempted to reach Paulet Island, where Nordenskjöld had built a small hut in 1903 and had laid in a food depot. On New Year's Day 1916 the party crossed the polar circle. The wrecked expedition pressed on further but just 100 kilometres from safety they had to alter direction afresh. The ice had become completely incalculable in its brittleness. Again and again it became more difficult to find old, firm pack ice for a camp site. Ever more frequently it happened that cracks suddenly gaped in the immediate vicinity of the tents.

Shackleton and Wild decided to get to the open sea as quickly as possible. They wanted to set course for Elephant Island. Their crew was never to be found wanting. The monotonous victuals, seal meat stew and roasted whale meat bacon they enlivened with readings from a volume of the *Encyclopaedia Britannica* which they continued to lug with them. On 14 April 1916, after sixteen months' odyssey on the ice sea, the men stepped for the first time on firm land again.

Elephant Island was no paradise. Luckily, however, there were seals and penguins. The food problem was thereby solved for the time being. Nevertheless there was little sense in hoping that a ship would pass by. They would have to organize their own rescue. The next inhabited spot was South Georgia. On 24 April 1916 Shackleton set out for it in a ship's boat and five men. He handed over command of the remaining shore party on Elephant Island to Frank Wild.

Wild, a survival specialist, knew that a happy outcome to the expedition depended on the unbroken will of all members to hold out. Accordingly, he organized everyday camp life. The two boats were turned upside down and converted into quarters. With much toil they were made winter proof. The biggest problem was condensation. In a single day 728 litres of water had to be scooped outside. Each Saturday and birthday was celebrated. For the feast a cocktail was brewed up, consisting of hot water, ginger, sugar and a teaspoonful of methylated spirits. They practised choral singing. A banjo had been preserved throughout all the dangers. It was a speciality of the crew of the *Endurance* to sing satirical verses, musically accompanied, with which the little weaknesses of individual expedition members were mercilessly laid bare. The victim then had a week to think up a suitable reply, in order to return the compliment on the following Saturday. The 'Boss', Shackleton, was expected back at any time. No one allowed himself to get careless. Discipline did not break down as food became scarcer. It was the beginning of August. The men, inventive and easily satisfied, boiled old seal bones. They discovered the use of seaweed as a vegetable and found it 'very tasty'. On 12 August 1916 Wild shared out the last of the meths. Henceforth they toasted each other with hot water flavoured with ginger. Slowly the winter came to an end. On 30 August at last they saw a sail come up over the horizon. 'Shack' was back. After 105 days of 'ice captivity' on Elephant Island the 'Boss' had come to fetch his lads.

Shackleton had not exactly had a pleasure trip. Just the opposite. But he had mastered all the difficulties. South Georgia lies 1,300 kilometres away from Elephant Island! In an open small boat 'Shack' sailed for weeks through a region that is notorious for its storms. The eternally cloud-shrouded sky rendered navigation more difficult. Certainly, there had been no alternative. 'Shack' took with him rations for only one month. Had he not reached his goal or a rescue ship in this time, all would have been up with him and with the crew waiting with Wild.

The first stage, right through the icebergs, 'Shack' and his Argonauts accomplished with dexterity. On the open sea their daily performance was about 100 kilometres per day. They had already done almost two-thirds of the journey when a storm overtook them which coated the whole boat in a layer of ice. The waves to which they were exposed exceeded everything that Shackleton had seen in his twenty-six years' seafaring. When one of their tanks sprang a leak, they were soon suffering from water shortage. They survived, just.

Nonetheless, on 8 May 1916 they sighted the coast of South Georgia, which in this area is to such a degree interspersed with cliffs, that at first they did not fancy landing. Faced with the onset of a hurricane, no other option remained to them, however. Again they found a channel through to the beach. Lucky. They landed. The saving whaling station lay 27 kilometres away. To reach it a 3,000-metre mountain ridge had to be crossed. Two of the men were so ill that they were not capable of it. Shackleton left a third man behind to care for them and marched with the other pair across the mountains. When Shackleton stepped into the station and introduced himself, there was an astonished silence. His first question was whether the war was over. No, it was not. Now, he had still to organize the rescue of his men. The terrible ice conditions in the Weddell Sea caused his first three attempts to fail. Only with the fourth ship, a Chilean government sailing vessel, which he had got hold of in Punta Arenas, did 'Shack' get through to Elephant Island. From the ship he counted the men who ran together to the shore. Only when he had reached the total of twenty-two did the worry fall from him. He was hugely relieved. In all the dangerous passages, over three years, he had not lost a single man.

Also dogged by bad luck was the sister expedition, the support team in the Ross Sea. The *Aurora* had reached the Ross Shelf Ice on 17 January 1915 and landed a group of ten men in addition to stores at Cape Evans. They settled into Scott's old hut. At the beginning of April 1915 a terrible storm drove the *Aurora*, together with the ice masses surrounding her, northwards. The cut-off party, of whom four died, did not suspect what had happened to Shackleton. They were only rescued on 10 January 1917. Meanwhile, as they were expecting Shackleton back from the Pole, they had under great stresses constructed food dumps on the Ross Shelf Ice as far as the Beardmore Glacier. All in vain. It was an adventure in the classic sense that brought nothing but personal danger for each individual. And that is enough.

1928 The 1920s saw in the Antarctic the stormy development of a new transport technique, flying. George Hubert Wilkins (1888–1958), an Australian adventurer, was the first to put it to the test in Antarctica. Like Shackleton, Wilkins had spent the First World War on the ice, having taken part as photographer during 1913–17 in an Arctic expedition. Shackleton hired him in 1921 for his last Antarctic enterprise, on which the 'Boss' was to die of a heart attack. In 1926 Wilkins flew from Alaska out into the Arctic. In 1928 he succeeded in winning the American newspaper tycoon, Randolph Hearst, as sponsor for his Antarctic plans and realizing his dream. With two Lockheed monoplanes he undertook, from Deception Island, the first flights over the Antarctic peninsula.

Simultaneously, Richard Byrd (1888–1957), who was the same age as Wilkins, started his Antarctic flights. This flying officer who had been highly decorated in the First World War came from one of the best families in the southern states of the USA. Already in 1926 he had achieved the first flight to the North Pole. When Amundsen, his companion, asked him what he proposed now, he answered promptly: your Pole. He wanted to fly to the South Pole.

1928/29   On 24 December 1928 Byrd's ship reached the edge of the Ross Shelf Ice. In Bay of Whales he constructed his base camp 'Little America'. His expedition was the best equipped that had ever set foot in Antarctica. Byrd had at his disposal three aircraft specially adapted for extreme cold. Also ninety-five dogs and fifty men. From 15 January 1929 test flights with the machines were carried out. Quickly four problems loomed up, for which the pilot had to be ready: starting the engines which constantly threatened to freeze up, icing of the wings, navigation, which on account of the proximity of the magnetic Pole proved exceedingly difficult; lastly, the bad weather with frequent interruptions of visibility. During the setting in of the Antarctic winter, one of the machines was destroyed on the ground during a snowstorm.

It was soon obvious that a direct flight to the Pole was too risky without intermediate stations. The Trans-Antarctica Mountains, which towered up to a height of 4,500 metres, had to be crossed, a flying ceiling which the three-engined Ford machines could not achieve heavily laden. Therefore a petrol dump for refuelling had to be constructed. Byrd planned to fly over the Axel Heiberg Glacier, then along the Amundsen route. At the foot of the mountains he must previously set up a fuel dump. On 19 November 1929 the depot's petrol drums stood in rank and file. On the way back to 'Little America' the fuel gave out and the machine had to make an emergency landing 160 kilometres from base. Because of the bad weather it was three days before the second machine could hurry to the aid of the stranded crew. On 28 November 1929 the ground station on the glacier announced over the radio that they had good weather. At once Byrd flew off with three companions. They crossed the Ross Shelf Ice, headed 700 kilometres in the direction of the Axel Heiberg Glacier, then decided spontaneously, and on sight, for the Liv Glacier, which seemed to be flatter. The mountain range bordering it, they flew over by the skin of their teeth by jettisoning ballast, two sacks of food which were to secure survival in case of an emergency landing. Wind and weather were on their side luckily. Without further difficulties they reached the Pole. They flew back without stopping and finally landed to refuel at the depot. After sixteen hours they were back again, tired out but happy, in 'Little America'. Their arrival in New York turned into a public festival, and Byrd was promoted to Rear-Admiral. After this successful Pole flight, a flight across Antarctica could be contemplated.

1934/35 Lincoln Ellsworth (1880–1951) was lucky enough to have a rich father and thus the freedom to realize his dreams. His inherited millions secured him independence. As a passionate flier he knew also the challenge that awaited him in the Antarctic. Ellsworth proposed to combine Shackleton's idea and Byrd's technique in a crossing of Antarctica by aircraft: 'The last great adventure!' He wanted to fly from Bay of Whales to the Weddell Sea and back again. This stretch was 5,500 kilometres. Ellsworth went shopping. First of all Hubert Wilkins organized the provisioning and equipping of the expedition. Flying experience brought in Bernt Balchen, Byrd's pilot, who was to steer Ellsworth's aircraft. Ellsworth economized neither on the ship, which he as a Western fan christened *Wyatt Earp*, nor on the aircraft, a special manufacture, which for its time flew at the remarkable speed of 370 kilometres per hour. Ellsworth gave it the name 'Polar Star'. In January 1934 he and his team set down on the Ross Shelf Ice.

Scarcely had the aircraft landed on the ice when the ice sheet disintegrated. The 'Polar Star' was salvaged but damaged. Ellsworth returned to the USA, had the machine repaired and set off for the second time. This time he set course for the Weddell Sea, so as to fly from there to Bay of Whales.

The expedition set up their base on Deception Island. However, bad luck dogged the millionaire. Immediately on first trying to start, a bit of frozen oil smashed the connecting rod in a cylinder. In camp there were all sorts of spare parts, except a spare connecting rod. Cursing, Ellsworth despatched the *Wyatt Earp* to South America to procure the necessary part. The airline Pan Am did its best. Ellsworth footed the bill. By the end of November 1934 the 'Polar Star' was ready once more.

Bad weather now interfered with Ellsworth's plans. For the whole of December the team was obliged to wait. At last on 3 January 1935

Ellsworth gave up, unnerved, and ordered the retreat. The weather promptly improved. Ellsworth and Balchen climbed aboard the aircraft. After some hours' flying Balchen suddenly turned away. He had observed cloud formations on the horizon which heralded a storm. To him that was risky. To his incensed employer he explained that he had no desire to commit suicide. This meant breaking off the expedition: Ellsworth was furious. By March 1935 the *Wyatt Earp* was back in the USA.

Regardless of the amounts which his obsession cost him, Ellsworth financed another attempt. He engaged a new pilot, Herbert Hollick-Kenyon from Britain, and in November 1935 they travelled to Antarctica. This time base camp was erected on Dundee Island. From there to Bay of Whales the best route one could follow was reckoned at 3,700 kilometres. They estimated they would need fourteen hours to fly there.

On 23 November 1935 the pair flew off. In fourteen hours non-stop they covered 2,900 kilometres. Then extremely bad visibility forced them to put down. They waited nineteen hours. However, after the second start they were able to fly for only half an hour. This second enforced wait on the ground lasted three days. When they took to the air for the third time their flight was to come to an end after an hour. A snowstorm pinned them down for eight days. With the first calm weather they dug the 'Polar Star' out of the snow and started a fourth time. With relief, they flew on for four hours. Two hundred kilometres still separated them from Bay of Whales. For the last time the two lone fliers set down on the ice desert to refuel.

Next day there was wonderful flying weather but their petrol ran out and, 16 kilometres from 'Little America', Ellsworth and his pilot made an emergency landing. Abruptly, the weather worsened, mist closed in. The real adventure began. For eight days the two 'adventurers' marched without orientation in visibility of 30 metres until at last they found the 'Little America' base. It was 15 December 1935. Three days later the *Wyatt Earp* arrived. The expedition was not cheap but had been successful. Ellsworth, when asked whether it had been worth so much money to him, replied that he didn't regret a single cent.

1946/47   In later years Antarctica became more and more the playground of 'games of conquest'. Technical know-how and political influences determined the journeys. Different nations carved themselves out on the map various large pieces of the continent and defended their rights; they maintained that with the claim they also held sovereignty. Previously, Goering had sent Dornier flying-boats to the Antarctic and had had marker poles with swastikas thrown out, to demonstrate the claims of the Third Reich.

After the end of the Second World War, the US Navy commissioned the biggest expedition of all time to the eternal ice, under the command of Richard Byrd. Thirteen ships, among which were ice-breakers and submarines, went to sea in 1946. They carried twenty-three aircraft and helicopters on deck and had a complement of 4,700 men. When the fleet of this undertaking, code-named 'High Jump', returned on 1 March 1947, the American pilots had made aerial photographs of 60 per cent of the Antarctic coastline. An area of 3.9 million square miles had been flown over.

1955/58   The age of the independent adventurer was manifestly over. What counted now was the massive input of the most modern technology, for which costs private sponsors no longer sufficed. Now rich industrial nations made provision in their budgets, in order to have a 'foothold' in Antarctica. Scientific research was often thereby a pretext to 'occupy' the inhospitable land.

The year 1957 was declared International Geophysical Year (IGY). Twelve countries took part and sixty research stations were set up in the Antarctic. Above all, the USA were committed. On 31 October 1956 Captain George Dufek (1903–77), who had already participated in Operation 'High Jump', landed his aircraft at the South Pole. He was the first person to set foot on this point since Scott. In March 1958 there were already seven American bases in the Antarctic, for which they had expended the remarkable sum of 245 million dollars. Whole arsenals of machines were stationed there, such as aircraft whose starting performances had been decidedly improved by rockets; crawler tractors, nicknamed Sno-cats; and converted tractors whose motors could cope with the extreme cold. The scope of expedition activity widened more and more through such technical finesse.

A refurbished tractor with which Hillary's group supported the Fuchs Expedition. Today it stands in the Antarctic section of Christchurch Museum.

Thus equipped, the desire was to apply the new techniques to the old challenges. Vivian Fuchs (b. 1908) organized the Commonwealth Trans-Antarctic Expedition for the IGY. This plan, to realize the old Shackleton idea with machine power, was so called because not only Queen Elizabeth II accepted the patronage and donated £100,000 but New Zealand, Australia and South Africa topped up Fuchs' coffers handsomely. This monster journey cost a vast sum in cash, logistics and technical extravagance.

With the aid of Sno-cats and special ice tractors, supplied and accompanied by aircraft, Fuchs intended, as it were, to 'waltz' across the Antarctic. The old plan made by Filchner and Shackleton, the land journey from the Weddell Sea to Ross Sea, must finally come to fruition.

To carry through this undertaking with machine power was above all a logistical affair. The engines of the special vehicles required massive amounts of fuel. Spare parts had to be made available, aircraft were employed for aerial reconnaissance. Where they could not get through with machines, they wanted to try with dogs. On the first voyage of Fuchs' ship *Theron*, his men unloaded 300 tons of materials alone.

In November 1955 Fuchs constructed a station on the Filchner Shelf Ice, which he named respectfully Shackleton Base. After overwintering, in January 1957 he reached a second depot 350 kilometres further south. By aerial reconnaissance, he established the best route to the Pole for his 'armoured trucks'.

Concurrently with the Fuchs group, the New Zealander Edmund Hillary (b. 1919), the first man to climb Everest, was working his way southwards from the Ross Shelf Ice on McMurdo Sound. He was to prepare the route for Fuchs with fuel and food dumps. In so doing Hillary followed a completely new route which led over the Skelton Glacier and Victoria Land to the Pole. On 14 October 1957 he departed with his armour-like, reinforced crawler tractors and, despite constant technical problems, reached the Pole on 4 January 1958. Only 90 litres of fuel remained in the tanks. It had taken him eighty-one days to cover the 1,600 kilometres.

Fuchs and his convoy had started their Antarctica traverse on 24 November 1957, arriving at the Pole on 19 January 1958, where he stayed five days in the American base. Hillary had flown back to McMurdo and remained there as emergency back-up. On 24 January 1958 Fuchs set out for McMurdo without great problems and, thanks to Hillary's dumps, he reached there on 2 March. Fuchs had covered 3,472 kilometres in ninety-nine days, corresponding to a daily average of 35 kilometres. With that the problem of the land crossing of Antarctica was officially resolved. Who in the Space Age would think of a traverse in the style of Scott?

1980/81   Twenty-two years passed before another Antarctic crossing was attempted. The British explorers Ranulph Fiennes, Charles Burton and Oliver Shepard had taken it upon themselves to circle the earth on longitude 0°, the Greenwich Meridian. Their so-called 'Trans-Globe' expedition took them also to the region of the South Pole. The zero meridian here runs not far from the South African base Sanae III, through Queen Maud Land to the South Pole. The trio used Ski-doos, motorized sledges with 640cc engines. Each machine could carry up to 500 kilos. The British were supplied by air drops. In sixty-seven days, they covered 3,600 kilometres, starting on 29 October 1980 and reaching New Zealand's Scott Base on McMurdo Sound in good shape on 11 January 1981. The greatest danger for them had been the drifted-over crevasses of the Antarctic glaciers.

1984/86   In the same year, 1981, Robert Swan (b. 1956) from Britain, made the decision to march to the South Pole 'in the footsteps of Scott'. His plan obviously appealed to his countrymen. Within three years he had found himself two partners, Roger Mear (b. 1950) and Gareth Wood (b. 1952), and 500 sponsors who altogether contributed around DM3,500,000. The age of historical adventure games had begun. It was the intention of the trio, seventy-five years after Scott's failure, to follow the old route to the Pole in the style of the turn of the century: on foot, without radio, without air support, totally self-reliant. In October 1984 they left for the Antarctic in a small trawler. Respectfully, in an allusion to Shackleton's last ship *Quest*, they named her *Southern Quest*. Swan and his people took their time, training for almost a year on the Ross Shelf Ice. They climbed Mount Erebus and tested mountain bikes in the darkness of the Antarctic winter. On 2 November 1985 they marched away at last with three sledges. Each sledge weighed 100 kilos, half as much as Scott's had done. This was not only attributable to the fact that modern equipment (sleeping-bags, tents, skis) weigh less than the corresponding items in Scott's time; it was because from the first they planned to end the expedition at the Pole. Swan wanted to fly back to McMurdo from there. Thus they would need less provisions because no dumps for the return march would have to be set up. At 5,200 per day, the calorie intake was much higher than on Scott's 1911/12 expedition.

The party covered the 1,450 kilometres in seventy days. Like Scott, they started on 2 November 1985 and arrived at the South Pole on 11 January 1986. Overall they experienced everything that had tormented Scott's team; snowstorms, extremely low temperatures, mist, sastrugi, crevasses. The three young disciples had the highest admiration for Scott's performance and were very glad not to have to retrace the route. The only piece of bad luck was that the *Southern Quest* had been crushed by pack ice meanwhile, ironically exactly on the day the Pole party came in sight of their goal. Swan, Mear and Wood were flown out on a US aircraft.

1986/87 At about the same time, Norway's Monica Kristensen had had the idea of repeating Amundsen's march to the Pole with the same means as he had used. Monica Kristensen (b. 1951), a Cambridge graduate in glaciology, christened her expedition '90 Degrees South'. Six years were devoted to preparation. She organized, raised over DM5,000,000 and purchased an old whaler. With her ship *Aurora*, likewise a reminder of Shackleton, the expedition left Oslo harbour in October 1986.

In Monica Kristensen the expedition had a woman as leader. Her three companions for the polar march all had ice experience. Specially to look after and drive the twenty-two sledge dogs, she had engaged two Danes, Jesper Andersen and Jacob Larsen, who had carried out several expeditions in Greenland. The careful planning was commendable because the Norwegian undertaking was more ambitious than the British concept. For Kristensen had to return from the Pole, like Amundsen, to Bay of Whales, as the Americans at the polar station categorically refused from the outset to provide return air transportation. Whosoever wants to operate in Antarctica must be completely self-sufficient. As the Antarctic summer set in late in 1986 and Kristensen had rejected an overwintering, she lost time from the start.

The group was not able to start until 17 December 1986. The undertaking became a race against time which Kristensen lost. It was planned that if they were not to winter in Antarctica, the *Aurora* must be reached again by the beginning of March at the latest. Despite all efforts the average daily performance of this dog-sledge expedition was less than 20 kilometres per day. Kristensen saw no chance of getting there and back. Still 440 kilometres from the Pole, she found herself compelled to give up and on 30 January 1987 the group turned back. They managed to reach the *Aurora* just in time before the pack ice closed in on her. Yet Kristensen and her male companions had covered almost 2,000 kilometres with the dog sledges, in the course of which food depots had been supplied by a small aircraft.

372

The Trans-Antarctica Expedition at the South Pole. From the left: Somers, Dahl, Steger, Etienne, Boyarsky, Funatsu. An international group for peace and environment.

1989/90 Will Steger (b. 1944) and Jean-Louis Etienne (b.1946) had taken upon themselves more than three times this distance in the 1989/90 Antarctic summer. Steger, mountaineer, adventurer and dog breeder from Minnesota, who could call on a rich experience with dog sledges in the Arctic, and Etienne, a French doctor and climber, who had marched alone and on skis with air support to the North Pole, wanted to kill several birds with one stone with their 'Trans-Antarctica' expedition. Their traverse was to be the longest possible, they were to serve world peace and ecology, above all, it was planned as a public relations spectacular with live television coverage and its own magazine. In a purely technical sense, the project was artificial. The traverse of Antarctica was not to follow the classic Weddell Sea–Ross Sea route. Steger and Etienne chose the longest possible stretch (6,450km), from the northern point of the Antarctic peninsula (Hope Bay), past Mount Vinson, highest peak on the continent, through the Thiel Mountains to the South Pole, then on through eastern

Antarctica, via the USSR station Vostok, through Wilkes Land and down to the Davis Sea where the USSR base Mirny lies. Besides the two initiators, there were four men – a Russian, a Chinese, a Japanese and a Briton. Each had his job and all six made up a perfect team. Thirty-six dogs, which were often replaced, pulled the three expedition sledges which were laden with a weight of 450 kilos most of the time. More than a dozen depots, set up by air, made supplies easier. The international quality of the group was to strengthen its international concern: before the expiry of the Antarctic Treaty in 1991, the attention of the world public was to be massively directed towards the threatened continent – with a modern dog-sledge adventure, the likes of which had no equal. Although the expedition claimed to be the first traverse of Antarctica without mechanical aids, it was from the outset dependent on technical help like snow vehicles and aircraft. Twelve depots were supplied by air-drops, five research stations used as staging posts. In these altogether 14 tons of provisions and dog food were stored. Exhausted and sick dogs were flown out to recover and replaced by fresh ones. The elaborate logistics cost almost DM20,000,000. Steger and Etienne raised the money from French industrialists, from an American dog food manufacturer, from sports gear firms and a television company.

Because of the distance, the expedition was compelled to set out on 17 July 1989 in the harshest weather conditions of the Antarctic winter. In September, with temperatures of −43°C., men and dogs were pinned down for thirteen days by a snowstorm. In spite of the delay they adhered to their timetable all through and reached the South Pole on 11 December 1989. From there to the Russian station Vostok, they used a route on which no man had been before. On 24 February 1990 finally they reached their ultimate goal, the USSR base Mirny on the Davis Sea, where their ship, the specially built *U.A.P.*, so named after a French insurance company which had likewise sponsored them, was waiting. Apart from a couple of frozen dogs there were no casualties to lament. In 213 days the expedition had covered 6,400 kilometres, a daily average of 30 kilometres. A splendid performance.

At the same time and in part parallel to 'Trans-Antarctica', their paths sometimes crossing, there took place the expedition fully described in the present book: the 'Würth-Antarktis-Transversale'. Reinhold Messner (b.1944), the South Tyrolean mountaineer and adventurer, who is the only person to have climbed all fourteen 8,000-metre peaks without artificial oxygen, and Arved Fuchs (b.1952), a German seaman and Arctic expert, who in the winter of 1984 had paddled a canoe around Cape Horn and who on 14 January 1989 had reached the North Pole on foot, as part of an international expedition led by Robert Swan, took up the old Filchner/Shackleton plan for an Antarctic crossing in its original form. They made it come true with two air-supplied dumps as their only compromise to 'by fair means'. Under their own steam, on foot they walked across the continent after an aircraft had taken them to the starting point. Through a personal stake, they demonstrated their commitment to an Antarctic 'World Park' in a very effective manner: no more motorized locomotion, no intensive depot flying, as required by the use of dog sledges, no leaving behind of rubbish. Thank to their self-imposed restrictions, Messner and Fuchs managed with costs of just DM1,000,000 for expedition expenses (excluding the production costs of the television film).

The original plan of starting for the South Pole from the edge of the Ronne Shelf Ice came to nothing when, time and again, their departure for the Antarctic had to be put back on account of bad weather conditions. When the pair at last landed at 'Patriot Hills', a camp run by the private organization 'Adventure Network', on the edge of the Ellsworth Mountains, they were already two weeks late. A further week was lost through shortage of aircraft fuel. On 13 November 1989 they set out for the Pole from a point on the mainland 500 kilometres inside the Ronne Shelf Ice. Each man pulled a sledge with an 80-kilo load (cooker, tent, fuel, food) behind him. Only two supply points were planned on the (as the crow flies) 2,450-kilometre route, the first in the Thiel Mountains, the second at the South Pole. On 6 December Messner and Fuchs arrived at the Thiel Mountains and replenished their food stocks. After a two-day rest stop, they continued on towards the Pole. The satellite navigation system GPS, really developed for sea voyages and now used for the first time on a land journey in Antarctica, was operated by Arved Fuchs and came through with flying colours. On 31 December 1989 they reached the American research station at the South Pole. They had coped with the first section of 1,050 kilometres in forty-eight days (22 kilometres per day). After three rest days, the pair replenished their supplies for the second and last time.

At the Pole they loaded their sledges with some 120 kilos, the maximum which they were able to pull under the hard Antarctic conditions. Based on a need for 5,200 calories per day, this worked out at rations for forty-five days. The fuel was to last more than fifty days. The weight–distance calculation was based on the premise that the 1,450 kilometres over the polar plateau, Mill and Beardmore glaciers and Ross Shelf Ice, in part the old Scott route, to the New Zealand Scott Base at McMurdo Sound, was to be done at a daily performance of 35 kilometres.

Despite the bad state of Fuchs' feet, the two ice travellers thought they could improve their speed by almost 50 per cent, by making use of the wind blowing from the Pole with kite sails. The calculation soon went awry. Difficult sections, lack of wind and bad snow slowed them down. The recommended route over the Mill Glacier proved itself to be ideal. On account of horrendous crevasses, however, the diagonal crossing of the Beardmore Glacier was extremely dangerous. Standstill or short stages they compensated with whole-day marches, the longest of which was 104 kilometres. At last a favourable wind got up and on 12 February 1990 they arrived, thin but well, at Scott Base. In ninety-two days they had covered 2,800 kilometres, an average of 30 kilometres per day.

For the first time in the history of Antarctica the ice continent had been traversed on foot without the help of dog sledges, as well as with the minimum of air support and in a fabulously short time. In 1911–12 Amundsen had achieved the same daily performance with his dog sledges. Steger and Etienne, despite constant dog changes and better equipment, did not much better. Fuchs and Hillary had been some 5 kilometres per hour faster with the gigantic material use of their snow tractors. Shackleton, the most successful ice traveller of former years and easily the earliest comparable with the present author, made 21 kilometres per day on his almost successful march to the Pole – pulling the provisions sledges himself over a long stretch like Fuchs and Messner.

VII Appendix

tenda a cupola | Prototipo
2 persone | mi serve per un
per l'Antartide | test a solda
| 4. - 9. 2. '89

raggio del
sole

nero

Paleria

(ne si
ma)

Cara Signora Ferrini,
quest'idea potrebbe essere nuova
e realizzabile per il futuro. Con
questo sistema posso collezionare il
calore del sole e asciugare + ri-
caldare la tenda In Antartide
abbiamo 24 ore di sole (basso).
È difficile soltanto trovare il
tro esterno, che deve essere trasparente
e forte (vento). La tenda deve essere
facilmente montabile. Paleria, tenda
Interna e poi quella esterna sopra
                Cordiali saluti

Minimum Equipment for South Pole

Cooking:

MSR-Cooker (¼-litre fuel tank) with cover
Petrol cans (lots), spare pumps
3 pots (coffee – 1¼ litre; cooking – 2½ litre; water – 3 litre)
Pocket lighters (2–3)
Plywood sheet 30× 40cm (to place under cooking area)
Toilet paper for cleaning, etc.; tissues (1 roll per person per week)
Plastic mug
Aluminium plate?
Spoon
Pocket-knife
Ladle
Brush

Clothing:

Paper underpants (3 per week)
Normal underpants (4 per month)
Net underwear 1×
Pile suit (two-part) 1×
Thin underwear 1×
Anorak with wolf fur (Goretex)
Overtrousers (not bib type) (Goretex) 1×
Balaclava – pile cap 1×
Mask – glasses 1×
Ordinary glasses 1×
Stockings (1 pair per week)
Fingerless gloves

Sketch and suggestion for our Antarctic tent. On all my expeditions I was able to develop new equipment ideas, thus originating plastic boots, scissor crampons, 'Ever-dry-rope'.

Shackleton's snow vehicle. With motorized transport sledges a modern Antarctic expedition is relatively problem-free, but on ecological grounds no longer defensible.

Arctic gloves 2×
Intermediate gloves 1×
Boots with inner boot 1×
Down jacket with vapour barrier (only North Pole)
Neopren stockings (1 pair)

General Equipment:

Tent
2× mats
1× Thermos (1 litre)
1× sleeping–bag
1× piss pot
1× sledge (+mat)
2× Magellan (GPS)
Maps
Skis with skins
Light ski sticks
Shovel

1 spare ski each
Medicine (plasters, strapping)
1× Argos?
Crampons
Ice-axe
Diary
1× recorder with micro/earphone
1 book per person
Spirits (1 litre per month)

Food:

Coffee (real)
Biscuits (3 packets per person)
Bacon and hard bread
Parmesan cheese (in plastic)
Carbohydrate breakfast
Hazelnuts (2 per person)
Vitamin C bars
Dried bananas
Dried fruit and nuts
Fruit slices
Soup (in plastic) (tomato, vegetable)
Tea
Freeze-dried food (rice, noodles, potatoes)
Pemmican
Olive oil (in plastic)
Butter (in plastic)
Noodles+ purée+ rice (ready mixed)
Chocolate

Luxuries:

Selection of spices and herbs
Whisky
Fishermens

Antarctic Cir

30°

Georg von Neumayer
(Germany)

60°

Elephant I.

King George I.

General Belgrano II
(Argentina)

Deception I.

Shackleton Ra.

GRAHAM LAND

Filchner Station
(Germany)

Filchner Ice Shelf

Adelaide I.

PALMER LAND

George VI Sound

Ronne Ice Shelf

Berkner I.

Pensacola
Mts.

Forrestal Ra.

U.S. Siple

ELLSWORTH LAND

De Gerlache Seamounts

90°

Ellsworth Mts.

Patriot Hills

Vinson-Massif
4897

Thiel Mts.

Amundsen
(USA

MARIE BYRD LAND

Amun

Axel Heiberg Gl.

KING

EDWARD VII LAND

120°

Bay of Wh

Amundsen ••••••••
Scott ....
Hillary-Fuchs ———
Trans-Antarctica ·—·—·
Messner-Fuchs ———

0   200   400   600km

150°